CONTENTS

ANSWERS

G-TELP

GRAMMAR

GENIUS

G-TELP 인증점수 획득을 위한 필수 문법서

G-TELP 문법의 최신 출제 경향 반영
최소 노력으로 최대 효과를 얻는 구성
왕초보를 위한 최단기 합격법 제시

공무원, 경찰, 군무원 수험자를 위한
G-TELP 학습서
개정판

ANSWERS

CHAPTER **1**

동사의
시제

EXERCISE

Ⅰ 괄호 안에서 문법적으로 올바른 것을 고르시오.

01 The CEO of the company (has exercised / is exercising / was exercising) at a gym **right now.**

→ 해당문장에 [right now (바로 지금)]가 있으므로 현재진행형이 적절하다.

해석 그 회사의 최고경영자는 지금 체육관에서 운동을 하고 있다.

02 The owner of the company (holds / is holding / holds) a welcoming ceremony in honor of Mr. Park **at the moment.**

→ 해당문장에 [at the moment (현재)]가 있으므로 현재진행형이 적절하다.

해석 그 회사의 소유주는 현재 박 선생님을 기리면서 환영회를 열고 있다.

03 The Human Resources Department (is holding / holds / has held) a special appreciation lunch for all employees **these days.**

→ 해당문장에 [these days (요즘)]가 있으므로 현재진행형이 적절하다.

해석 인사과는 요즘에 모든 직원을 위한 특별 감사오찬을 가질 것이다.

04 The New Rangton Chronicles (was offering / offers / is offering) discounts to the general public in an attempt to increase its circulation **at this time.**

→ 해당문장에 [at this time (현재)]가 있으므로 현재진행형이 적절하다.

해석 뉴랭클 크로니클은 현재 일반대중에게 발행부수를 늘리려는 시도로 할인을 제공하고 있다.

05 Private education spending (had been increasing / has been increasing) by 2 trillion won each year **since 2000.**

→ 해당문장에 [since 2000 (2000년 이후로)]가 있으므로 현재완료진행형이 적절하다.

해석 사교육비는 2000년 이후 매년 2조원씩 증가해 왔다.

06 A team of researchers (have been studying / are studying) dolphins in Florida, the United States for 30 years now.

→ 해당문장에 [for 30 years now (지금까지 30년 동안)]가 있으므로 현재완료진행형이 적절하다.

해석 한 연구팀은 현재 미국 플로리다 주에서 30년간 돌고래를 연구해왔다.

07 The nation (has been improving / was improving) its transparency score since 1999, when it was given a mark of 3.8 out of a possible 10 points.

→ 해당문장에 [since 1999 (1999년 이후로)]가 있으므로 현재완료진행형이 적절하다.

해석 한국의 투명성 점수는 10점 만점에 3.8점을 받은 1999년부터 상승하기 시작했다.

08 Even though Russell (swims / swam / <u>has been swimming</u> / had swum) since he was 9, he has not yet perfected his strokes.

> → 해당문장에 [since he was 9 (그가 9살 때 이후로)]가 있으므로 현재완료진행형이 적절하다.

> 해석 러셀은 비록 9 살부터 수영을 해왔지만 그는 아직 수영법을 완성하지 못했다.

Ⅲ 다음 빈칸에 들어갈 가장 올바른 것을 고르시오.

01 **Currently** VNC Solutions _____ for talented computer professionals who have at least three years of experiences in the programming field.

> → 해당문장에 [Currently (현재)]가 있으므로 현재진행형이 적절하다.

> 해석 현재 VNC 솔루션은 현재 프로그래밍 분야에서 최소 3년의 경력을 가지고 있는 재능 있는 컴퓨터 전문가를 찾고 있는 중이다.

(a) was currently looking
(b) has currently been looking
(c) has currently looked
(d) <u>is currently looking</u>

02 A survey of Torino restaurants shows that Japanese restaurants _____ popularity **for over five years now**.

> → 해당문장에 [for over five years now(지금까지 5년 넘는 기간 동안)]가 있으므로 현재완료진행형이 적절하다.

> 해석 토리노 식당들엔 대한 조사는 현재 일본식당들은 5년이 넘는 동안 인기를 얻고 있다는 것을 보여준다.

(a) <u>have been gaining</u>
(b) were gaining
(c) gained
(d) had been gaining

EXERCISE

I 괄호 안에서 문법적으로 올바른 것을 고르시오.

01 Busan had been considered the early favorite, but Jeju's chances (are increasing / were increasing) rapidly **as the decision neared.**

> → 해당문장에 시간부사절[as the decision **neared** (결정이 다가오면서)]의 시제가 과거이므로 과거진행형이 적절하다.
>
> 해석 당초 부산이 유력시 되었지만 결정이 다가오면서 제주도의 가능성이 급격히 높아지고 있다.

02 **One research examined 10 participants** who experienced the strange phenomenon while they (were watching / had watched / are watching) ASMR videos.

> → 해당문장의 주절[One research **examined** 10 participants]의 시제가 과거이므로 부사절의 시제는 과거진행형이 적절하다.
>
> 해석 한 연구는 ASMR 영상을 보는 동안 이상한 현상을 경험한 10명의 참가자들을 조사했다.

03 The woman's husband (was waiting / is waiting) outside the investigation room **at that exact moment,** and the prosecutor claims that she was the one who seduced him.

> → 해당문장에 [at that exact moment (그 당시에)]가 있으므로 과거진행형이 적절하다.
>
> 해석 그 당시 조사실 밖에서 그 여성의 남편은 기다리고 있었다. 그리고 검사는 그녀가 그를 유혹한 사람이었다고 주장한다.

04 American Airlines (was looking for / has been looking for) a new, fuel-efficient aircraft with plenty of cargo space to handle its Caribbean routes **last year.**

> → 해당문장에 [last year (작년에)]가 있으므로 과거진행형이 적절하다.
>
> 해석 작년에 아메리칸 항공이 캐러비안 노선을 다루기 위해 연료 효율이 좋고 풍부한 화물 적재 공간을 가지고 있는 새로운 항공기를 찾고 있었다.

05 **When Russell finally arrived at Busan,** he (has travelled / had been travelling) **for over two months.**

> → 해당문장의 부사절[When Russell finally **arrived** at Busan]의 시제가 과거시제이고, 주절에 [for over two months (두 달 넘게 동안)]가 있으므로 과거완료진행형이 적절하다.
>
> 해석 러셀 마침내 부산에 도착했을 때, 그는 두 달 넘게 여행을 해오는 중이었다.

06 We (had been playing / has been raining / were raining) soccer **for an hour when it started to rain.**

> → 해당문장의 부사절[when it **started** to rain]의 시제가 과거시제이고, 주절에 [for an hour (한 시간 동안)]가 있으므로 과거완료진행형이 적절하다.
>
> 해석 비가 오기 시작했을 때 우리는 한 시간 동안 축구하고 있는 중이었다.

07 Bella (<u>had been working out</u> / was working out / has worked out) **for 30 minutes when she realized** that she was in the wrong gym.

> **→** 해당문장의 부사절[when she **realized** ~]의 시제가 과거시제이고, 주절에 [for 30 minutes (30분 동안)]가 있으므로 과거완료진행형이 적절하다.

> **해석** 벨라는 30분 동안 운동을 하고 나서야 체육관을 잘못 찾아왔다는 것을 깨달았다.

08 **By the time Russell woke up this morning,** he (is sleeping / <u>had been sleeping</u> / has been sleeping) for about 10 hours.

> **→** 해당문장의 부사절[By the time Russell **woke up** this morning]의 시제가 과거시제이고, 주절에 [for about 10 hours (약 10시간 동안)]가 있으므로 과거완료진행형이 적절하다.

> **해석** 러셀이 오늘 아침에 일어났을 때 그는 약 10시간동안 잠을 자고 있었다.

🔲 다음 빈칸에 들어갈 가장 올바른 것을 고르시오.

01 While cyber terror attacks _____ increasingly intelligent and sophisticated, **an establishment of a pan-governmental control tower and reinforcement of security awareness among businesses was urgent.**

> **→** 해당문장의 주절[an establishment of a pan-governmental control tower and reinforcement of security awareness among businesses **was** urgent]의 시제가 과거이므로 부사절의 시제는 과거진행형이 적절하다.

> **해석** 사이버테러가 점차 지능화되고 정교해지고 있는 가운데 범정부차원의 컨트롤타워 구축과 기업들 사이에서 보안 의식 강화가 시급한 실정이었다.

(a) wold become   (b) has been becoming

(c) had become   (d) <u>were becoming</u>

02 Mr. Gardner is widely respected not only for his contributions to the country's economic progress but also for its involvement in the social service. He _____ in the service **for over 30 years before he died last year.**

> **→** 해당문장의 부사절[before he **died** last year]의 시제가 과거시제이고, 주절에 [for over 30 years (30년 넘게 동안)]가 있으므로 과거완료진행형이 적절하다.

> **해석** 가드너씨는 그 나라의 경제발전에 기여한 것뿐만 아니라 사회복지서비스에 참여한 것으로 널리 존경받는다. 그는 작년에 죽기 전까지 30년 넘게 그 활동에 참여했었다.

(a) was participating   (b) <u>had been participating</u>

(c) had participated   (d) has been participating

EXERCISE

I 괄호 안에서 문법적으로 올바른 것을 고르시오.

01 This time next week, I (will be lying / am lying / have been lying) on the beach in Bali.

→ 해당문장에 [This time next week (다음 주 이맘때쯤)]가 있으므로 미래진행형이 적절하다.

해석 다음 주 이맘때쯤 나는 발리의 해변에서 누워있을 것이다.

02 By the time Russell arrives tomorrow afternoon, we (will have played / are playing / will be playing) tennis.

→ 해당문장의 부사절[By the time Russell **arrives tomorrow afternoon**]내의 시제가 현재다. 시간부사절의 현재시제는 미래를 나타내므로 주절은 미래진행형이 적절하다.

해석 내일 오후 러셀이 도착했을 때는 우리는 테니스를 치고 있을 것이다.

03 The chefs (are preparing / will be preparing / were preparing) many dishes **when the restaurant opens later this evening.**

→ 해당문장의 부사절[when the restaurant **opens** later this evening]내의 시제가 현재다. 시간부사절의 현재시제는 미래를 나타내므로 주절은 미래진행형이 적절하다.

해석 그 식당이 오늘 저녁에 오픈할 때는 요리사들이 많은 요리를 준비하고 있는 중일 것이다.

04 If you need to contact me, I (stay / will be staying / have stayed) at the TG hotel until Saturday.

→ 해당문장의 부사절[If you **need** to contact me]내의 시제가 현재다. 조건부사절의 현재시제는 미래를 나타내므로 주절은 미래진행형이 적절하다.

해석 만약 나에게 연락을 하고 싶다면, 나는 토요일까지 TG 호텔에 머물고 있을 것이다.

05 By the time Russell is finished with his work, Bella (will have been cleaning / has been cleaning / will be cleaning) her room **for two hours.**

→ 해당문장의 부사절[By the time Russell **is** finished with his work]내의 시제가 현재이다. 주절에 [for two hours (두 시간 동안)]가 있으므로 주절은 미래완료진행형이 적절하다.

해석 러셀이 일을 마칠 때쯤에는 벨라는 두 시간 동안 자신의 방을 청소하고 있는 중일 것이다.

06 The students (will wait / will have been waiting / are waiting) **for half an hour when their teacher enters the classroom.**

→ 해당문장의 부사절[when their teacher **enters** the classroom]내의 시제가 현재이다. 주절에 [for half an hour (30분 동안)]가 있으므로 주절은 미래완료진행형이 적절하다.

해석 선생님에 교실로 들어오셨을 때 학생들은 30분 동안 기다리고 있는 중일 것이다.

07 **By the end of the year,** the company (will promote / is promoting / <u>will have been promoting</u>) their products **for three months.**

> → 해당문장의 부사구[By the end of the year (올해 말까지)]와 [for three months (3달 동안)]가 있으므로 미래완료진행형이 적절하다.

> 해석 올해 말까지 그 기업은 자신의 상품들을 3달 동안 홍보를 해오고 있을 것이다.

08 **When Russell moves next month,** he (<u>will have been living</u> / is living / had been living) in his house **for five years.**

> → 해당문장의 부사절[When Russell **moves** next month]내의 시제가 현재이다. 주절에 [for five years (5년 동안)]가 있으므로 주절은 미래완료진행형이 적절하다.

> 해석 러셀이 다음 달에 이사를 갈 때는 그는 그의 집에서 5년 동안 살아오고 있는 중일 것이다.

Ⅲ 다음 빈칸에 들어갈 가장 올바른 것을 고르시오.

01 **By the end of the century,** people _____ new technologies that we can't imagine now.

> → 해당문장에 [By the end of the century (이번 세기 말에는)]가 있으므로 미래진행형이 적절하다.

> 해석 이번 세기말에는 사람들은 지금은 우리가 상상하지도 못하는 새로운 기술품들을 즐기고 있을 것이다.

(a) had been enjoying
(b) had enjoyed
(c) <u>will be enjoying</u>
(d) will enjoy

02 Bella and her friends plan to work out in the gym together until 7 pm. **By the time they leave,** they _____ **for three hours.**

> → 해당문장의 부사절[By the time they **leave**]내의 시제가 현재이다. 주절에 [for three hours (3시간 동안)]가 있으므로 주절은 미래완료진행형이 적절하다.

> 해석 벨라와 친구들은 저녁 7시까지 체육관에서 운동을 할 계획이다. 그들이 떠날 때쯤에는 세 시간 동안 운동을 해오고 있는 중일 것이다.

(a) are working out
(b) <u>will have been working out</u>
(c) have been worked out
(d) had worked out

01 Currently we _____ someone to oversee the construction of the new facility to ensure that the contractors do their work appropriately.

ⓐ are looking for
ⓑ will look for
ⓒ look for
ⓓ has been looking for

> 정답 ⓐ

> 해석 현재 우리는 하청업자들이 자신들의 일을 적절하게 하는 것을 보장하기 위해 새로운 시설에 대한 건설을 감독할 사람을 찾고 있다.

> → 해당문장에 현재진행 부사어구[Currently(현재)]가 있으므로 현재진행형이 적절하다.

02 Trade with Asia's most populous country, China, _____ at a double-digit pace **since such figures were compiled in 1998**.

ⓐ expands
ⓑ is expanding
ⓒ has been expanding
ⓓ will expand

> 정답 ⓒ

> 해석 아시아에서 가장 인구가 많은 중국과의 교역은 1998년 통계수치를 수집을 시작한 이래로 두 자릿수의 속도로 확대되어 왔다.

> → 해당문장에 현재완료진행 부사어구[since such figures were compiled in 1998]가 있으므로 현재완료진행형이 적절하다.

03 These rats _____ much concern **lately** because they are very destructive to their surrounding environment.

ⓐ would arouse
ⓑ have been arousing
ⓒ arouse
ⓓ will arouse

> 정답 ⓑ

> 해석 이 쥐들은 주변 환경에 많은 피해를 주기 때문에 최근 많은 우려를 야기해 왔다.

> → 해당문장에 현재완료진행부사어구[lately (최근에)]가 있으므로 현재완료진행형이 적절하다.

04 **Last year** alone some 36,000 Koreans _____ in schools in China while more than 60,000 Chinese took Korean as a second language.

ⓐ <u>were studying</u>
ⓑ will be studying
ⓒ have studied
ⓓ are studying

정답 ⓐ

해석 지난 한 해에만 약 3만 6천명의 한국인들이 중국 내 학교에서 유학 중에 있었고, 6만 명이상의 중국인들이 한국어를 제 2 외국어로 선택했다.

→ 해당문장에 과거진행부사어구[Last year (작년)]가 있으므로 과거진행형이 적절하다.

05 **In the future,** the government _____ on a comprehensive plan to further open the service sector to foreign competition.

ⓐ is working
ⓑ had worked
ⓒ has been working
ⓓ <u>will be working</u>

정답 ⓓ

해석 앞으로 정부가 서비스 부문을 해외로부터의 경쟁에 더욱 개방하는 종합적인 계획을 수립할 것이라고 말했다.

→ 해당문장에 미래진행부사어구[In the future (앞으로)]가 있으므로 미래진행형이 적절하다.

06 Bella who is now seventeen years old began collecting dolls when she was ten years old. **By the end of this year,** Bella _____ dolls **for 8 years.**

ⓐ has collected
ⓑ <u>will have been collecting</u>
ⓒ is collecting
ⓓ would collect

정답 ⓑ

해석 벨라는 지금 17 살인데 10살 때부터 인형을 모으기 시작했다. 올해 말이면 벨라는 8년 동안 인형을 모으고 있는 중일 것이다.

→ 해당문장에 미래완료진행부사어구[By the end of this year(올해 말까지)]와 [for 8 years (8년 동안)]가 있으므로 미래완료진행형이 적절하다.

07 Mr. Smith immigrated to Korea with his family 10 years ago. **Since last year,** Mr. Smith _____ at the Seoul University in Korea.

ⓐ lectures
ⓑ has been lecturing
ⓒ had been lecturing
ⓓ will have lectured

해석 스미스씨는 10년 전에 가족과 함께 한국으로 이민 왔다. 작년부터 스미스씨는 한국의 서울대학에서 강의를 해 오고 있다.

→ 해당문장에 현재완료진행부사어구[Since last year (작년부터)]가 있으므로 현재완료진행형이 적절하다.

08 Public concern about the possible paralysis of up to 100 hospitals nationwide _____ as public and private hospitals unions move to start large-scale strikes from today.

ⓐ will now rise
ⓑ was now be rising
ⓒ is now rising
ⓓ has now risen

해석 공사립 병원 노조들이 오늘부터 대규모 파업을 시 작할 움직임을 보이고 있어 전국적으로 100여개의 병원이 마비되지 않을까 하는 국민의 우려가 증가하고 있다.

→ 해당 선택지에 현재진행부사어구[now(지금)]가 있 으므로 현재진행형이 적절하다.

09 According to a recent UN report, **by the year 2040,** 15 percent of the world's population _____ from malaria, a serious disease carried by mosquitoes which causes periods of fever

ⓐ will be suffering
ⓑ would suffer
ⓒ is suffering
ⓓ has suffered

해석 유엔 보고서에 따르면 2040년까지 세계인구의 15%가 모기에 의해서 전염되는 열을 동반하는 심각한 질 병인 말라리아로 고통 받을 것이다.

→ 해당문장에 미래진행부사어구[by the year 2040 (2040년 까지)]가 있으므로 미래진행형이 적절하다.

10 **Yesterday,** the Bastille Day, celebrating the French Revolution, thousands of tourists _____ the last minutes of fireworks along the beaches of Nice, a popular vacation city of France.

ⓐ were watching
ⓑ have watched
ⓒ will be watching
ⓓ had been watching

정답 ⓐ

해석 '바스티유의 날'인 어제 프랑스 혁명을 기념하는 수천 명의 관광객들이 프랑스의 유명 휴가지인 니스의 해변에서 마지막 불꽃놀이를 보고 있었다.

→ 해당문장에 과거진행부사어구[Yesterday (어제)]가 있으므로 과거진행형이 적절하다.

11 Russell's family went on a trip to Vietnam for vacation. When they arrived at Hanoi airport, there was nobody for them. They _____ **for 20 minutes before their tour guide finally arrived.**

ⓐ are waiting
ⓑ will wait
ⓒ had been waiting
ⓓ have waited

정답 ⓒ

해석 러셀의 가족은 베트남으로 휴가여행을 갔다. 하노이공항에 도착했을 때 아무도 없었다. 여행가이드가 마침내 도착했을 때는 그들은 20동안 기다리고 있었다.

→ 해당문장의 부사어구[before their tour guide finally arrived]의 시제가 과거시제이고, 주절에 [for 20 minutes (20분 동안)]가 있으므로 과거완료진행형이 적절하다.

12 I _____ in the train **when I woke up** because of the loud noise and saw a man throwing something and starting a fire.

ⓐ would have slept
ⓑ was sleeping
ⓒ have slept
ⓓ am sleeping

정답 ⓑ

해석 시끄러운 소리에 깨어나서 한 남자가 뭔가를 던지며 불을 지르는 것을 보았을 때, 나는 열차에서 자고 있었다.

→ 해당문장에 과거진행부사어구[when I woke up]가 있으므로 과거진행형이 적절하다.

13 James and his team, who specialize in developing training solutions for multinational corporations, _____ with the marine experts at the London Aquarium **for the last 10 years.**

ⓐ had been working
ⓑ are working
ⓒ work
ⓓ **have been working**

정답 ⓓ

해석 다국적 기업을 위한 교육 솔루션 개발을 전문으로 하고 제임스와 그의 팀은 지난 10년 동안 그들은 런던 수족관의 해양 전문가들과 작업해왔다.

→ 해당문장에 현재완료진행부사어구[for the last 10 years]가 있으므로 현재완료진행형이 적절하다.

14 **Back in the early 1920s** in the United States, radio broadcast _____ very popular, and radios were fast-selling items.

ⓐ **was becoming**
ⓑ becomes
ⓒ has become
ⓓ will be becoming

정답 ⓐ

해석 과거 1920년대 초 미국에서는 라디오 방송이 점점 큰 인기를 얻게 되었고, 라디오는 매우 잘 팔리는 품목이었다.

→ 해당문장에 과거진행부사어구[Back in the early 1920s (과거 1920년대 초)]가 있으므로 과거진행형이 적절하다.

15 Russell has just returned from a long Education trip, and has brought a lot of teaching materials with him. I wanted to visit him, but I am concerned he _____ for classes with them, **when I get to his home.**

ⓐ prepared
ⓑ **will be preparing**
ⓒ had prepared
ⓓ prepares

정답 ⓑ

해석 러셀은 긴 교육여행에서 돌아왔고 많은 교육 자료들을 가지고 왔다. 나는 그를 방문하고 싶지만 내가 그의 집에 도착했을 때 그는 수업준비를 하고 있는 중 일까봐 걱정된다.

→ 해당문장의 부사절[when I **get** to his home]내의 시제가 현재다. 시간부사절의 현재시제는 미래를 나타내므로 주절은 미래진행형이 적절하다.

16 My parents bought my little brother, Jack, a cute toy car. He started playing with the toy car and hasn't put it aside yet. He _____ **for five hours by dinnertime.**

ⓐ plays

ⓑ was playing

ⓒ will have been playing

ⓓ has played

해석 나의 부모님께서 나의 남동생인 잭에게 귀여운 장난감 자동차를 하나 사주었다. 그는 그 장난감 자동차를 가지고 놀기 시작해서 아직 치워두지 않았다. 그는 저녁시간까지면 5시간동안 놀고 있는 중일 것이다.

→ 해당문장에 미래완료진행부사어구[by dinnertime (저녁시간까지)]와 [for five hours (5시간 동안)]가 있으므로 미래완료진행형이 적절하다.

17 **When I wrote my thesis on cell phones,** I realized everyone _____ around wormholes in his or her pockets.

ⓐ carried

ⓑ was carrying

ⓒ would carried

ⓓ will carry

해석 제가 핸드폰에 관한 논문을 쓸 때, 나는 모든 사람들이 자기 주머니에 구멍이 있다는 것을 알게 되었습니다.

→ 해당문장에 과거진행부사어구[When I wrote my thesis on cell phones]가 있으므로 주절은 과거진행형이 적절하다.

18 The population of the rural areas in the country _____ rapidly **since 1995,** which has contributed to high levels of poverty there.

ⓐ was soaring

ⓑ will soar

ⓒ has been soaring

ⓓ had soared

해석 1995년 이래로 그 나라의 시골 지역 인구는 빠르게 증가해오는 중이고, 그것은 그곳에서 높은 빈곤율의 원인이 되어 왔다.

→ 해당문장에 현재완료진행부사어구[since 1995 (1995년 이후로)]가 있으므로 현재완료진행형이 적절하다.

19 According to the Education Ministry, **these days** students _____ bigger because of junk food and little exercise.

ⓐ will be becoming
ⓑ have become
ⓒ are becoming
ⓓ became

해석 교육부에 따르면 정크푸드와 운동을 거의 하지 않는 것 때문에 학생들의 체격이 더 커지고 있다.

→ 해당문장에 현재진행부사어구[these days (요즘)]가 있으므로 현재진행형이 적절하다.

20 Nevertheless, the average retirement age _____ **since 2006,** when it was recorded at 56.9.

ⓐ will slowly increase
ⓑ slowly increased
ⓒ has slowly been increasing
ⓓ would slowly increase

해석 그럼에도 불구하고 56.9세를 기록한 2006년부터 평균 정년이 서서히 높아졌다.

→ 해당문장에 현재완료진행부사어구[since 2006 (2006년 이후로)]가 있으므로 현재완료진행형이 적절하다.

MEMO

ANSWERS

CHAPTER 2

가정법

EXERCISE

D 괄호 안에서 문법적으로 올바른 것을 고르시오.

01 If Bella **had** time, she (will / would) go with us.

→ 가정절의 동사가 과거[had]이므로 현재 또는 미래사건에 대한 가정법 과거문장이다. 따라서 주절은 조동사의 과거형[would] 가 적절하다.

해석 만약 벨라가 시간이 있다면 우리와 함께 갈 것이다.

02 If I (know / had known / knew) the man's phone number, I **might call** him.

→ 주절의 동사가 [조동사의 과거형 + 동사원형(might call)]이므로 현재 또는 미래의 사실에 대한 것이다. 따라서 가정절의 동사 는 과거형[knew]가 적절하다.

해석 만약 내가 그 남자의 전화번호를 알고 있다면 그에게 전화할 것이다

03 If I **had** enough money, I (will buy / would buy / would have bought) a new car.

→ 가정절의 동사가 과거[had]이므로 현재 또는 미래사건에 대한 가정법 과거문장이다. 따라서 주절은 [조동사의 과거형 + 동사원 형(would buy)]가 적절하다.

해석 만약 내가 충분한 돈을 가진다면 나는 새 자동차를 살 것이다.

04 If the girls **came** here, they (would enjoy / would have enjoyed) themselves.

→ 가정절의 동사가 과거[came]이므로 현재 또는 미래사건에 대한 가정법 과거문장이다. 따라서 주절은 [조동사의 과거형 + 동사 원형(would enjoy)]가 적절하다.

해석 만약 그 소녀들이 이곳에 온다면 그들은 재미있게 놀 것이다.

05 If this room **were** tidy, I (could find / found / find) things easily.

→ 가정절의 동사가 과거[were]이므로 현재 또는 미래사건에 대한 가정법 과거문장이다. 따라서 주절은 [조동사의 과거형 + 동사 원형(could find)]가 적절하다.

해석 만약 이 방이 정돈되어 있다면 나는 물건을 쉽게 찾을 텐데.

06 If she **were** to appear at the party, everyone (would be / would have been) very surprised.

→ 가정절의 동사가 과거[were]이므로 현재 또는 미래사건에 대한 가정법 과거문장이다. 따라서 주절은 [조동사의 과거형 + 동사 원형(would be)]가 적절하다.

해석 만약 그녀가 파티에 나타난다면 모든 사람을 매우 놀랄 것이다.

07 If my grandfather (were / had been) still alive, he **would be** a hundred today.

→ 주절의 동사가 [조동사의 과거형 + 동사원형(would be)]이므로 현재 또는 미래의 사실에 대한 것이다. 따라서 가정절의 동사 는 과거형[were]이 적절하다.

해석 만약 나의 할아버지가 아직도 살아 있다면 오늘날 그는 백세일 텐데.

08 If I **knew** enough about the machine, I (<u>would mend</u> / mended / mend) it myself.

> → 가정절의 동사가 과거[knew]이므로 현재 또는 미래사건에 대한 가정법 과거문장이다. 따라서 주절은 [조동사의 과거형 + 동사원형(would mend)]가 적절하다.

> 해석 만약 내가 그 기계에 대해 충분히 안다면 내가 그것을 고칠 텐데.

09 You (<u>would know</u> / would have known) the answer if you **finished** reading the book.

> → 가정절의 동사가 과거[finished]이므로 현재 또는 미래사건에 대한 가정법 과거문장이다. 따라서 주절은 [조동사의 과거형 + 동사원형(would know)]가 적절하다.

> 해석 네가 그 책을 다 읽는다면 너는 정답을 알 것이다.

10 We **might** soon **be making** a profit if all (<u>went</u> / go) according to the plan.

> → 주절의 동사가 [조동사의 과거형 + 동사원형(might be making)]이므로 현재 또는 미래의 사실에 대한 것이다. 따라서 가정절의 동사는 과거형[went]가 적절하다.

> 해석 모든 것이 계획대로 진행되면 우리는 곧 이익을 낼 것이다.

🔲 다음 빈칸에 들어갈 가장 올바른 것을 고르시오.

01 Jack is tired at school, which makes it hard for him to concentrate on the work. If I **were** him, I _____ some relax right now.

> → 가정절의 동사가 과거[were]이므로 현재 또는 미래사건에 대한 가정법 과거문장이다. 따라서 주절은 [조동사의 과거형 + 동사원형(would get)]가 적절하다.

> 해석 잭은 학교에서 피곤해서 일에 집중하는 것을 어렵게 만든다. 내가 그라면 지금 당장 휴식을 취할 것이다.

(a) <u>would get</u>   (b) am getting

(c) get   (d) had got

02 We all haven't decided to go fishing this Sunday because it is expected to rain. If the weather **were** not rainy, we _____ fishing.

> → 가정절의 동사가 과거[were]이므로 현재 또는 미래사건에 대한 가정법 과거문장이다. 따라서 주절은 [조동사의 과거형 + 동사원형(could go)]가 적절하다.

> 해석 비가 올 것이기 때문에 우리 모두는 이번 주 일요일에 낚시를 가는 것을 결정하지 못했다. 만약 비가 오지 않는다면 우리는 낚시를 갈 수 있을 텐데.

(a) will go   (b) go

(c) would have gone   (d) <u>could go</u>

EXERCISE

D 괄호 안에서 문법적으로 올바른 것을 고르시오.

01 If the weather (was / were / had been) fine, we **would have gone** on a picnic.

→ 주절의 동사가 [조동사의 과거형 + have pp(would have gone)]이므로 과거의 사실에 대한 것이다. 따라서 가정절의 동사는 과거완료형[had been]이 적절하다.

해석 만약 날씨가 좋았다면 우리는 피크닉을 갔을 것이다.

02 If he **had taken** more money out of the bank, he (could have bought / bought / could buy) the shoes.

→ 가정절의 동사가 과거완료[had taken]이므로 과거사건에 대한 가정법 과거완료문장이다. 따라서 주절은 [조동사의 과거형 + have pp(could have bought)]가 적절하다.

해석 만약에 그가 은행에서 더 많은 돈을 인출했다면 그는 그 신발을 구매할 수 있었을 것이다.

03 If he **had set** the alarm clock, he (wouldn't have overslept / won't oversleep / won't have overslept).

→ 가정절의 동사가 과거완료[had set]이므로 과거사건에 대한 가정법 과거완료문장이다. 따라서 주절은 [조동사의 과거형 + have pp(would have overslept)]가 적절하다.

해석 만약 그가 자명종을 설정했다면 그는 늦잠을 자지 않았을 것이다.

04 **Had I known** you were coming to Busan, I (went / would go / would have gone) to the station to meet you.

→ 가정절의 동사가 과거완료[had known]이므로 과거사건에 대한 가정법 과거완료문장이다. 따라서 주절은 [조동사의 과거형 + have pp(would have gone)]가 적절하다. 참고로 해당문장은 가정절의 접속사[if]가 생략된 문장이므로, 가정절의 주어와 동사가 도치[Had I]가 되어 있다.

해석 만약 네가 부산으로 오고 있었다는 것을 알았다면 나는 너를 만나러 역에 갔을 것이다.

05 Tom (would have cooked / had cooked) a Thai food if he **had found** the proper ingredients last night.

→ 가정절의 동사가 과거완료[had found]이므로 과거사건에 대한 가정법 과거완료문장이다. 따라서 주절은 [조동사의 과거형 + have pp(would have cooked)]가 적절하다.

해석 만약 탐이 지난밤에 적절한 재료를 찾았다면 태국음식을 요리했을 것이다.

06 **Had** the clerk **known** the great news, he (would have let / would let)you know immediately.

→ 가정절의 동사가 과거완료[had known]이므로 과거사건에 대한 가정법 과거완료문장이다. 따라서 주절은 [조동사의 과거형 + have pp(would have let)]가 적절하다. 참고로 해당문장은 가정절의 접속사[if]가 생략된 문장이므로, 가정절의 주어와 동사가 도치 [Had the clerk]가 되어 있다.

해석 만약 점원이 그 엄청난 소식을 알았다면 그는 너에게 즉시 알려주었을 것이다.

07 If there (<u>had not been</u> / weren't / wasn't) Newton, the law of gravitation **would not have been** discovered.

> → 주절의 동사가 [조동사의 과거형 + have pp(would not have been)]이므로 과거의 사실에 대한 것이다. 따라서 가정절의 동사는 과거완료형[had not been]가 적절하다.

> 해석 뉴턴이 없었다면 중력법칙은 발견되지 않았을 것이다.

08 If it **hadn't snowed,** I (would go / <u>would have gone</u>) out with my friends then.

> → 가정절의 동사가 과거완료[hadn't snowed]이므로 과거사건에 대한 가정법 과거완료문장이다. 따라서 주절은 [조동사의 과거형 + have pp(would have gone)]가 적절하다.

> 해석 만약 눈이 내리지 않았다면 나는 그때 나의 친구들과 외출 할 수 있었을 텐데.

09 If it (<u>hadn't rained</u> / didn't rain) yesterday, I **might not have stayed** at home.

> → 주절의 동사가 [조동사의 과거형 + have pp(might not have stayed)]이므로 과거의 사실에 대한 것이다. 따라서 가정절의 동사는 과거완료형[hadn't rained]가 적절하다.

> 해석 만약 어제 비가 오지 않았다면 나는 집에 있지 않았을 텐데.

10 If I hadn't paid my electricity bill last month, I (<u>would</u> / will) have been in the dark.

> → 가정절의 동사가 과거완료[hadn't paid]이므로 과거사건에 대한 가정법 과거완료문장이다. 따라서 주절은 [조동사의 과거형 + have pp(would have been)]가 적절하다. 즉, 해당문장에선 조동사의 과거형[would]가 적절하다.

> 해석 만약 지난달에 전기요금을 내지 않았다면 나는 어둠속에 있었을 텐데

Ⅲ 다음 빈칸에 들어갈 가장 올바른 것을 고르시오.

01 Russell quit his job three months ago and still can't get a new one. If he _____ how difficult it is to get a job, he **would not have quit** it in the first place.

> → 주절의 동사가 [조동사의 과거형 + have pp(would not have quit)]이므로 과거의 사실에 대한 것이다. 따라서 가정절의 동사는 과거완료형[had known]이 적절하다.

> 해석 러셀은 3달 전에 직장을 그만뒀고 여전히 새로운 직장을 얻을 수가 없다. 만약 그가 직장을 얻는 것이 얼마나 어려운지 알았다면 처음부터 그만두지 않을 것이다.

(a) knew
(b) <u>had known</u>
(c) has known
(d) would know

02 Bella will leave for England to study English. But she is actually fonder of Spanish. If she **had been given** the chance to select the language to study, she _____ Spanish.

> → 가정절의 동사가 과거완료[had been given]이므로 과거사건에 대한 가정법 과거완료문장이다. 따라서 주절은 [조동사의 과거형 + have pp(would have chosen)]이 적절하다.

> 해석 벨라는 영어를 공부하러 영국으로 떠날 것이다. 그러나 그녀는 실제로 스페인어를 더 좋아한다. 만약 그녀가 공부할 언어를 선택할 기회가 주어졌다면 그녀는 스페인어을 선택했을 것이다.

(a) would choose
(b) chooses
(c) <u>would have chosen</u>
(d) had chosen

01 John has always owned his own house. If he **earned** a lot of money, he _____ a house and live a happy life.

ⓐ building
ⓑ would build
ⓒ builds
ⓓ will build

정답 ⓑ

해석 존은 항상 자신의 집을 갖기를 원했다. 만약 그가 많은 돈을 번다면 그는 집을 지어서 행복한 삶을 살 것이다.

→ 가정절의 동사가 과거[earned]이므로 현재 또는 미래사건에 대한 가정법 과거문장이다. 따라서 주절은 [조동사의 과거형 + 동사원형(would build)]가 적절하다.

02 Jenny Nelson didn't do well in school and was not interested in her study. If she **had been** a better student in the past, she _____ a top candidate for an entry-level position at ENR then.

ⓐ is
ⓑ was
ⓒ would be
ⓓ would have been

정답 ⓓ

해석 제니 넬슨은 학교에서 잘하지 못했고, 학업에도 관심이 없었다. 만약 그녀가 과거에 더 나은 학생이었다면, 그때 그녀는 ENR의 하급직 자리를 위한 아마 가장 뛰어난 지원자였을 것이다.

→ 가정절의 동사가 과거완료[had been]이므로 과거사건에 대한 가정법 과거완료문장이다. 따라서 주절은 [조동사의 과거형 + have pp(would have been)]가 적절하다.

03 Daniel neglected equations when preparing for the math contest. **Had** Daniel **remembered** a few more equations, he _____ the math contest that he competed in last month.

ⓐ would win
ⓑ won
ⓒ would have won
ⓓ winning

정답 ⓒ

해석 다니엘은 수학 경시대회를 준비할 때 방정식을 소홀히 했다. 만약 다이엘이 조금 더 많은 방정식을 암기했더라면, 그는 아마 지난달에 참가했던 수학경시대회에서 우승을 했을 것이다.

→ 가정절의 동사가 과거완료[had remembered]이므로 과거사건에 대한 가정법 과거완료문장이다. 따라서 주절은 [조동사의 과거형 + have pp(would have won)]가 적절하다. 참고로 해당문장은 가정절의 접속사[if]가 생략된 문장이므로, 가정절의 주어와 동사가 도치[Had Daniel]가 되어 있다.

04 The employees in the company had been looking forward to the company picnic. However, not many employees attended it. If Ms. Watson **had distributed** the flyers to all of the employees, attendance at the company picnic _____ much greater.

ⓐ would have been
ⓑ is
ⓒ being
ⓓ will be

정답 ⓐ

해석 그 회사의 직원들은 회사 야유회를 고대해 왔다. 그러나, 그리 많은 직원들이 참석하지는 않았다. 만약 왓슨 씨가 모든 직원들에게 전단지를 더 많이 배포했더라면, 회사 야유회의 참석률은 아마 더 높았을 것이다.

→ 가정절의 동사가 과거완료[had distributed]이므로 과거사건에 대한 가정법 과거완료문장이다. 따라서 주절은 [조동사의 과거형 + have pp(would have been)]가 적절하다.

05 Gyasa Industries **would have** to create a more powerful motor if it _____ to compete effectively in the lawn mower market at this stage.

ⓐ wanted
ⓑ wants
ⓒ will want
ⓓ would want

정답 ⓐ

해석 Gyasa Industries가 현 단계의 잔디 깎는 기계시장에서 효율적으로 경쟁하길 원한다면, 좀 더 강력한 모터를 개발해야 한다.

→ 주절의 동사가 [조동사의 과거형 + 동사원형(would have)]이므로 현재 또는 미래의 사실에 대한 것이다. 따라서 가정절의 동사는 과거형[wanted]이 적절하다.

06 Please do not keep the computer printer outside. If the computer printer _____ sudden changes in the temperature, condensation **might occur** and result in the possibility of unsuccessful prints.

ⓐ experiences
ⓑ experienced
ⓒ experiencing
ⓓ may experience

정답 ⓑ

해석 그 컴퓨터 프린터를 야외에서 보관하지 마세요. 그 컴퓨터 프린트가 급격한 기온 변화를 당하게 되면, 응축이 발생하여 불량인쇄를 초래할 수 있다.

→ 주절의 동사가 [조동사의 과거형 + 동사원형(might occur)]이므로 현재 또는 미래의 사실에 대한 것이다. 따라서 가정절의 동사는 과거형[experienced]가 적절하다.

07 If the hoses **were not connected** tightly, they _____, causing an enormous amount of gasoline to be spilled into the ocean and polluting plants and marine wildlife.

ⓐ broke
ⓑ break
ⓒ would have broken
ⓓ would break

정답 ⓓ

해석 만약 호스가 단단히 연결되어 있지 않다면 차열되어 버릴 것이며 엄청난 양의 가솔린이 바다로 유출되어 식물과 해양생물들을 오염시킬 것이다.

→ 가정절의 동사가 과거[were not connected]이므로 현재 또는 미래사건에 대한 가정법 과거문장이다. 따라서 주절은 [조동사의 과거형 + 동사원형(would break)]가 적절하다.

08 We didn't realize that Russell had studied and conducted Marketing for over 10 years. **Had** we **known** about his extensive background in the field, we _____ him far more consideration for the position.

ⓐ are giving
ⓑ would have given
ⓒ will have given
ⓓ gave

정답 ⓑ

해석 우리는 러셀이 10년 넘게 마케팅을 연구하고 실행했다는 것을 알지 못했다. 우리가 그 분야에서 그의 방대한 경력에 관해 알았다면, 그 직책에 대해 그에게 훨씬 더 많은 고려를 했었을 것이다.

→ 가정절의 동사가 과거완료[had known]이므로 과거사건에 대한 가정법 과거완료문장이다. 따라서 주절은 [조동사의 과거형 + have pp(would have given)]가 적절하다. 참고로 해당문장은 가정절의 접속사[if]가 생략된 문장이므로, 가정절의 주어와 동사가 도치[Had we]가 되어 있다.

09 If anyone **spent** more than usual on inventory this quarter, we _____ to reduce his or her budget by twenty percent next quarter as a punitive measure.

ⓐ would have
ⓑ have
ⓒ had had
ⓓ will have

정답 ⓐ

해석 누구라도 이번 분기에 평소보다 더 많은 재고를 사용한다면, 이에 대한 제재로 다음 분기에는 당사자의 예산을 20%를 줄여야만 할 것이다.

→ 가정절의 동사가 과거[spent]이므로 현재 또는 미래사건에 대한 가정법 과거문장이다. 따라서 주절은 [조동사의 과거형 + 동사원형(would have)]가 적절하다.

10 There is much traffic in the rush hour around the company. If they **lived** closer to the company, they _____ to work instead of driving a car.

ⓐ walk
ⓑ would walk
ⓒ would have walked
ⓓ walking

정답 ⓑ

해석 러시아워동안 회사 주변에는 많은 차량으로 교통이 정체된다. 그들이 회사에 더 가까이 산다면, 자동차를 운전하는 것 대신에 걸어서 출근할 것이다.

→ 가정절의 동사가 과거[lived]이므로 현재 또는 미래 사건에 대한 가정법 과거문장이다. 따라서 주절은 [조동사의 과거형 + 동사원형(would walk)]가 적절하다.

11 A number of builders are against the plan to construct apartments near the river because of the weak ground. If the builders _____ able to convince the board that the site is unsuitable, the planning department **would have** to locate a new one.

ⓐ to be
ⓑ will be
ⓒ were
ⓓ would be

정답 ⓒ

해석 많은 시공업체들은 취약지반을 이유로 그 강 근처에 아파트를 건설하는 계획에 반대한다. 시공업체들이 그 장소가 적합하지 않다고 이사회를 설득시킬 수 있다면 설계부서는 새로운 장소를 찾아야 할 것이다.

→ 주절의 동사가 [조동사의 과거형 + 동사원형(would have)]이므로 현재 또는 미래의 사실에 대한 것이다. 따라서 가정절의 동사는 과거형[were]이 적절하다.

12 If one of the apartments _____ vacant before the end of next week, we **would call** you for an appointment to view it with one of our real estate agents.

ⓐ becomes
ⓑ became
ⓒ had become
ⓓ has become

정답 ⓑ

해석 다음 주말 이전에 그 아파트 중 하나가 비게 되면, 저희 부동산 중개인 중 한분과 둘러볼 수 있는 약속을 잡기 위해 전화를 드리겠습니다.

→ 주절의 동사가 [조동사의 과거형 + 동사원형(would call)]이므로 현재 또는 미래의 사실에 대한 것이다. 따라서 가정절의 동사는 과거형[became]이 적절하다.

13 **Had** we **known** that the company was going to perform so outstandingly well, we _____ our shares away at such a low price.

ⓐ hadn't given
ⓑ wouldn't have given
ⓒ haven't given
ⓓ won't have given

해석 그 회사가 그렇게 탁월한 실적을 낼 줄 알았다면 우리가 그렇게 낮은 가격에 주식을 양도하지 않았을 것이다.

→ 가정절의 동사가 과거완료[had known]이므로 과거사건에 대한 가정법 과거완료문장이다. 따라서 주절은 [조동사의 과거형 + have pp(wouldn't have given)]가 적절하다. 참고로 해당문장은 가정절의 접속사[if]가 생략된 문장이므로, 가정절의 주어와 동사가 도치[Had we]가 되어 있다.

14 Economists are predicting that foreign investors **would sell** their stocks if the Indonesian economy _____ to decline.

ⓐ continues
ⓑ had continued
ⓒ is continuing
ⓓ continued

해석 만일 인도네시아의 경제가 계속 침체를 보이면 해외 투자자들이 주식을 매도해 버릴 것이라고 경제전문가들이 예상을 하고 있다.

→ 주절의 동사가 [조동사의 과거형 + 동사원형(would sell)]이므로 현재 또는 미래의 사실에 대한 것이다. 따라서 가정절의 동사는 과거형[continued]이 적절하다.

15 The current office is not attractive because it is limited and distractive. If the company **had moved** to its new office last year, the more spacious work areas, the upgraded cafeteria and the pleasant location _____ productivity by at least ten percent.

ⓐ were improving
ⓑ would have improved
ⓒ had improved
ⓓ would improve

해석 현 사무실은 공간이 좁고, 산만해서 매력적이지 않다. 지난 해 그 기업이 새로운 사무실로 옮겼다면, 더 넓은 업무 공간, 개선된 카페테리아, 쾌적한 위치가 최소 10%의 생산성을 개선시켰을 것이다.

→ 가정절의 동사가 과거완료[had moved]이므로 과거사건에 대한 가정법 과거완료문장이다. 따라서 주절은 [조동사의 과거형 + have pp(would have improved)]가 적절하다.

16 Many small businesses are having difficulties surviving due to the recession. If the government **reduced** the number of small business loans and grants under this situation, many small firms _____ bankrupt before next spring.

ⓐ would go
ⓑ can go
ⓒ went
ⓓ might have gone

해석 많은 소기업들은 경기불황 때문에 생존에 어려움을 겪고 있다. 이러한 상황에서 만일 정부가 소기업 대출과 보조금의 수를 줄이면, 많은 소규모 기업들은 다음 봄 이전에 파산을 하게 될 것이다.

→ 가정절의 동사가 과거[reduced]이므로 현재 또는 미래사건에 대한 가정법 과거문장이다. 따라서 주절은 [조동사의 과거형 + 동사원형(would go)]가 적절하다.

17 There was a report that most toys of the company had improperly been made with toxic substances. We **would not have given** the toys to the children at the day care center, if we _____ that they were recalled because of toxicity concerns.

ⓐ know
ⓑ had known
ⓒ would know
ⓓ knew

해석 그 기업의 대부분의 장난감들이 독성물질로 부적절하게 만들어졌다는 보도가 있었다. 그 장난감이 독성문제로 리콜 되었다는 것을 알았더라면, 우리는 그것들을 탁아소에 있는 아이들에게 나누어 주지 않았을 것이다.

→ 주절의 동사가 [조동사의 과거형 + have pp(would not have given)]이므로 과거의 사실에 대한 것이다. 따라서 가정절의 동사는 과거완료형[had known]가 적절하다.

18 She was in two minds about running for a political office, so that she was passive about the campaign. If she _____ an aggressive campaign, she **would have won** the election.

ⓐ has run
ⓑ could run
ⓒ ran
ⓓ had run

해석 그녀는 공직에 출마하는 것에 대해서 망설였다. 그래서 그녀는 선거운동에 소극적이었다. 만약 그녀가 공격적인 선거운동을 했다면 그녀는 선거에서 승리했을 것이다.

→ 주절의 동사가 [조동사의 과거형 + have pp(would won)]이므로 과거의 사실에 대한 것이다. 따라서 가정절의 동사는 과거완료형[had run]이 적절하다.

19 As nursing technology continues to change rapidly, nurses need to continuously update their knowledge and skills. If they _____ such efforts, the public's health **could be jeopardized**.

    ⓐ didn't make
    ⓑ hadn't make
    ⓒ haven't make
    ⓓ aren't making

정답 ⓐ

해석 간호기술이 계속해서 빠르게 변화함에 따라 간호사들은 계속해서 지식과 기술을 업데이트해야 합니다. 만약 그런 노력을 하지 않는다면, 대중의 건강은 위험에 빠질 수 있습니다.

→ 주절의 동사가 [조동사의 과거형 + 동사원형(could be jeopardized)]이므로 현재 또는 미래의 사실에 대한 것이다. 따라서 가정절의 동사는 과거형[didn't make]이 적절하다.

20 You may believe that not many of your students are interested in economics. Actually, most of them _____ an interest in that subject if they **learned** it in an engaging way.

    ⓐ could take
    ⓑ are taking
    ⓒ have taken
    ⓓ took

정답 ⓐ

해석 경제학에 관심이 있는 학생들이 많지 않다고 생각할 수 있습니다. 실제로 관심을 끄는 방식으로 경제학을 배우면, 대부분의 학생들은 그 과목에 관심을 가질 수 있습니다.

→ 가정절의 동사가 과거[learned]이므로 현재 또는 미래사건에 대한 가정법 과거문장이다. 따라서 주절은 [조동사의 과거형 + 동사원형(could take)]가 적절하다.

ANSWERS

관계사

EXERCISE

Ⅰ 괄호 안에서 문법적으로 올바른 것을 고르시오.

01 The river [(<u>which</u> / who) flows through London] is called the Thames.

> → 선행사[The river]가 사물이고 뒤에 주어가 없는 불완벽한 문장이다. 따라서 주격관계대명사[which]가 적절하다.

> 해석 런던을 관통해 흐르는 강은 테임즈 강이라고 불린다.

02 About 95% of us experience jealousy at some stage in our lives. This is **the basic emotion** [(<u>which</u> / who / whom) touches man in every human relationship].

> → 선행사[The basic emotion]가 사물이고 뒤에 주어가 없는 불완벽한 문장이다. 따라서 주격 관계대명사[which]가 적절하다.

> 해석 우리의 약 95퍼센트가 우리 삶의 어떤 단계에서 질투를 경험한다. 이것은 모든 인간관계에서 인간에게 영향을 미치는 기본적인 감정이다

03 From other countries in 1998 United States attracted **more than 450,000 students**, [(<u>who</u> / that / which) poured more than $7 billion into American economy].

> → 선행사[450,000 students]가 사람이고 뒤에 주어가 없는 불완벽한 문장이므로 주격 관계대명사[who]가 적절하다. 참고로 [, (comma)]가 있어서 관계대명사[that]은 적절하지 않다.

> 해석 미국은 1998년에 다른 나라로부터 45만 명 이상의 학생들을 불러들였는데, 그들은 미국 경제에 70억 달러 이상을 쏟아 부었다.

04 The particular stream [(who / <u>that</u>) serves as their journey's end] is almost invariably the same one in which they were born.

> → 선행사[The particular stream]가 사물이고 뒤에 주어가 없는 불완벽한 문장이다. 따라서 선행사가 사람이나 사물 모두 취할 수 있는 관계대명사[that]이 적절하다.

> 해석 여행의 종착지 역할을 하는 이 특별한 강은 그들이 태어난 곳과 거의 변함없이 일치한다.

05 He's always **a really rude man**, [(that / <u>who</u>) looks down on others].

> → 선행사[a really rude man]가 사람이고 뒤에 주어가 없는 불완벽한 문장이므로 주격관계대명사[who]가 적절하다. 또한 [, (comma)]가 있어서 관계대명사[that]은 적절하지 않다.

> 해석 그는 항상 정말 무례한 사람이다. 그는 다른 사람들을 무시한다.

06 The rapid melting of Arctic ice has become **an undeniable phenomenon**, [(when / that / who / <u>which</u>) suggests that fear of global warming is warranted].

> → 선행사[an undeniable phenomenon]가 사물이고 뒤에 주어가 없는 불완벽한 문장이므로 주격 관계대명사[which]가 적절하다. 참고로 [, (comma)]가 있어서 관계대명사[that]은 적절하지 않다.

> 해석 북극 얼음의 급격한 해빙은 부인할 수 없는 현장이 되었는데, 그것은 지구온난화의 공포가 확실시 된다는 것을 나타낸다.

07 It was **a rainy day,** [(that / <u>which</u>) was a great pity].

> → 선행사[a rainy day]가 사물이고 뒤에 주어가 없는 불완벽한 문장이다. 따라서 주격관계대명사[which]가 적절하다. 참고로 [, (comma)]가 있어서 관계대명사[that]은 적절하지 않다.

> 해석 비가 오는 날이었다, 그것은 대단한 유감이었다.

08 **His brother** [(<u>who</u> / which) is just seventeen] has already passed his driving test.

> → 선행사[His brother]가 사람이고 뒤에 주어가 없는 불완벽한 문장이다. 따라서 주격관계대명사[who]가 적절하다.

> 해석 오직 17세의 그의 동생이 이미 운전시험에 합격했다.

Ⅲ 다음 빈칸에 들어갈 가장 올바른 것을 고르시오.

01 In 1863 American President Abraham Lincoln made Thanksgiving **an official annual holiday,**

_____.

> → 선행사[an official annual holiday]가 사물이고 뒤에 주어가 없는 불완벽한 문장이다. 따라서 관계대명사[which]가 적절하다. 참고로 [, (comma)]가 있어서 관계대명사[that]은 적절하지 않다.

> 해석 1863년 미국의 대통령 아브라함 링컨은 추수감사절을 공휴일로 만들었다. 그것은 지금 매년 11월 4번째 목요일에 경축되고 있다.

(a) <u>which is now celebrated on the 4th Thursday of November each year</u>

(b) who is now celebrated on the 4th Thursday of November each year

(c) when is now celebrated on the 4th Thursday of November each year

(d) that is now celebrated on the 4th Thursday of November each year

02 Money related to English teaching around the world in 1998 was about $ 10 billion. That total includes money spent for teaching, books, other materials, and tuition of **students**

_____.

> → 선행사[students]가 사람이고 뒤에 주어가 없는 불완벽한 문장이므로 주격관계대명사[who]가 적절하다.

> 해석 1998년에 전 세계에서 영어를 가르치는 데 관련된 돈은 약 100억 달러였다. 그 총액에는 수업, 책, 다른 자료, 그리고 영어를 사용하는 국가에서 공부를 하는 학생들의 수업료에 지불된 돈이 포함되어 있다.

(a) <u>who were studying in English speaking countries</u>

(b) whom were studying in English speaking countries

(c) when were studying in English speaking countries

(d) which were studying in English speaking countries

EXERCISE

I 괄호 안에서 문법적으로 올바른 것을 고르시오.

01 The man [(<u>whom</u> / which / whose) you met yesterday on the way here] is my brother.

→ 선행사[The man]가 사람이고 뒤에 목적어가 없는 불완벽한 문장이다. 따라서 목적격 관계대명사[whom]이 적절하다.

해석 어제 이곳으로 오는 길에 당신이 만났던 남자는 나의 동생이다.

02 They have **lots of vitamin a and protein** [(who / whom / <u>which</u>) we use to prevent and delay skin from aging].

→ 선행사[lots of vitamin a and protein]가 사물이고 뒤에 목적어가 없는 불완벽한 문장이다. 따라서 목적격 관계대명사[which]가 적절하다.

해석 그것들에는 피부노화를 예방하고 지연시키기 위해 그들이 우리가 사용하는 많은 비타민 A와 단백질이 있다.

03 She is **a model figure** [(<u>whom</u> / which) many Korea's future scientists look up to].

→ 선행사[a model figure]가 사람이고 뒤에 목적어가 없는 불완벽한 문장이다. 따라서 목적격 관계대명사[whom]이 적절하다.

해석 그녀는 한국의 많은 과학 꿈나무들이 똑 같이 되기를 원하며 우러러보는 인물이다.

04 The car [(<u>that</u> / whom) I can lend you right now] is that yellow one.

→ 선행사[The car]가 사물이고 뒤에 목적어가 없는 불완벽한 문장이다. 따라서 선행사가 사람이나 사물 모두 취할 수 있는 관계대명사[that]이 적절하다.

해석 지금 내가 너에게 빌려줄 수 있는 그 자동차는 저기 노란색 것이다.

05 I've stood at the deathbed of **several famous people**, [(<u>whom</u> / which / that) you would know].

→ 선행사[several famous people]가 사람이고 뒤에 목적어가 없는 불완벽한 문장이다. 따라서 목적격 관계대명사[whom]이 적절하다. 또한 [, (comma)]가 있어서 관계대명사[that]은 적절하지 않다.

해석 저는 여러분이 아실만한 몇몇 유명한 사람들이 세상을 떠나는 순간에 서 있었습니다.

06 This means it makes a person buy **a product** [(<u>that</u> / when / who) he doesn't really need] — it may be a new type of telephone, or a new TV set.

→ 선행사[a product]가 사물이고 뒤에 목적어가 없는 불완벽한 문장이다. 따라서 선행사가 사람이나 사물 모두 취할 수 있는 관계대명사[that]이 적절하다.

해석 이 의미는 그것은 사람이 정말로 살 필요가 없는 상품(그것은 새로운 타입의 전화기나 새 TV 같은 것일 수 있다)을 사게 만든다는 것이다.

07 If you compare our, perhaps, 90 years here to the age of **this planet** [(that / who / when) we call home], you will see we are only here in a blink.

> → 선행사[this planet]가 사물이고 뒤에 목적어가 없는 불완벽한 문장이다. 따라서 선행사가 사람이나 사물 모두 취할 수 있는 관계대명사[that]이 적절하다.

> 해석 아마 이 세상에서의 90년을 우리가 살고 있는 이 행성의 나이와 비교하면 우리가 시간상으로 단지 한 순간밖에 이곳에 있지 않다는 것을 알 것이다.

08 Watts plays **an unemployed actress** [(whom / which / whose) King Kong falls in love with].

> → 선행사[an unemployed actress]가 사람이고 뒤에 목적어가 없는 불완벽한 문장이다. 따라서 목적격 관계대명사[whom]이 적절하다.

> 해석 왓츠는 킹콩이 사랑하는 실직한 영화배우로 나온다.

▋▋ 다음 빈칸에 들어갈 가장 올바른 것을 고르시오.

01 Difficulties with culture shock are often related to an individual's ability to speak the language of **the country** _____.

> → 선행사[the country]가 사물이고 뒤에 목적어가 없는 불완벽한 문장이다. 따라서 선행사가 목적격 관계대명사[which]가 적절하다.

> 해석 문화적 충격의 어려움은 종종 살고 있는 나라의 언어를 말할 수 있는 개인의 능력과 관련 있다.

(a) when he or she is inhabiting

(b) whom he or she is inhabiting

(c) which he or she is inhabiting

(d) whose he or she is inhabiting

02 Many analysts share the view that this pattern has moved from Japan to Korea and is now in **China,** _____.

> → 선행사[the country]가 사물이고 뒤에 목적어가 없는 불완벽한 문장이다. 따라서 선행사가 목적격 관계대명사[which]가 적절하다. 또한 [, (comma)]가 있어서 관계대명사[that]은 적절하지 않다.

> 해석 많은 애널리스트들은 이러한 패턴이 일본에서 한국으로 넘어왔으며 이제는 많은 패션리더들이 일을 하는 중국에서도 나타났다는 견해에 공감한다.

(a) whom a lot of fashion leaders work in

(b) which a lot of fashion leaders work in

(c) that a lot of fashion leaders work in

(d) when a lot of fashion leaders work in

EXERCISE

■ 괄호 안에서 문법적으로 올바른 것을 고르시오.

01 A park [(<u>where</u> / when) a number of people will enjoy themselves] will have been constructed completely by next year.
> → 관계사 뒤에 문장이 완벽하고 선행사[A park]가 장소명사이므로 장소의 관계부사[where]가 적절하다.
> 해석 많은 사람들이 즐길 한 공원이 내년까지 완공될 것이다.

02 London [(<u>where</u> / when) there are numbers of buildings and people] is one of the best cities in the world.
> → 관계사 뒤에 문장이 완벽하고 선행사[London]가 장소명사이므로 장소의 관계부사[where]가 적절하다.
> 해석 많은 건물과 사람들이 있는 런던은 세계최고의 도시 중의 하나이다.

03 All changed in **October, 1984,** [(where / <u>when</u> / that) NBC-TV showed a five-minute report on the famine].
> → 관계사 뒤에 문장이 완벽하고 선행사[October, 1984]가 시간 명사이므로 시간의 관계부사[when]가 적절하다.
> 해석 모든 것이 NBC-TV가 기근에 관한 5분짜리 기사를 방송했던 1984년 10월에 변했다.

04 We look forward to **the time** [(where / <u>when</u>) the power to love will replace the love of power]. Then will our world know the blessings of peace.
> → 관계사 뒤에 문장이 완벽하고 선행사[the time]가 시간 명사이므로 시간의 관계부사[when]가 적절하다.
> 해석 우리는 사랑의 힘이 권력에 대한 사랑을 대체하게 될 때를 갈망한다. 그때가 되면 우리세상은 평화의 축복을 알게 될 것이다.

05 The Jeju Uprising refers to the incident on **April 3, 1948,** [(where / <u>when</u>) countless Jeju citizens were killed during armed conflict].
> → 관계사 뒤에 문장이 완벽하고 선행사[April 3, 1948]가 시간 명사이므로 시간의 관계부사[when]가 적절하다.
> 해석 제주 4.3 사건은 1948년 4월 3일에 무력 충돌로 인해 수많은 제주도민들이 죽은 사건을 일컫는다.

06 As a result, human ancestors were forced to live near **mountains and hills** [(<u>where</u> / when / which) there were ample sources of food and water].
> → 관계사 뒤에 문장이 완벽하고 선행사[mountains and hills]가 장소명사이므로 장소의 관계부사[where]가 적절하다.
> 해석 그 결과, 인류는 먹을 것과 물이 더 풍부한 산 근처에서 살게 되었다.

07 They sold **the house** [(<u>where</u> / when / who) their parents had lived for 20 years].
> → 관계사 뒤에 문장이 완벽하고 선행사[the house]가 장소명사이므로 장소의 관계부사[where]가 적절하다.
> 해석 그들은 그들의 부모님들이 20년을 살아왔던 집을 팔았다.

08 Following "Falling in Love", the girl group will be releasing a new single every month until **October** [(where / when / which) they will release a new album].

> → 관계사 뒤에 문장이 완벽하고 선행사[October]가 시간 명사이므로 시간의 관계부사[when]가 적절하다.

> 해석 소녀 그룹은 새로운 앨범을 발매 하는 10월까지 "Falling in Love"에 이어서 매달 새로운 싱글 앨범을 발매 할 것이다.

Ⅲ 다음 빈칸에 들어갈 가장 올바른 것을 고르시오.

01 Baseball games are cancelled or delayed when it rains heavily and it is difficult to play baseball during **winter** _____.

> → 관계사 뒤에 문장이 완벽하고 선행사[winter]가 시간 명사이므로 시간의 관계부사[when]가 적절하다.

> 해석 비가 많이 오면 야구 경기는 취소되거나 지연되고 날씨가 춥고 눈이 오는 겨울 동안에는 야구하기가 힘들다.

(a) where the weather is cold and snowy

(b) when the weather is cold and snowy

(c) which the weather is cold and snowy

(d) who the weather is cold and snowy

02 In these days when so many human beings are compelled to live in **enormous cities** _____, that love of nature is more necessary than ever.

> → 관계사 뒤에 문장이 완벽하고 선행사[enormous cities]가 장소명사이므로 장소의 관계부사[where]가 적절하다.

> 해석 너무나 많은 사람들이 자연이 인간보다 위대하다는 사실을 너무 쉽게 잊어버리게 되는 거대한 도시에 살 수 밖에 없는 오늘날에는 자연에 대한 그런 사랑이 어느 때보다 더 필요하다.

(a) which they so easily forget the fact that nature is greater than man

(b) when they so easily forget the fact that nature is greater than man

(c) whom they so easily forget the fact that nature is greater than man

(d) where they so easily forget the fact that nature is greater than man

01 The Korean university, _____, announced Friday that the 35-year-old lawmaker-elect had committed plagiarism in his doctoral thesis.

ⓐ which the 2004 Olympic gold medalist in taekwondo did his doctoral work in 2007

ⓑ who the 2004 Olympic gold medalist in taekwondo did his doctoral work in 2007

ⓒ where the 2004 Olympic gold medalist in taekwondo did his doctoral work in 2007

ⓓ that the 2004 Olympic gold medalist in taekwondo did his doctoral work in 2007

정답 ⓒ

해석 2004년 올림픽 태권도 금메달리스트가 2007년 박사과정을 공부했던 국민대학교는 금요일에 그 35세의 국회의원 당선자는 박사학위 논문을 표절 하였다고 발표하였다.

→ 관계사 뒤에 문장이 완벽하고 선행사[The Korean university]가 장소명사이므로 장소의 관계부사[where]가 적절하다.

02 Roman gladiatorial combat is thought to have originated as **a religious event** _____. The symbolic death of the gladiators was believed to honor the fallen.

ⓐ when was held at funerals

ⓑ who was held at funerals

ⓒ where was held at funerals

ⓓ which was held at funerals

정답 ⓓ

해석 로마 검투사들의 결투는 장례식의 종교 의식에서 유래되었다고 보여 진다. 사람들은 검투사의 상징적인 죽음이 고인을 명예로이 한다고 믿었다.

→ 선행사[a religious event]가 사물이고 뒤에 주어가 없는 불완벽한 문장이다. 따라서 주격 관계대명사[which]가 적절하다.

03 A new study found a doubling of the rate of prescribing antipsychotic drugs to young patients from 2000 to 2007, _____.

ⓐ when some patients had received a proper mental health assessment.

ⓑ which some patients had received a proper mental health assessment.

ⓒ where some patients had received a proper mental health assessment.

ⓓ that some patients had received a proper mental health assessment.

정답 ⓐ

해석 새로운 연구는 2000년에서 2007년까지 나이 어린 환자들에게 처방된 항정신병약의 양이 두 배로 증가했지만 그 환자들 중 40%만이 제대로 된 정신 건강 평가를 받았다는 사실을 발견했다.

→ 관계사 뒤에 문장이 완벽하고 선행사[2000 to 2007]가 시간 명사이므로 시간의 관계부사[when]가 적절하다.

04 The Anglo-Saxons eventually divided their occupied area, 'Engla Land', into **seven kingdoms,** _____.

ⓐ when was eventually united as England in the tenth century

ⓑ whom was eventually united as England in the tenth century

ⓒ that was eventually united as England in the tenth century

ⓓ which was eventually united as England in the tenth century

정답 ⓓ

해석 '앵글라 랜드'를 7개의 왕국으로 분할하였는데, 이들 왕국들은 결국 10세기에 '잉글랜드'로 통일되었다.

→ 선행사[seven kingdoms]가 사물이고 뒤에 주어가 없는 불완벽한 문장이다. 따라서 주격 관계대명사 [which]가 적절하다.

05 Come to 'Neighbors', Vancouver's trendiest new restaurant. Located in the heart of the city center, 'Neighbors' is the place _____.

ⓐ which service is as important as the food we serve

ⓑ where service is as important as the food we serve

ⓒ when service is as important as the food we serve

ⓓ that service is as important as the food we serve

정답 ⓑ

해석 밴쿠버에서 최고로 세련된 새 식당 '네이버스'로 오세요. 도심 한가운데 위치한 '네이버스'는 저희가 제공하는 음식만큼이나 서비스도 중요하게 생각하는 곳입니다.

→ 관계사 뒤에 문장이 완벽하고 선행사[the place]가 장소명사이므로 장소의 관계부사[where]가 적절하다.

06 The greatest annual domestic spending in a household with teenagers is **the expense related to school,** _____.

ⓐ which involves tuition fees, uniforms, books, and other equipment

ⓑ whose involves tuition fees, uniforms, books, and other equipment

ⓒ when involves tuition fees, uniforms, books, and other equipment

ⓓ who involves tuition fees, uniforms, books, and other equipment

정답 ⓐ

해석 십대 자녀를 둔 가정의 연가 지출의 가장 큰 부분을 차지하는 것은 학교관련 비용인데, 학비, 교복, 교재, 기타 기기에 들어가는 비용이 여기에 포함된다.

→ 선행사[the expense related to school]가 사물이고 뒤에 주어가 없는 불완벽한 문장이다. 따라서 주격 관계대명사[which]가 적절하다.

07 People _____ believe that part-time jobs help teenagers become more responsible with money.

ⓐ whom are for teenagers having part-time jobs

ⓑ when are for teenagers having part-time jobs

ⓒ where are for teenagers having part-time jobs

ⓓ who are for teenagers having part-time jobs

해석 청소년들이 파트타임으로 일하는 것에 찬성하는 사람들은 파트타임으로 하는 일이 청소년들이 돈에 대해 책임감을 가질 수 있게 한다고 믿는다.

→ 선행사[People]가 사람이고 뒤에 주어가 없는 불완벽한 문장이다. 따라서 주격 관계대명사[who]가 적절하다.

08 Each of the different theme parks within Lotte World is a whirlwind of excitement, _____.

ⓐ that is going to sweep you off your feet

ⓑ which is going to sweep you off your feet

ⓒ when is going to sweep you off your feet

ⓓ who is going to sweep you off your feet

해석 롯데월드 내에 있는 다양한 테마파크들은 하나하나 모두 즐거움의 소용돌이이며 당신을 즐거움에 푹 빠지게 할 것이다.

→ 선행사[a whirlwind of excitement]가 사물이고 뒤에 주어가 없는 불완벽한 문장이다. 따라서 주격 관계대명사[which]가 적절하다.

09 Before Wegener proposed the Pangaea theory, scientists believed in the existence of **land bridges between America and Africa**, _____.

ⓐ where had since been eroded away.

ⓑ that had since been eroded away.

ⓒ which had since been eroded away.

ⓓ who had since been eroded away.

해석 베게너가 판게아 이론을 제안하기 전의 과학자들은 미국 대륙과 아프리카 대륙을 연결해주는 다리가 존재했다가 후에 침식돼 사라진 것이라고 믿었다.

→ 선행사[land bridges between America and Africa]가 사물이고 뒤에 주어가 없는 불완벽한 문장이다. 따라서 주격 관계대명사[which]가 적절하다.

10 At the theater playing the popular musical Cats, **the people** _____ in an endlessly long line wished they had come sooner to buy their tickets.

ⓐ which are waiting
ⓑ that are waiting
ⓒ whom are waiting
ⓓ where are waiting

정답 ⓑ

해석 인기 뮤지컬 (캐츠)가 공연되는 극장에서 끝없이 긴 줄에서 순서를 기다리는 사람들은 더 일찍 와서 표를 살 걸 하고 후회를 하였다.

→ 선행사[the people]가 사람이고 뒤에 주어가 없는 불완벽한 문장이다. 따라서 선행사가 사람이나 사물 모두 취할 수 있는 관계대명사[that]이 적절하다.

11 The renowned watercolor painting depicts the artist's motherland with **strokes** _____ and reach into our senses so that we, too, can see the things his mind houses.

ⓐ when enliven each image
ⓑ where enliven each image
ⓒ that enliven each image
ⓓ who enliven each image

정답 ⓒ

해석 그 유명한 수채화는 그림 속의 이미지들에 생동감을 불어 넣고 우리의 감각에 닿을 수 있는 붓질로 그 미술가의 조국을 묘사하고 있어서, 우리 또한 그의 마음이 담고 있는 것들을 볼 수 있다.

→ 선행사[strokes]가 사물이고 뒤에 주어가 없는 불완벽한 문장이다. 따라서 선행사가 사람이나 사물 모두 취할 수 있는 관계대명사[that]이 적절하다.

12 After a memorable journey, you will often want to go back to the photos taken along the way for the intensity of **the feelings** _____.

ⓐ where they convey
ⓑ who they convey
ⓒ which they convey
ⓓ whom they convey

정답 ⓒ

해석 잊지 못할 여행이 끝난 후, 당신은 종종 그때 찍었던 사진들을 다시 꺼내어 보면 그 사진들이 전하는 강렬한 감정들을 다시 느끼고 싶어 할 것이다.

→ 선행사[the feelings]가 사물이고 뒤에 목적어가 없는 불완벽한 문장이다. 따라서 목적격 관계대명사[which]가 적절하다.

13 A new term "the Hispanic paradox" was coined because Hispanics have a lower median family income than whites and are less likely than whites to have a college education – **factors** _____.

ⓐ who are generally associated with better health

ⓑ whom are generally associated with better health

ⓒ when are generally associated with better health

ⓓ which are generally associated with better health

해석 라틴 아메리카계 사람들이 일반적으로 더 나은 건강 상태와 관련돼 있는 요인들인 가구당 평균 수입과 대학 교육을 받을 가능성이 백인들 보다 적기 때문에 "히스패닉 파라독스"라는 신조어가 만들어졌다.

→ 선행사[factors]가 사물이고 뒤에 주어가 없는 불완벽한 문장이다. 따라서 주격관계대명사[which]가 적절하다.

14 Since foreclosure practices are similar from bank to bank, analysts now expect other lenders to follow suit and proceed with **a wave of foreclosures** _____.

ⓐ that could further depress the housing market

ⓑ where could further depress the housing market

ⓒ when could further depress the housing market

ⓓ whose could further depress the housing market

정답 ⓐ

해석 담보권행사의 실태는 은행마다 비슷하기 때문에, 분석가들은 이에 따라 다른 대출기관들도 이 선례를 따라 주택시장을 더운 침체시킬 수 있는 대규모의 담보 처분을 대대적으로 추진한다고 현재 예측한다.

→ 선행사[a wave of foreclosures]가 사물이고 뒤에 주어가 없는 불완벽한 문장이다. 따라서 선행사가 사람이나 사물 모두 취할 수 있는 관계대명사[that]이 적절하다.

15 We have no choice but to try to overhaul our daycare system because **the grandparents** _____ now live far away.

ⓐ whose used to be around the corner

ⓑ who used to be around the corner

ⓒ where used to be around the corner

ⓓ whom used to be around the corner

정답 ⓑ

해석 예전에는 가까운 곳에 살던 조부모들께서 지금은 멀리 살고 계시기 때문에, 우리에게는 보육 제도를 철저히 보완하는 것 외에 다른 선택은 없습니다.

→ 선행사[the grandparents]가 사람이고 뒤에 주어가 없는 불완벽한 문장이다. 따라서 주격 관계대명사[who]가 적절하다.

16 The history of the Miss Korea contest goes back to **the late 1950s,** _____ after the Korean War.

ⓐ that Korea was still suffering from hardships

ⓑ when Korea was still suffering from hardships

ⓒ where Korea was still suffering from hardships

ⓓ whom Korea was still suffering from hardships

정답 ⓑ

해석 미스코리아 대회의 역사는 한국이 아직 한국 전쟁으로 인한 고난으로 고통 받고 있던 1950년대 후반으로 거슬러 올라간다.

→ 관계사 뒤에 문장이 완벽하고 선행사[the late 1950s]가 시간 명사이므로 시간의 관계부사[when]가 적절하다.

17 Afterwards, depending on the public's reaction, the playground may be developed by putting more facilities like **benches and equipment** _____.

ⓐ which owners and dogs can use

ⓑ who owners and dogs can use

ⓒ when owners and dogs can use

ⓓ where owners and dogs can use

정답 ⓐ

해석 그 후, 대중들의 반응에 따라 놀이터는 의자 같은 시설과, 반려견들과 견주들이 사용 할 수 있는 용품들을 더 넣으며 발전할 수도 있다

→ 선행사[benches and equipment]가 사물이고 뒤에 목적어가 없는 불완벽한 문장이다. 따라서 목적격 관계대명사[which]가 적절하다.

18 The huge storm striking the Philippines has one confirmed fatality - a man that drowned in a river - and is expected to plunge a day later into **China** _____ from a coastal province.

ⓐ which authorities have evacuated 100,000 people

ⓑ that authorities have evacuated 100,000 people

ⓒ where authorities have evacuated 100,000 people

ⓓ when authorities have evacuated 100,000 people

정답 ⓒ

해석 필리핀을 강타한 거대한 폭풍은 강물에 익사한 한명의 확인된 사망자를 낳았으며, 당국이 해안지방으로부터 10만 명을 대피시킨 중국을 다음날 덮칠 것으로 예상됩니다.

→ 관계사 뒤에 문장이 완벽하고 선행사[China]가 장소 명사이므로 장소의 관계부사[where]가 적절하다.

19 The core early event was Napoleon Bonaparte's 1798 military expedition accompanied by a team of 150 scholars, _____.

ⓐ whose studied and recorded all aspects of Egypt

ⓑ whom studied and recorded all aspects of Egypt

ⓒ who studied and recorded all aspects of Egypt

ⓓ that studied and recorded all aspects of Egypt

정답 ⓒ

해석 핵심적인 초기 사건은 이집트의 모든 측면을 연구하고 기록한 150명의 학자들과 동반한 1798년의 나폴레옹 보나파르트의 군사원정이었다.

→ 선행사[a team of 150 scholars]가 사람이고 뒤에 주어가 없는 불완벽한 문장이다. 따라서 주격 관계대명사[who]가 적절하다.

20 Sign up for a new credit card with HCB Bank and receive up to 1,000 bonus air miles. Note that **customers** _____ are also eligible for lower interest rates.

ⓐ whom sign up for it before July 30

ⓑ where sign up for it before July 30

ⓒ whose sign up for it before July 30

ⓓ who sign up for it before July 30

정답 ⓓ

해석 HCB은행의 신용카드를 만드시고, 최대 1,000포인트의 항공 마일리지를 받으세요. 7월 30일 이전에 가입하시는 분들에게는 더 낮은 이자율이 적용된다는 점을 기억하세요.

→ 선행사[customers]가 사람이고 뒤에 주어가 없는 불완벽한 문장이다. 따라서 주격 관계대명사[who]가 적절하다.

ANSWERS

CHAPTER 4

준동사

EXERCISE

I 괄호 안에서 문법적으로 올바른 것을 고르시오.

01 Would you **mind** (<u>turning</u> / to turn / turned) on the radio?

→ 타동사[mind]는 동명사를 목적어로 취하는 동사이므로 [turning]이 적절하다.

해석 라디오 볼륨을 높여도 되겠습니까?

02 We should **postpone** (<u>deciding</u> / to decide / decided) on the matter until we have more information.

→ 타동사[postpone]는 동명사를 목적어로 취하는 동사이므로 [deciding]이 적절하다.

해석 우리는 충분한 정보를 더 얻을 때까지 우리는 그 문제에 대한 결정을 보류해야 한다.

03 The fringe benefits **prevent** many an employee **from** (to quit / <u>quitting</u> / quit) his or her job.

→ 전치사[from]는 동명사를 목적어로 취하므로 [quitting]이 적절하다.

해석 복지혜택 때문에 많은 직원들이 그들의 직장을 그만두지 않는다.

04 Night owls who sleep in late often miss the opportunity to **go** (having hiked / <u>hiking</u> / to hike) or see a beautiful sunrise.

→ 관용어구[go ~ing (~하러 가다)]로 동명사[hiking]이 적절하다.

해석 늦게까지 자는 밤늦도록 자지 않는 사람들은 종종 하이킹을 가거나 아름다운 일출을 볼 기회를 놓친다.

05 (To make / Having made / <u>Making</u>) **much money** is not the aim of my life but the course.

→ 본주어자리는 동명사[Making]가 적절하다.

해석 많은 돈을 버는 것이 나의 삶의 목표가 아니라 과정이다.

06 The professor **acknowledged** (plagiarize / <u>plagiarizing</u> / to plagiarize) the thesis of someone else.

→ 타동사[acknowledged]는 동명사를 목적어로 취하는 동사이므로 [plagiarizing]이 적절하다.

해석 그 교수는 다른 사람의 논문을 표절한 것을 인정했다.

07 The company said that it wants to **avoid** (<u>encouraging</u> / to encourage / encourage) the killing of endangered elephants.

→ 타동사[avoid]는 동명사를 목적어로 취하는 동사이므로 [encouraging]이 적절하다.

해석 이 기업은 멸종 위기에 처한 코끼리의 살육을 부추기는 것을 피하길 원한다고 말했다.

08 He's a bit of a fool, but I **can't help** (liking / like / to like) him.

> → 관용어구[can't help ~ing (~하지 않을 수 없다)]로 동명사[liking]이 적절하다.

> 해석 그는 약간 모자라지만 나는 그를 좋아하지 않을 수 없다.

Ⅲ 다음 빈칸에 들어갈 가장 올바른 것을 고르시오.

01 Aggressive behavior **involves** _____ your thoughts and feelings and defending your rights in a way that openly violates the rights of others.

> → 타동사[involves]는 동명사를 목적어로 취하는 동사이므로 [expressing]이 적절하다.

> 해석 공격적인 행동은 당신의 생각과 감정을 표현하되 다른 사람들의 권리를 공공연히 침해가지 않은 방식으로 당신의 권리를 방어하는 것을 포함한다.

(a) having expressed   (b) expressing

(c) to be expressing   (d) to express

02 Many teens play games and send messages online, which are activities that don't **require** _____ books.

> → 타동사[require]는 동명사를 목적어로 취하는 동사이므로 [reading]이 적절하다.

> 해석 많은 십대들은 온라인에서 게임을 하고 메시지를 보내는데, 이것은 많은 양의 읽기를 필요로 하지 않는 활동이다.

(a) reading   (b) to read

(c) having read   (d) to be reading

EXERCISE

Ⅰ 괄호 안에서 문법적으로 올바른 것을 고르시오.

01 It no longer seems necessary (graduating / **to graduate** / graduate) **from college to get a job in Korea.**

→ 가주어·진주어 구문에서 진주어는 [to]부정사가 온다. 따라서 [to graduate]이 적절하다.

해석 한국에서 직장을 구하기 위해서는 대학을 졸업하는 것은 더 이상 필수적이지 않은 것 같다.

02 (Buying / To be buying / **To buy**) **a house,** he and his wife tried to save money.

→ 문맥상 부사적 용법의 목적(~하기 위하여)이다. 이 경우 [to]부정사 [To buy]가 적절하다.

해석 집을 사기위해서 그와 그의 아내는 돈을 모으려고 노력했다.

03 According to a legend, a king once placed a heavy stone in the roadway. Then he hid and **waited** (to see / see / having seen) who would remove it.

→ 타동사[wait]는 [to]부정사를 목적어로 취하는 동사이므로 [to see]가 적절하다.

해석 한 전설에 의하면 어떤 왕이 길에 큰 바위를 갖다 놓고 누가 이 바위를 치우나 하고 숨어서 엿보았다고 한다.

04 In a business, efficiency is very important and **allows** companies (to be / being / having been) more competitive.

→ 타동사[allow]는 5형식 구조에서 [to]부정사를 목적보어로 취한다. 따라서 [to be]가 적절하다.

해석 사업에서는 효율성이 아주 중요하고 기업들이 더욱 경쟁력 있게 해준다.

05 The toy company **warns** you (to be keeping / kept / to keep) this toy knife away from children.

→ 타동사[warn]는 5형식 구조에서 [to]부정사를 목적보어로 취한다. 따라서 [to keep]가 적절하다.

해석 그 장난감 회사는 당신에게 이 장난감 칼을 어린이들이 만질 수 없게 하라고 경고한다.

06 Many companies **tend** (hiring / to be hiring / to hire) people who have had previous working experience.

→ 타동사[tend]는 [to]부정사를 목적어로 취하는 동사이므로 [to hire]가 적절하다.

해석 많은 회사들은 예전 근무 경험이 있던 사람들을 고용하는 경향이 있다.

07 North Korea earlier **refused** (discussing / to discuss / to have discussed) a peace or unification agenda.

→ 타동사[refuse]는 [to]부정사를 목적어로 취하는 동사이므로 [to discuss]가 적절하다.

해석 북한은 전에 평화나 통일에 대한 사항을 논의 하는 것을 거부했습니다.

08 They say the South Korean government **needs** (<u>to improve</u> / to improving / improving) living conditions outside of Seoul.

> → 타동사[need]는 [to]부정사를 목적어로 취하는 동사이므로 [to improve]가 적절하다.

> 해석 그들은 한국 정부가 서울 바깥 지역의 생활 조건을 개선할 필요가 있다고 말한다.

Ⅲ 다음 빈칸에 들어갈 가장 올바른 것을 고르시오.

01 The San Francisco board of supervisors voted against Happy Meal and **asked** any other restaurant not _____ toys with a meal that does not meet certain nutritional requirements.

> → 타동사[ask]는 5형식 구조에서 [to]부정사를 목적보어로 취한다. 따라서 [to give away]가 적절하다.

> 해석 샌프란시스코 감리위원회는 해피밀에 반대 투표했고, 그 어떤 음식점도 어떤 영양 요구량을 충족하지 못하는 음식과 함께 장난감을 선물로 나누어 주지 않을 것을 요구했다.

(a) having given away

(b) to giving away

(c) <u>to give away</u>

(d) giving away

02 This removal of both live and dead vegetation reduces the remaining plants' competition for water, sun light, nutrients, and space, **allowing** them _____ stronger.

> → 타동사[ask]는 5형식 구조에서 [to]부정사를 목적보어로 취한다. 따라서 [to grow]가 적절하다.

> 해석 살아있고 죽은 초목의 제거는 물, 햇빛, 영양분, 그리고 공간에 대한 남아 있는 식물들의 경쟁을 줄여서 그들로 하여금 더 강하게 자라게 한다.

(a) growing

(b) to have grown

(c) <u>to grow</u>

(d) having grown

EXERCISE

I 괄호 안에서 문법적으로 올바른 것을 고르시오.

01 We must ask whether genetic information should be collected at all and who should **be able** (seeing / <u>to see</u> / to be seeing) and use it.

> → 관용어구[be able to R (~할 수 있다)]로 [to]부정사 [to see]가 적절하다.
>
> 해석 우리는 유전자 정보가 수집이 되어야 하고 누가 그것을 보고 사용할 수 있는지를 물어야한다.

02 The machine's capabilities are **too numerous** (<u>to list</u> / listing / to have listed) completely.

> → 관용어구[too + 형용사·부사 to R (너무 ~해서 ~할 수 없다)]로 [to]부정사 [to list]가 적절하다.
>
> 해석 그 기계의 기능은 너무나 많아서 완벽하게 열거할 수가 없다.

03 When citizens **are required** (voting / <u>to vote</u> / to be voting), they become more interested in candidates and policies.

> → 타동사[require]의 수동2형식 문장이다. 즉, [be required to R (~해야 하다. ~할 것을 요구받다)]로 [to]부정사 [to vote]가 적절하다.
>
> 해석 국민들이 의무적으로 투표를 해야 한다면, 그들은 후보자들과 정책에 더욱 관심을 가지게 된다.

04 Russell bought **many books** (<u>to read</u> / reading / having read) during his vacation.

> → 문맥상 앞의 명사[many books]를 수식해 주는 형용사적 용법이다. 이 경우 [to]부정사 [To read]가 적절하다.
>
> 해석 러셀은 휴가동안 읽을 책을 많이 구매했다.

05 Please **remember** (<u>to turn off</u> / turning off / turn off) the TV before you go to bed.

> → 타동사[remember]은 [to R]와 동명사를 모두 목적어로 취할 수 있다. 즉, [remember to R (~할 것을 기억하다)]와 [remember ~ing (~했던 것을 기억하다)]이다. 해당문장의 문맥상 '~할 것을 기억하다'로 [to] 부정사 [to turn off]가 적절하다.
>
> 해석 자러가기 전에 TV를 끄는 것을 기억하세요.

06 The world will **be willing** (helped / <u>to help</u> / to be helping / helping) North Korea only when it genuinely tries (<u>to come</u> / coming / to have come) out of isolation.

> → 관용어구[be willing to R (기꺼이 ~하다)]로 [to]부정사 [to help]가 적절하다.
>
> → 타동사[try]는 [to R]와 동명사를 모두 목적어로 취할 수 있다. 즉, [try to R (~하려고 노력하다)]와 [try ~ing (시험 삼아 ~해보다)]이다. 해당문장의 문맥상 '~하려고 노력하다'로 [to] 부정사 [to come]이 적절하다.
>
> 해석 북한이 진정으로 고립에서 나오려고 한다면 세계는 기꺼이 도와줄 것이다.

07 Many people often **forget** (<u>to take</u> / taking / take / to be taking) their documents, clothes and jewelry when they got off the subway train.

> → 타동사[forget]은 [to R]와 동명사를 모두 목적어로 취할 수 있다. 즉, [forget to R (~할 것을 잊다)]와 [forget ~ing (~했던 것을 잊다)]이다. 해당문장의 문맥상 '~할 것을 잊다'로 [to] 부정사 [to take]가 적절하다.
>
> 해석 많은 사람들은 종종 지하철에서 내릴 때 서류, 옷, 보석류들을 챙겨가는 것을 잊는다.

08 Most people believe that all workers should **be allowed** (<u>to protest</u> / protesting / to be protesting) against unfair conditions.

> → 타동사[allow]의 수동2형식 문장이다. 즉, [be allowed to R (~하는 것이 허용되다)]로 [to]부정사 [to protest]가 적절하다.

> 해석 많은 사람들은 모든 노동자들은 부당한 조건에 맞서 항의하는 것이 허용되어야 한다고 믿는다.

Ⅲ 다음 빈칸에 들어갈 가장 올바른 것을 고르시오.

01 More and more Americans are planning to **try** _____ smoking because they are afraid that it may be harmful to their health.

> → 타동사[try]는 [to R]와 동명사를 모두 목적어로 취할 수 있다. 즉, [try to R (~하려고 노력하다)]와 [try ~ing (시험 삼아 ~해보다)]이다. 해당문장의 문맥상 '~하려고 노력하다'로 [to] 부정사 [to stop]이 적절하다.

> 해석 점점 더 많은 미국인들이 담배 피는 것을 끊으려는 계획을 하고 있다. 왜냐하면 흡연이 건강에 해로울 것이라는 우려하기 때문이다.

(a) having stopped   (b) stopping

(c) to be stopping   (d) <u>to stop</u>

02 Lottery fever has hit the United States, and more and more states are beginning to use lotteries as a means of raising revenue. On the surface this seems **an easy way** _____ money.

> → 문맥상 앞의 명사[an easy way]를 수식해 주는 형용사적 용법이다. 이 경우 [to]부정사 [To raise]가 적절하다.

> 해석 복권 추첨 열기가 미국을 강타하고 있고 점점 더 많은 미국의 주에서 세입을 늘리는 수단으로 복권을 이용하기 시작하고 있다. 겉보기에 이것은 돈을 늘리는 손쉬운 방법처럼 보일 수 있다.

(a) <u>to raise</u>   (b) to have raised

(c) raising   (d) being raising

01 City planners **have been asked** _____ a series of neighborhood forums that community leaders believe will increase public support for the new traffic corridor.

ⓐ initiating
ⓑ to initiate
ⓒ to be initiating
ⓓ initiated

〔 정답 〕 ⓑ

〔 해석 〕 도시 계획자들은 지역사회 지도자들이 새로운 교통 경로에 대한 대중의 지지를 높일 것이라고 믿는 일련의 주민 토론회를 시작할 것을 요구받았다.

→ 타동사[ask]의 수동2형식 문장이다. 즉, [be asked to R (~하는 것이 요구되다)]로 [to]부정사 [to initiate]가 적절하다.

02 The Louvre Museum in Paris added extra security to protect the Mona Lisa after someone **tried** _____ the priceless painting.

ⓐ to be damaging
ⓑ damaging
ⓒ being damaging
ⓓ to damage

〔 정답 〕 ⓓ

〔 해석 〕 파리의 루브르 박물관은 누군가가 귀중한 그림을 훼손하려한 이후에 모나리자를 보호하기 위한 추가적인 보안조치를 취했다.

→ 타동사[try]는 [to R]와 동명사를 모두 목적어로 취할 수 있다. 즉, [try to R (~하려고 노력하다)]와 [try ~ing (시험 삼아 ~해보다)]이다. 해당문장의 문맥상 '~하려고 노력하다'로 [to] 부정사 [to damage]가 적절하다.

03 After performing at three concerts in Chicago, we allowed the members of the school band some time off so that they could **go** _____.

ⓐ sightsee
ⓑ to sightsee
ⓒ having sightseen
ⓓ sightseeing

〔 정답 〕 ⓓ

〔 해석 〕 시카고에서 세 번의 공연을 하고 난 뒤, 우리는 학교 밴드 멤버들이 관광을 하러 갈 수 있도록 휴식 시간을 주었다.

→ 관용어구[go ~ing (~하러 가다)]로 동명사 [sightseeing]이 적절하다.

04 _____worried, anxious, and nervous is a normal part of everyday life. Everyone has concerns or feels anxious from time to time.

ⓐ To feel
ⓑ Being feeling
ⓒ Feeling
ⓓ Felt

정답 ⓒ

해석 걱정스럽고 불안하고 긴장을 느끼는 것은 일상생활의 정상적인 한 부분이다. 누구나 때때로 걱정을 하거나 불안해한다.

→ 본주어자리는 동명사[Feeling]이 적절하다.

05 Central to the development of natural philosophy was the recovery of classical authors, most importantly the work of Aristotle. Humanists quickly realized the power of the printing press **for** _____ their knowledge.

ⓐ to spread
ⓑ to be spreading
ⓒ spreading
ⓓ having spread

정답 ⓒ

해석 자연철학의 발전에 중심에는 고전 작가들의 복원, 가장 중요한 것은 아리스토텔레스의 작품의 복원이었다. 인문학자들은 자신들의 지식을 퍼뜨리는 인쇄기의 힘을 빠르게 인식했다

→ 전치사[for]는 동명사를 목적어로 취하므로 [spreading]이 적절하다.

06 When he was young, Bradbury **enjoyed** _____ books by fantasy writer Edgar Allen Poe, which influenced his later writing.

ⓐ to have read
ⓑ reading
ⓒ to read
ⓓ having read

정답 ⓑ

해석 브래드 버리는 어릴 적 환상소설 작가인 에드가 엘런 포가 쓴 책들을 즐겨 읽었는데, 이는 그의 이후 소설에 영향을 줬다.

→ 타동사[enjoy]는 동명사를 목적어로 취하는 동사이므로 [reading]이 적절하다.

07 Is there a simple way of easing the stress of driving? According to a new study, there is. The researchers noted that _____ **to music while driving** helps relieve the stress that affects heart health.

ⓐ listening
ⓑ listens
ⓒ to listen
ⓓ having listened

정답 ⓐ

해석 운전의 스트레스를 덜어줄 간단한 방법이 있을까? 새로운 연구에 따르면, 있다. 연구원들은 운전하면서 음악을 듣는 것이 심장 건강에 영향을 미치는 스트레스를 덜어주는 데 도움이 된다고 말했다.

→ 본주어자리는 동명사[listening]이 적절하다. 참고로 해당문장은 동사[noted]의 목적절내의 본주어 자리이다.

08 The protests became known as Fridays for Future. Since Thunberg began her protests, more than 60 countries **have promised** _____ their carbon footprints by 2050.

ⓐ eliminating
ⓑ to eliminate
ⓒ to be eliminating
ⓓ eliminate

정답 ⓑ

해석 이 시위는 '미래를 위한 금요일'로 알려지게 되었다. 툰버그가 항의를 시작한 이후 60여 개국이 2050년까지 탄소 발자국 (온실 효과를 유발하는 이산화탄소의 배출량)을 없애겠다고 약속했다

→ 타동사[promise]는 [to]부정사를 목적어로 취하는 동사이므로 [to eliminate]가 적절하다.

09 Distinguishing between effectiveness and efficiency is much more than an exercise in semantics. Effectiveness **entails** _____ a stated objective.

ⓐ promptly to achieve
ⓑ promptly achieving
ⓒ promptly to have achieved
ⓓ promptly achieved

정답 ⓑ

해석 효과성과 효율성사이를 구별하는 것은 의미론에서 연습이상의 것이다. 이 두 용어들 사이의 관계는 중요하고 그것은 경영자들에게 끊임없는 딜레마를 제공한다. 효과성은 언급된 목적을 즉시 이루어내는 것을 함의한다.

→ 타동사[entail]는 명사를 목적어로 취하는 동사이므로 [promptly achieving]이 적절하다.

10 Loneliness and lack of self-esteem are among the most obvious conditions which can be alleviated **by** _____ with an animal friend.

ⓐ living
ⓑ to live
ⓒ having lived
ⓓ to have lived

정답 ⓐ

해석 외로움과 자존감 부족은 반려동물과 함께 생활함으로써 완화될 수 있는 가장 확실한 질환에 속한다.

→ 전치사[by]는 동명사를 목적어로 취하므로 [living]이 적절하다.

---

11 _____ responsibility to those you trust can not only make your organization run more smoothly but also free up more of your time so you can focus on larger issues.

ⓐ Giving away
ⓑ To give away
ⓒ Having given away
ⓓ To be giving away

정답 ⓐ

해석 신뢰하는 사람들에게 책임을 넘겨주는 것은 당신의 조직을 더 원활하게 운영되게 할 뿐 아니라, 더 많은 당신의 시간을 자유롭게 해주면서 더 중요한 문제에 집중할 수 있도록 해준다.

→ 본주어자리는 동명사[Giving away]이 적절하다.

---

12 Through the ages, industrious individuals have continuously created **conveniences** _____ life easier. From the Invention of the wheel to the light bulb, inventions have propelled society forward.

ⓐ making
ⓑ to be making
ⓒ to make
ⓓ makes

정답 ⓒ

해석 모든 시대를 통틀어 부지런한 사람들은 삶을 더 쉽게 만드는 편리한 것들을 계속해서 만들어왔다. 바퀴의 발명에서부터 백열전구에 이르기까지, 발명품은 사회를 앞으로 나아가게 했다.

→ 문맥상 앞의 명사[conveniences]를 수식해 주는 형용사적 용법이다. 이 경우 [to]부정사 [To make]가 적절하다.

13 If you get sick yourself, keep your towels and dishes separate from everyone else's. **Try** _____ things that belong to others. Don't touch other people, and don't shake hands.

ⓐ not having touched

ⓑ not to touch

ⓒ not touching

ⓓ not to be touched

해석 만약 당신이 아프다면, 수건과 식기들을 다른 사람들과 따로 사용하라. 다른 사람들의 물건들을 만지지 말도록 해라. 다른 사람들과 접촉하지 말고, 악수하지 않도록 노력해라.

→ 타동사[try]는 [to R]와 동명사를 모두 목적어로 취할 수 있다. 즉, [try to R (~하려고 노력하다)]와 [try ~ing (시험 삼아 ~해보다)]이다. 해당문장의 문맥상 '~하려고 노력하다'로 [to] 부정사 [not to touch]가 적절하다.

14 As of 2012, the Paralympic Games included events in more than 20 different sports, some of which **allowed** athletes _____ wheelchairs during competition.

ⓐ being used

ⓑ used

ⓒ to use

ⓓ to be using

해석 2012년부터 세계장애인 올림픽 경기는 20여개 이상의 다양한 경기가 포함되었고 몇몇은 운동선수로 하여금 경기 중 휠체어를 사용하는 것을 허용한다.

→ 타동사[allow]는 5형식 구조에서 [to]부정사를 목적보어로 취한다. 따라서 [to use]가 적절하다.

15 Based on the updated airline policy, now passengers must **remember** _____ before a flight because food and drinks are not allowed onboard a plane.

ⓐ eating

ⓑ to eat

ⓒ being eating

ⓓ to have eaten

해석 새로운 항공사 정책에 근거하여. 이제는 승객들은 비행기에 탑승 중에는 음식이나 음료가 허용되지 않기 때문에 항공 여행 전에 먹어야 하는 것을 기억해야 한다.

→ 타동사[remember]은 [to R]와 동명사를 모두 목적어로 취할 수 있다. 즉, [remember to R (~할 것을 기억하다)]와 [remember ~ing (~했던 것을 기억하다)]이다. 해당문장의 문맥상 '~할 것을 기억하다'로 [to]부정사 [to eat]가 적절하다.

16 You respect the people with whom you're speaking and **are authentically willing** _____ them courteously even if you disagree with their positions.

ⓐ treating
ⓑ to treat
ⓒ to treating
ⓓ treat

정답 ⓑ

해석 당신은 당신이 이야기 하고 있는 사람들을 존중하고 비록 당신이 그들의 입장에 동의하지 않더라도 진정으로 그들을 예의바르게 대하려고 한다.

→ 관용어구[be willing to R (기꺼이 ~하다)]로 [to]부정사 [to treat]가 적절하다.

17 *Natural Gas World* subscribers will receive accurate and reliable key facts and figures about what is going on in the industry, so they **are fully able** _____ what concerns their business.

ⓐ having discerned
ⓑ discerns
ⓒ discerning
ⓓ to discern

정답 ⓓ

해석 Natural Gas World 구독자들은 그 산업에서 어떤 일이 벌어지고 있는 지에 관한 정확하고 신뢰할 수 있는 주요 사실들과 수치들을 받게 될 것이다. 따라서 그들은 자신의 사업에 관련된 것들을 완전히 식별할 수 있다.

→ 관용어구[be able to R (~할 수 있다)]로 [to]부정사 [to discern]가 적절하다.

18 Have you ever tried to catch a fish under water and missed? We **tend** _____ of our line of sight as a straight line, but light bends due to refraction at the air-water surface.

ⓐ thinking
ⓑ to think
ⓒ to be thinking
ⓓ thought

정답 ⓑ

해석 당신은 물속의 물고기를 잡으려 했으나 놓친 적이 있습니까? 우리는 우리의 시선을 직선이라고 생각하는 경향이 있지만 공기와 물이 만나는 표면에서의 굴절 때문에 빛은 구부러진다. 당신이 굴절을 고려하지 않는다면 물고기는 당신이 생각하는 곳에 있지 않다.

→ 타동사[tend]는 [to]부정사를 목적어로 취하는 동사이므로 [to think]가 적절하다.

19 The defense chief **proposed** _____ defense ministerial talks between the two countries every year instead of every two years and holding working-level talks twice a year.

ⓐ to hold
ⓑ holding
ⓒ having held
ⓓ held

정답 ⓑ

해석 국방부 장관은 양국 간 장관급 국방 회담을 내 2년마다가 아닌 매년 개최하고 실무자급 회의는 일 년에 두 차례 열 것을 제안했다.

→ 타동사[propose]는 동명사를 목적어로 취하는 동사이므로 [holding]이 적절하다.

20 Globalization leads more countries to open their markets, allowing them _____ goods and services freely at a lower cost with greater efficiency.

ⓐ trading
ⓑ to be trading
ⓒ to trade
ⓓ having traded

정답 ⓒ

해석 세계화는 더 많은 국가들이 그들의 시장을 개방하도록 유도한다, 그리고 그들이 상품과 서비스를 더 큰 효율성과 더 낮은 비용으로 자유롭게 거래하도록 한다.

→ 타동사[allow]는 5형식 구조에서 [to]부정사를 목적보어로 취한다. 따라서 [to trade]가 적절하다.

MEMO

ANSWERS

CHAPTER

5

조동사

EXERCISE

■ 괄호 안에서 문법적으로 올바른 것을 고르시오.

01 Russell has been in quite a few countries. He (<u>can</u> / will / might) speak three languages.

> **→** 문맥상 능력이므로 [can(~할 수 있다)]가 적절하다.
>
> **해석** 러셀은 적지 않은 나라에서 살았다. 그는 3개 국어를 할 수 있다.

02 I am looking for Bella. I think she (<u>might</u> / can / will) be watching TV in her room.

> **→** 문맥상 추측이므로 [might(~일지도 모른다)]가 적절하다.
>
> **해석** 나는 벨라를 찾고 있다. 나는 그녀가 그녀의 방에서 TV를 보고 있을 지도 모른다고 생각한다.

03 My grandmother loved music. She (<u>could</u> / may / will) play the violin very well then.

> **→** 문맥상 과거의 능력이므로 [could(~할 수 있었다)]가 적절하다.
>
> **해석** 나의 할머니는 음악을 좋아하셨다. 그 당시에는 그녀는 바이올린을 아주 잘 연주할 수 있었다.

04 Jack says that we (<u>can</u> / will / must / shall) borrow his houses as long as we leave it clean and tidy.

> **→** 문맥상 허가이므로 [can(~해도 된다)]가 적절하다.
>
> **해석** 잭은 우리가 집을 깨끗하고 단정하게 유지한다면 그의 집을 빌려도 된다고 말한다.

05 Unmarried and highly paid, they (may / <u>can</u> / might / must) afford to spend money on luxury brand goods.

> **→** 문맥상 능력이므로 [can(~할 수 있다)]가 적절하다.
>
> **해석** 미혼이면서 고액 연봉을 받기 때문에 그들은 사치품에 사는 데 돈을 쓸 수 있다.

06 An adult (<u>might</u> / shall / would) need a translator to understand what they are talking about.

> **→** 문맥상 추측이므로 [might(~일지도 모른다)]가 적절하다.
>
> **해석** 어른들은 아이들이 무엇에 대해 얘기하는지 이해하기 위해 번역사가 필요할 지도 모른다.

07 Currently citizens (<u>may</u> / would / will) visit the museum from 9 a.m. to 6 p.m. excluding Mondays.

> **→** 문맥상 허가이므로 [may(~해도 된다)]가 적절하다.
>
> **해석** 현재 시민들은 월요일을 제외한 아침 9시부터 저녁 6시까지 그 박물관을 방문해도 된다.

08 When Jack gets a job, I (<u>might</u> / must / will) get the money back that I lent him but I am not sure.

> → 문맥상 추측이므로 [might(~일지도 모른다)]가 적절하다.

> 해석 잭이 직장을 얻었을 때, 빌려줬던 돈을 받을 수 있을지도 모른다. 그러나 확신할 수는 없다.

Ⅲ 다음 빈칸에 들어갈 가장 올바른 것을 고르시오.

01 Many people worry that the next generation _____ respond wisely when others maliciously try to distort our history.

> → 문맥상 추측이므로 [may(~일지도 모른다)]가 적절하다.

> 해석 많은 사람들은 다른 이들이 악의적으로 우리의 역사를 왜곡시키려 할 때 다음 세대들이 현명하게 대처할 수 없을 수도 있다는 것에 대해 우려한다.

(a) shall not   (b) should not

(c) <u>may not</u>   (d) will not

02 When the weather is nice, all the roofs will stay opened so that spectators _____ enjoy the nice weather.

> → 문맥상 능력이므로 [can(~할 수 있다)]가 적절하다.

> 해석 날씨가 좋으면, 관중들이 좋은 날씨를 즐길 수 있도록 모든 지붕들을 계속 열어놓을 수 있다.

(a) might   (b) <u>can</u>

(c) must   (d) would

EXERCISE

Ⅰ 괄호 안에서 문법적으로 올바른 것을 고르시오.

01 I am too tired to walk home. I think I (will / shall / may) take a taxi.

→ 문맥상 주어의 의지이므로 [will(~할 것이다)]가 적절하다.

해석 나는 너무 피곤해서 집에 걸어갈 수 없다. 나는 택시를 타고 가야겠다.

02 To get there on time, we (will / must / might) leave home by 8, 30.

→ 문맥상 강한의무이므로 [must(반드시 ~해야 한다)]가 적절하다.

해석 정각에 그곳에 도착하기 위해서는 우리는 8시 30분까지 집을 떠나야 한다.

03 Bella needs a change. She (should / will / may) go away for a few days.

→ 문맥상 조언, 충고이므로 [should(~하는 것이 좋다, 해야 한다)]가 적절하다.

해석 벨라는 기분전환이 필요하다. 그녀는 몇 일간 여행을 가는 것이 좋다.

04 Russell (will / ought to / shall) give her another opportunity to get the suitable job.

→ 문맥상 주어의 의지이므로 [will(~할 것이다)]가 적절하다.

해석 러셀은 적당한 직업을 얻을 수 있는 또 다른 기회를 그녀에게 줄 것이다.

05 We (must / will / could) do something dramatic if we want to save ourselves from going under.

→ 문맥상 강한의무이므로 [must(반드시 ~해야 한다)]가 적절하다.

해석 만약에 우리가 파산하지 않으려면, 우리는 극적인 무엇인가를 해야 한다.

06 In order to avoid such heartburn or indigestion, one (should / will / shall) try to eat regularly and slowly.

→ 문맥상 조언, 충고이므로 [should(~하는 것이 좋다, 해야 한다)]가 적절하다.

해석 속쓰림이나 소화불량을 피하기 위해서 음식을 규칙적으로 천천히 식사하는 습관을 가지도록 노력해야 한다.

07 That man on the motorcycle isn't wearing a helmet. That's dangerous. He (should / will / may) be wearing a helmet.

→ 문맥상 의무이므로 [should (~해야 한다)]가 적절하다.

해석 오토바이를 타고 있는 저 남자는 헬멧을 쓰고 있지 않다. 그것은 위험하다. 그는 헬멧을 써야 한다.

08 Since there are a lot of people using smart phones and tablet PCs, webcomics (can / will / should) continue to increase in popularity.

→ 문맥상 미래이므로 [will(~할 것이다)]가 적절하다.

해석 스마트폰과 태블릿PC를 사용 하는 사람이 많기 때문에 웹툰의 인기는 계속해서 상승할 것이다.

🏛 다음 빈칸에 들어갈 가장 올바른 것을 고르시오.

01 For the better society, the government _____ focus on things like making more bicycle roads, putting up more lights, etc.

> **→** 문맥상 의무이므로 [should (~해야 한다)]가 적절하다.

> **해석** 더 나은 사회를 위해서 정부는 더 많은 자전거 도로를 만들고, 더 많은 등을 세우는 것과 같은 일들에 집중을 해야 한다.

(a) could

(b) should

(c) would

(d) may

02 In order to use the playground, a dog _____ have an identification tag with the owner's contact information and the owner is responsible for cleaning up the dog's waste.

> **→** 문맥상 강한의무이므로 [must(반드시 ~해야 한다)]가 적절하다.

> **해석** 운동장을 이용하기 위해선, 개는 주인의 연락처가 있는 인식표가 있어야 하며 견주는 개의 배설물을 치워야 하는 책임이 있다.

(a) must

(b) can

(c) will

(d) shall

EXERCISE

I 괄호 안에서 문법적으로 올바른 것을 고르시오.

01 As we become more electronically dependent, it is **crucial** that we (have / will have / had) the ability to feel that our information is safe.

→ 이성적 판단형용사[crucial (중요한)]의 진주어는 당위절로 항상 동사원형으로 나타내야 한다. 따라서 [have]가 적절하다.

해석 우리가 더 전자적으로 의존함에 따라, 점점 더 늘어날수록 우리의 정보가 안전하다고 생각하는 능력을 지니는 건 아주 중요하다.

02 It is **necessary** that an employee (finishes / finish) his work on time.

→ 이성적 판단형용사[necessary(필수적인)]의 진주어는 당위절로 항상 동사원형으로 나타내야 한다. 따라서 [finish]가 적절하다.

해석 직원이 제시간에 그의 일을 마치는 것은 필수적이다.

03 It is **imperative** that the CEO (understand / understands) the present conditions.

→ 이성적 판단형용사[imperative (필수적인)]의 진주어는 당위절로 항상 동사원형으로 나타내야 한다. 따라서 [understand]가 적절하다.

해석 CEO가 현재의 상황을 이해해야하는 것은 필수적이다.

04 The nurses **asked** that the hospital (not be / was not / won't be) closed.

→ 당위동사[ask (요구하다)]의 목적절은 당위절로 해당절에 동사를 반드시 동사원형으로 나타내야 한다. 따라서 [not be]가 적절하다.

해석 간호사들은 병원이 폐쇄되면 안 된다고 요구했다

05 The airline recommended we (be / were / has been) at the airport two hours before our flight.

→ 당위동사[recommend (권장하다)]의 목적절은 당위절로 해당절에 동사를 반드시 동사원형으로 나타내야 한다. 따라서 [be]가 적절하다.

해석 항공사는 우리가 비행기가 출발하기 두 시간 전에는 공항에 도착하는 것을 권장했다.

06 It is **vital** that every runner (is drinking / drink / drinks) water during the marathon.

→ 이성적 판단형용사[vital (중요한)]의 진주어는 당위절로 항상 동사원형으로 나타내야 한다. 따라서 [drink]가 적절하다.

해석 모든 경주자는 마라톤 하는 동안에 물을 마시는 것은 중요하다.

07 I forgot my daughter's birthday last year, so it is really **important** that I (will remember / remember / has remembered) it this year.

→ 이성적 판단형용사[important (중요한)]의 진주어는 당위절로 항상 동사원형으로 나타내야 한다. 따라서 [lose]가 적절하다.

해석 나는 삭년에 나의 딸이 생일을 잊었다. 그래서 올해에는 그것을 기억하는 것은 정말 중요하다.

08 It is **important** that Russell (<u>lose</u> / lost / has lost / loses) weight for better health.

> → 이성적 판단형용사[important (중요한)]의 진주어는 당위절로 항상 동사원형으로 나타내야 한다. 따라서 [lose]가 적절하다.

> 해석 러셀은 더 나은 건강을 위해서 살을 빼야하는 것이 중요하다.

09 The police **ordered** that all weapons (will be / <u>be</u> / were) handed in immediately.

> → 당위동사[order (명령하다)]의 목적절은 당위절로 해당절에 동사를 반드시 동사원형으로 나타내야 한다. 따라서 [be]가 적절하다.

> 해석 경찰은 모든 무기는 즉시 제출되어야 한다고 명령했다.

10 We **insisted** that the money (is / was / has been / <u>be</u>) available to all students in financial difficulties.

> → 당위동사[insist (주장하다)]의 목적절은 당위절로 해당절에 동사를 반드시 동사원형으로 나타내야 한다. 따라서 [be]가 적절하다.

> 해석 우리는 그 돈은 재정적 위기에 처한 모든 학생들에게 이용 가능해야 한다고 주장했다.

Ⅲ 다음 빈칸에 들어갈 가장 올바른 것을 고르시오.

01 They **advised** that investors carefully _____ the current situation of the market before making any hasty investment decisions.

> → 당위동사[advise (권하다, 충고하다)]의 목적절은 당위절로 해당절에 동사를 반드시 동사원형으로 나타내야 한다. 따라서 [watch]가 적절하다.

> 해석 그들은 성급한 투자 결정을 내리기 전에 투자자들이 시장 상황을 면밀히 살펴볼 것을 권하고 있다.

(a) will watch   (b) are watching

(c) watched   (d) <u>watch</u>

02 The members of the board strongly **recommend** that Russell _____ on the duties of CEO until a permanent replacement can be found.

> → 당위동사[recommend (권장하다)]의 목적절은 당위절로 해당절에 동사를 반드시 동사원형으로 나타내야 한다. 따라서 [take]가 적절하다.

> 해석 이사진들은 러셀이 정식 후임자를 찾을 때까지 최고경영자의 책무를 맡아야 한다고 강력히 권고한다.

(a) <u>take</u>   (b) will take

(c) has taken   (d) takes

01 The management team **asked** that all shipments _____ until inventories subsides to manageable levels.

ⓐ are suspended
ⓑ be suspended
ⓒ will be suspended
ⓓ have been suspended

정답 ⓑ

해석 경영진은 재고가 어느 정도 줄어들 때까지 모든 출하를 보류해 줄 것을 요청했다.

→ 당위동사[ask (요구하다)]의 목적절은 당위절로 해당절에 동사를 반드시 동사원형으로 나타내야 한다. 따라서 [be suspended]가 적절하다.

02 Even under devastating circumstances, we _____ make our lives more pleasant by paying attention to simple amenities, such as being polite to others.

ⓐ might
ⓑ can
ⓒ will
ⓓ shall

정답 ⓑ

해석 힘든 상황에서조차도 다른 사람들에게 예의 바르게 행동하는 것과 같은 간단한 예절에 관심을 기울이면 삶을 좀 더 즐겁게 만들 수 있다.

→ 문맥상 능력이므로 [can(~할 수 있다)]가 적절하다.

03 The company has been prospering by selling environment-friendly products which helps make us safe. It _____ be profit-oriented, but it plays an important role in helping conserve the environment.

ⓐ will
ⓑ would
ⓒ must
ⓓ may

정답 ⓓ

해석 그 기업은 우리를 안전하게 하는데 도움을 주는 환경 친화적인 상품을 판매함으로써 번영해왔다. 그 기업은 이윤을 지향하는지는 모르겠지만 환경보호를 돕는데 중요한 역할을 한다.

→ 문맥상 추측이므로 [may(~일지도 모른다)]가 적절하다.

04 Some experts **insist** that expectations of growth and the models of growth in FinTech _____ a bit unrealistic, due mostly to demographics and the nature of money.

ⓐ have been
ⓑ be
ⓒ are
ⓓ would be

해석 일부 전문가들은 대게 인구 통계와 돈의 성질 때문에 핀테크가 성장할 기대와 성장모델이 약간은 비현실적이라고 주장한다.

→ 당위동사[insist (주장하다)]의 목적절은 당위절로 해당절에 동사를 반드시 동사원형으로 나타내야 한다. 따라서 [be]가 적절하다.

05 It **is recommended** that all the transactions involving the property _____ subject to the written approval of the committee.

ⓐ were
ⓑ will be
ⓒ be
ⓓ had been

해석 자산에 관련된 모든 거래는 위원회의 서면 승인을 받아야 하도록 권고되었다.

→ 당위동사[recommend (권고하다)]의 수동태 구문이다. 이 경우에도 진주어는 당위절로 해당절에 동사를 반드시 동사원형으로 나타내야 한다. 따라서 [be]가 적절하다.

06 It is **imperative** that the science communities in the 3rd worlds _____ systematized ways of amassing knowledge.

ⓐ will make
ⓑ have made
ⓒ make
ⓓ are making

해석 제 3세계의 과학 공동체는 지식을 축적하는 체계적인 방법을 만드는 것이 필수적이다.

→ 이성적 판단형용사[imperative (필수적인)]의 진주어는 당위절로 항상 동사원형으로 나타내야 한다. 따라서 [make]가 적절하다.

07 Air Force officials believed that bad weather, mechanical problems of the ageing aircraft or pilots' suffering from vertigo _____ have led to the accidents.

ⓐ must
ⓑ should
ⓒ might
ⓓ can

정답 ⓒ

해석 공군 관계자는 악천후와 노후 항공기의 기계적 결함 또는 조종사의 현기증이 사고로 이어졌을 것으로 믿고 있다.

→ 문맥상 추측이므로 [might(~일지도 모른다)]가 적절하다.

---

08 To protect computers from malware, anti-virus programs _____ be installed and scheduled regularly to clean the computer and check for malware.

ⓐ would
ⓑ should
ⓒ will
ⓓ might

정답 ⓑ

해석 악성코드로부터 컴퓨터를 보호하기 위해 사람들은 백신 프로그램을 설치하여 해야 하고 악성코드를 검사하고 컴퓨터를 깨끗 하게하기 위해 정기적으로 이 백신 프로그램을 실행해야 한다.

→ 문맥상 의무이므로 [should(~해야 하다)]가 적절하다.

---

09 Farmers' interest groups like the Korean Advanced Farmers Federation *have been proposing* that the government _____ further protective measures against a wider rice market opening.

ⓐ has offered
ⓑ offer
ⓒ offers
ⓓ is offering

정답 ⓑ

해석 한국농업경영인중앙연합회와 같은 농민 이익단체들은 정부가 쌀시장 개방 확대에 대해 추가적인 보호대책을 제시할 것을 제의해 왔다.

→ 당위동사[propose (제의하다)]의 목적절은 당위절로 해당절에 동사를 반드시 동사원형으로 나타내야 한다. 따라서 [offer]가 적절하다.

10 South Korea yesterday denied outright that the United States **had requested** that the Seoul government _____ a crackdown against illegal financial activities by North Korea.

ⓐ join
ⓑ is joining
ⓒ will join
ⓓ joined

해석 한국은 어제 미국정부가 북한에 의한 불법적인 금융거래 단속에 함께 해 줄 것을 요구했다는 것은 단도직입적으로 부인했다.

→ 당위동사[request (요구하다)]의 목적절은 당위절로 해당절에 동사를 반드시 동사원형으로 나타내야 한다. 따라서 [join]이 적절하다.

11 Real fans must support celebrities through good times and bad times, and everyone _____ remember that they give us the gift of entertainment.

ⓐ can
ⓑ may
ⓒ will
ⓓ must

정답 ⓓ

해석 진정한 팬은 좋을 때건 나쁠 때건 그들을 지지해야 하며, 모든 사람은 그들이 우리에게 오락이라는 선물을 준다는 사실을 잊지 말아야 한다.

→ 문맥상 강한의무이므로 [must(반드시 ~해야 한다)]가 적절하다.

12 Despite the city's denial, the ruling party **demanded** that the mayor _____ a public apology for his remarks last Friday.

ⓐ offered
ⓑ has offered
ⓒ is offering
ⓓ offer

정답 ⓓ

해석 그 도시의 부인에도 불구하고, 지난 금요일에 여당은 시장이 자신의 발언에 대해 공식 사과할 것을 요구했다.

→ 당위동사[demand (요구하다)]의 목적절은 당위절로 해당절에 동사를 반드시 동사원형으로 나타내야 한다. 따라서 [offer]가 적절하다.

13 A researcher at Samsung Economic Research Institute **suggested** that Korea _____ on strengthening its R&D environment to attract investors.

ⓐ is focusing
ⓑ focus
ⓒ has focused
ⓓ would focus

14 Unlike teenagers who receive money from their parents, teenagers who have part-time jobs ____ save money and use it more responsibly.

ⓐ ought to
ⓑ shall
ⓒ will
ⓓ should

15 A change in the value of the 10,000 won bill, the highest-denomination banknote in the nation, shows that it is necessary that 100,000 won bills _____.

ⓐ have been issued
ⓑ will be issued
ⓒ are issued
ⓓ be issued

16 Because Asian economies have succeeded on the strength of an open international economy, it is important that they now _____ to further expand the global economic system.

ⓐ contribute
ⓑ contributed
ⓒ are contributing
ⓓ may contribute

[정답] ⓐ

[해석] 아시아 국가들은 개방적 국제경제에 힘입어 성공했기 때문에 이제는 세계경제 시스템이 더욱 확대되도록 기여하는 것이 중요하다.

[→] 이성적 판단형용사[important (중요한)]의 진주어는 당위절로 항상 동사원형으로 나타내야 한다. 따라서 [contribute]가 적절하다.

17 The medical specialists diagnosed her with a severe form of fear of emotional attachment and **recommended** that they _____ her in a separate house and stop further contact.

ⓐ are placing
ⓑ have placed
ⓒ place
ⓓ would place

[정답] ⓒ

[해석] 그 의학 전문가들은 그녀를 감정적 애착에 대한 심각한 형태의 두려움으로 진단했으며, 그녀를 분리된 집에 있게 하고, 추가적인 접촉을 중단하라고 권고했다.

[→] 당위동사[recommend (권고하다)]의 목적절은 당위절로 해당절에 동사를 반드시 동사원형으로 나타내야 한다. 따라서 [place]가 적절하다.

18 An official that if a wild boar is encountered, it is **best** that you _____ back from it and added the animals usually become aggressive when disturbed.

ⓐ stepped
ⓑ are stepping
ⓒ step
ⓓ have stepped

[정답] ⓒ

[해석] 한 관계자는 멧돼지와 우연히 마주치게 되면 당신은 그것에서 물러나는 것이 최고라고 말했고, 동물들은 괴롭힘을 당하면 더 공격적이 된다고 덧붙였다.

[→] 이성적 판단형용사[best (최고인)]의 진주어는 당위절로 항상 동사원형으로 나타내야 한다. 따라서 [step]가 적절하다.

19 Our puppy, Rocky, had finally come back home. He has been missing for over two weeks. We are still wondering where he _____ have been during his absence.

ⓐ can
ⓑ might
ⓒ will
ⓓ should

정답 ⓑ

해석 우리 강아지 록키가 마침내 집으로 돌아왔다. 그는 2주 넘게 실종되었다. 우리는 여전히 록키가 없어진 동안 어디에 있었는지 궁금해 하고 있다.

→ 문맥상 과거이 추측이므로 [might have pp (~였을지도 모른다.)]가 적절하다. 참고로 [should have pp (~했어야 했다.)] 이다.

20 From colonial times, unmarried women had enjoyed many of the same legal rights as men, although custom **required** that they _____ early.

ⓐ were marrying
ⓑ have been marrying
ⓒ marry
ⓓ married

정답 ⓒ

해석 식민지 시대부터 미혼 여성들은 비록 사회 관습상 일찍이 결혼해야 했지만, 남성들과 동일한 법적 권리를 많이 누려왔다.

→ 당위동사[requir (요구하다)]의 목적절은 당위절로 해당절에 동사를 반드시 동사원형으로 나타내야 한다. 따라서 [marry]가 적절하다.

MEMO

ANSWERS

CHAPTER **6**

연결사

EXERCISE

🔲 괄호 안에서 문법적으로 올바른 것을 고르시오.

01 All drivers should carry a spare tire in good condition and an emergency kit (despite / in case / although / however) they have a breakdown.

> → 문맥상 조건의 의미이므로 조건접속사[in case (~할 경우에 대비하여)]가 적절하다.
>
> 해석 모든 운전자들은 차량이 고장 나는 것을 대비해서 상태가 좋은 여분의 타이어와 비상 용구함을 가지고 있어야 한다.

02 Suicide rates are rapidly increasing in Korea, (while / if / once / even if) they are decreasing throughout the developed nations.

> → 문맥상 대조의 의미이므로 대조접속사[while (반면에)]가 적절하다.
>
> 해석 선진국에서는 자살률이 감소하고 있는 반면에, 한국에서는 자살율이 급격히 증가하고 있다.

03 A number of doctors study hard (so that / afterward / unless) they can keep abreast of all the latest developments in medicine.

> → 문맥상 목적의 의미이므로 목적접속사[so that (~할 수 있도록)]가 적절하다.
>
> 해석 많은 의사들이 의학에서의 모든 최신의 발전에 뒤떨어지지 않기 위해서 열심히 공부한다.
> (keep abreast of ~에 뒤지지 않게 하다/ ~에 대한 최근정황을 알다)

04 The administration's approval rating falls (in spite of / whenever / so that) the president's speech grows distant from reality.

> → 문맥상 시간의 의미이므로 시간접속사[in case (~할 때마다)]가 적절하다.
>
> 해석 대통령의 연설이 현실과 거리가 멀어질 때마다 정부의 지지율이 떨어진다.

05 Scientists have found out in a recent study that (before / wherever / no matter how / while) **low-fat** the milk may be, it does not affect weight loss.

> → 문맥상 양보의 의미이고 형용사[low-fat]을 바로 동반하는 유일한 양보접속사[no matter how (아무리 ~할지라도)]가 적절하다.
>
> 해석 최근 연구에서 과학자들은 아무리 우유가 저지방이라고 할지라도, 그 우유는 체중 감소에 영향을 주지 않는다.

06 The driver will not be able to focus on driving, (if / unless / until) you disturb the driver.

> → 문맥상 조건의 의미이므로 조건접속사[if (만약 ~라면)]가 적절하다.
>
> 해석 운전자를 방해하면 운전자는 운전에 집중할 수가 없다.

07 There can be no true liberty (unless / although / if) there is economic liberty.

> → 문맥상 부정조건의 의미이므로 부정조건접속사[unless (만약 ~가 아니라면)]가 적절하다.
>
> 해석 경제적 자유가 없다면 진정한 자유가 있을 수 없다.

08 The National Health Association approved a series of graphic anti-smoking ads, (when / during / <u>despite</u> / even though) the controversy surrounding them.

> **→** 해당문장은 바로 뒤에 명사[the controversy]가 이어지고, 문맥상 양보의 의미이므로 양보전치사[despite (~에도 불구하고)]가 적절하다.

> **해석** 국립보건원은 그것들을 둘러싸고 있는 논란에도 불구하고 생생한 일련의 금연광고들을 승인했다.

🔢 다음 빈칸에 들어갈 가장 올바른 것을 고르시오.

01 The judge is frustrated that a mistrial must be declared _____ the jury cannot reach a decision regarding the defendant's guilt or innocence.

> **→** 문맥상 이유의 의미이므로 이유접속사[because (왜냐하면, ~때문에)]가 적절하다.

> **해석** 판사는 배심원단이 피고의 유죄나 무죄에 대해 평결을 내릴 수 없었기 때문에 무효재판이 선언되어야 하는 것이 실망스러웠다.
> mistrial 미결정 심리, 무효재판

(a) however   (b) as long as

(c) instead   (d) <u>because</u>

02 Firefighters are people whose job is to put out fires and rescue people. _____ fires, firefighters save people and animals from car wrecks, collapsed buildings, stuck elevators and many other emergencies.

> **→** 해당문장은 바로 뒤에 명사[fires]가 이어지고, 문맥상 첨가의 의미이므로 첨가전치사[besides (~외에도)]가 적절하다.

> **해석** 소방관은 화재를 진압하고 사람들을 구조하는 일을 하는 사람들이다. 화재사건 외에도, 소방관들은 사고 난 자동차, 붕괴된 건물, 꼼짝 못하는 엘리베이터와 많은 다른 응급상황으로 부터 사람들과 동물들을 구조한다.

(a) While   (b) <u>Besides</u>

(c) Since   (d) Despite

EXERCISE

I 괄호 안에서 문법적으로 올바른 것을 고르시오.

01 Bella had written many letters seeking admission to medical schools for over two years. (In addition / In other words / Finally), she was accepted by a medical school in Philadelphia.

→ 문맥상 결론의 의미이므로 결론의 접속부사[finally (마침내)]가 적절하다.

해석 벨라는 2년이 넘게 의과대학 입학을 요청하는 많은 편지를 썼다. 마침내 그녀는 필라델피아의 한 의과대학으로부터 입학허가를 받았다.

02 The use of cameras and video cameras is permitted in all permanent collection galleries. (In other words / However / Therefore / Regardless), flash photography is not permitted inside museums.

→ 문맥상 앞문장과의 역접의 의미이므로 역접의 접속부사[however (그러나)]가 적절하다.

해석 카메라와 비디오카메라의 사용은 모든 상시 전시관에서는 허용됩니다. 그러나 플레쉬 사용은 박물관내에서는 허용되지 않습니다.

03 People in today's society are interested in diets and eating healthily. (On the other hand / Regardless / Therefore), they refrain from eating unhealthy or high calorie foods.

→ 문맥상 앞 문장에 대한 결과의 의미이므로 결과의 접속부사[therefore (그러므로)]가 적절하다.

해석 현대 사회의 사람들은 다이어트와 건강하게 먹는 것에 대해 관심이 있다. 그러므로 건강에 좋지 않은 음식이나 칼로리가 높은 음식을 먹는 것을 삼간다.

04 The cruel sights touched off thoughts that, (otherwise / therefore / likewise), wouldn't have entered her mind.

→ 문맥상 역접의 의미이므로 역접의 접속부사[otherwise (그렇지 않다면)]가 적절하다

해석 그 잔인한 광경은 그러지 않다면 그녀의 마음에 들어오지 않았을 생각을 떠올리게 했다.

05 For over 50 years, no Spanish children were born in any of the higher altitudes. (For example / On the contrary / Consequently), the Indians were fertile in the same climate.

→ 문맥상 스페인 아이와 원주민 아이를 대조하는 의미이므로 대조의 접속부사[on the contrary (대조적으로)]가 적절하다

해석 50년 동안 고지대에서는 한 명의 스페인 아이도 태어나지 않았다. 대조적으로 원주민들은 똑같은 기후 에서 아이를 많이 낳았다.

06 The rapid growth of suburbs has created many problems. (For example / However / In contrast), numerous suburbs have had trouble raising enough money for such essential services as police and fire protection.

→ 문맥상 앞 문장에 대한 예시가 이어지므로 예시의 접속부사[for example (예를 들면)]가 적절하다.

해석 교외지역의 급속한 성장이 많은 문제를 야기했다. 예를 들어, 많은 교외 지역에서 경찰이나 소방 같은 필수적인 서비스를 갖추기 위해 재원을 충분히 확보하는데 어려움을 겪고 있다.

07 In 1857 she and her sister managed to open the first hospital for women and children. (Accordingly / Besides / In short), she established the first medical school for women.

> → 문맥상 앞 문장에 언급한 업적을 첨가하는 내용이므로 첨가의 접속부사[besides (게다가)]가 적절하다

> 해석 1857년 그녀와 그녀의 여동생은 다른 여성의사와 함께 여성과 아동을 위한 최초의 병원을 마침내 열었다. 게다가 그녀는 최초의 여성 의과대학을 설립했다.

▮▮ 다음 빈칸에 들어갈 가장 올바른 것을 고르시오.

01 In studying Chinese calligraphy, one must learn something of the origins of Chinese language and of how they were originally written. _____, except for those brought up in the artistic traditions of the country, its aesthetic significance seems to be very difficult to apprehend.*

> → 문맥상 앞문장과의 역접의 의미이므로 역접의 접속부사[however (그러나)]가 적절하다.

> 해석 중국 서예를 공부하는데 있어서, 중국 언어의 기원과 원래는 어떻게 쓰여 졌는지에 대한 것을 배워야만 한다. 그러나, 그 국가(중국)의 예술적 전통에서 자란 사람들을 제외하면, 그 미적 중요성은 이해하기 매우 어려운 듯하다.

(a) Furthermore   (b) Therefore

(c) As a result   (d) However

02 Instead of asking "Am I a good person?" you may want to ask "What good do I do in the world?" Grushcow's temple puts these beliefs into action inside and outside their community. _____, they sponsored two refugee families from Vietnam to come to Canada in the 1970s.

> → 문맥상 앞 문장에 대한 예시가 이어지므로 예시의 접속부사[for instance (예를 들면)]가 적절하다.

> 해석 "나는 선한 사람인가?"라고 묻지 말고 "세상에서 나는 어떤 선행을 행할까?"라고 물어보고 싶을 것이다. 그루시카우의 회당은 지역사회 안팎에서 이런 믿음을 행동으로 옮긴다. 예를 들어, 1970년대에 그들은 캐나다로 오기위해 베트남에서 온 두 난민 가족들을 후원했다.

(a) Eventually   (b) Hence

(c) For instance   (d) In conclusion

01 After Francesca made a case for staying 1 at home _____ the summer holidays, ⓑ an uncomfortable silence fell on the dinner table. Robert was not sure if it was the right time for him to tell her about his grandiose plan.

ⓐ similarly
ⓑ during
ⓒ while
ⓓ Because of

정답 ⓑ

해석 Francesca가 여름휴가 동안에 집에 있자고 강력히 제안한 후에 거북한 침묵이 저녁 식사 시간에 내려앉았다. 로버트는 지금 그녀에게 자신의 웅장한 계획에 대해서 말해야 할지 확신하지 못했다.

→ 해당문장은 바로 뒤에 명사[the summer holidays]가 이어지고, 문맥상 시간의 의미이므로 시간전치사[during (~동안에)]가 적절하다.

02 The world may be a different place, and 2 you will likely be a different person. So ⓑ try to anticipate these changes, both in the world and yourself, _____ you consider a job path.

ⓐ in other words
ⓑ when
ⓒ although
ⓓ because

정답 ⓑ

해석 세상은 다른 곳이 될지도 모르고 당신도 아마도 다른 사람일 것입니다. 그래서 진로를 고려할 때 세상과 당신들에서 이러한 변화들을 예상하려고 노력하세요.

→ 문맥상 시간의 의미이므로 시간접속사[when (~할 때)]가 적절하다.

03 Law enforcement personnel must have 3 probable cause to believe that the ⓐ owner of the property has been involved in criminal activity, _____ law enforcement personnel can search or seize private property.

ⓐ before
ⓑ while
ⓒ since
ⓓ however

정답 ⓐ

해석 법 집행관이 사유 재산을 수색하고 압수할 수 있기 전에 그 부지의 소유주가 범죄에 연루되어있다고 믿을 수 있는 개연성 있는 근거가 있어야 한다.

→ 문맥상 시간의 선후사건을 의미하므로 시간접속사[before (~전에)]가 적절하다.

04 Thunderstorms are extremely common4 in many parts of the world, _____,ⓒ throughout most of North America. Updrafts of warm air set off these storms.

ⓐ therefore
ⓑ furthermore
ⓒ for example
ⓓ hence

정답 ⓒ

해석 폭풍우는 전 세계 각 지역에서 예를 들면 북미 전역에서 매우 흔한 것이다. 따뜻한 공기의 상승기류가 이런 폭풍을 시작하게 한다.

→ 문맥상 앞 문장에 대한 예시가 이어지므로 예시의 접속부사[for example (예를 들면)]가 적절하다

05 A manuscript written by hand is a5 unique and unreproducible object.ⓐ _____, print with its standard format and type, introduced exact mass reproduction.

ⓐ However
ⓑ Therefore
ⓒ Consequently
ⓓ Even though

정답 ⓐ

해석 손으로 작성된 원고는 유일하고 복제 불가능한 물건이다. 하지만, 그것의 표준 형식과 유형을 가진 인쇄술은 정확한 대량 복제를 도입했다.

→ 문맥상 앞문장과의 역접의 의미이므로 역접의 접속부사[however (그러나)]가 적절하다.

06 The campaign to eliminate pollution6 will turn out to be absolutely futileⓑ _____ it has the understanding and full cooperation of the public who is concerned about the environmental pollution.

ⓐ if
ⓑ unless
ⓒ as soon as
ⓓ Besides

정답 ⓑ

해석 환경오염에 대해서 걱정하는 대중의 이해와 전폭적인 협조가 없다면 오염을 없애는 캠페인은 완전히 쓸모가 없을 것이다.

→ 문맥상 부정조건의 의미이므로 부정조건접속사 [unless (만약 ~가 아니라면)]가 적절하다.

07 The white-tailed deer was one of the 7 first animals to be protected by federal ⓑ legislation. _____ unlike the passenger pigeon, white-tailed deer were not in much need of protection.

ⓐ Nevertheless
ⓑ But
ⓒ Likewise
ⓓ Hence

해석 흰 꼬리 사슴은 연방법으로 보호받는 최초의 동물 중 하나였다. 그러나 여행 비둘기와는 달리 흰 꼬리 사슴은 보호할 필요가 별로 없었다.

→ 문맥상 앞의 내용과 대조하고 있으므로 대조구조를 이룰 수 있는 등위접속사[but (그러나)]가 적절하다.

08 If you turn a doorknob that has always 8 turned easily and it won't move, you ⓐ will turn the knob harder, and may pull it up or push it down. _____, you may shove or kick the door.

ⓐ Eventually
ⓑ However
ⓒ Otherwise
ⓓ Accordingly

정답 ⓐ

해석 항상 쉽게 열렸던 손잡이를 돌리고, 그것이 움직이지 않는다면, 당신은 손잡이를 더욱 세게 돌리다가, 당겨보기도 하고 밀어보기도 할 것이다. 결국 문을 밀치고 발로 찰 수도 있을 것이다.

→ 문맥상 결론의 의미이므로 결론의 접속부사[eventually (결국)]가 적절하다.

09 In what seems almost a miraculous 9 way, poetry brightens up words that ⓒ looked dull and ordinary. _____, poetry is perpetually recreating language.

ⓐ For example
ⓑ By contrast
ⓒ In other words
ⓓ Soon

정답 ⓒ

해석 거의 기적같이, 시는 재미없고, 평범해 보였던 말들을 밝게 빛나게 해준다. 다시 말하면, 시는 끊임없이 언어를 재창조하는 것이다.

→ 문맥상 앞의 문장을 다시 언급하고 있으므로 재언급의 접속부사[in other words (다시 말하면)]가 적절하다.

10 Children are susceptible for the effects of television _____ their minds are growing, developing, and learning much faster than those of adults.

ⓐ although
ⓑ before
ⓒ because
ⓓ when

10

정답 ⓒ

해석 어린이들은 TV의 영향을 쉽게 받는다. 왜냐하면 아이들의 마음은 어른들의 마음보다 훨씬 더 빠르게 성장하고, 발달하고, 배우고 있기 때문이다.

→ 문맥상 이유의 의미이므로 이유접속사[because(왜냐하면, ~때문에)]가 적절하다.

11 Aggressive drivers react foolishly in several dangerous ways. One way is to cut off another motorists and tailgate the other car. _____ cutting off and tailgating other cars, they often use rude language or gestures to show their anger.

ⓐ Therefore
ⓑ Besides
ⓒ Despite
ⓓ But

11

정답 ⓑ

해석 난폭 운전자들은 여러 가지 위험한 방식으로 다른 운전자들에 대해서 어리석게 대처 한다. 한 가지 방식은 다른 운전자들의 길을 막아버리는 것이다. 또 다른 방식은 다른 차 뒤를 바짝 따라가는 것이다. 길을 막고 차 뒤에 바짝 붙는 것에 덧붙여, 난폭 운전자들은 그들의 화를 표출하기 위해 무례한 말이나 행동을 종종 사용한다.

→ 해당문장은 바로 뒤에 동명사[cutting off and tailgating other cars]가 이어지고, 문맥상 첨가의 의미이므로 첨가전치사[besides (~외에도)]가 적절하다.

12 In our country, child labor was abrogated fifty years ago. _____, in some countries, where people are usually in a poor condition, people are still using it.

ⓐ In the other hand
ⓑ At last
ⓒ Instead
ⓓ Likewise

12

정답 ⓐ

해석 우리나라에서는 아동노동은 50년 전에 폐지되었다. 반면에 대게 열악한 상황에 있는 일부 국가에서는 사람들이 여전히 아동노예를 이용하고 있다.

→ 문맥상 우리나라와 다른 나라의 아동노예에 대한 대조를 하고 있으므로 대조 접속부사[in the other hand (반면에)]가 적절하다.

13 5 cents in 1972 had more market value 13 than 5 cents today. In this situation, ⓑ the actual costs can't legitimately be compared. _____, the costs have to be compared after they've been adjusted for inflation.

ⓐ For instance
ⓑ Hence
ⓒ Likewise
ⓓ Eventually

정답 ⓑ

해석 1972년도의 5센트는 오늘날 5센트보다 더 높은 시장가격을 가지고 있기 때문이다. 이와 같은 상황에서 실제가격은 타당하게 비교될 수는 없다. 오히려 그 비용은 물가상승에 맞추어 조정된 후에 비교되어져야 한다.

→ 문맥상 결과의 의미이므로 결과접속부사[hence(그래서)]가 적절하다.

14 The Mona Lisa and Michelangelo's 14 David are reproduced so often that we ⓒ may feel we know them _____ we have never been to Paris or Florence.

ⓐ because
ⓑ when
ⓒ even if
ⓓ despite

정답 ⓒ

해석 모나리자와 미켈란젤로의 다비드상은 너무 자주 복제되어서 심지어 우리가 파리나 플로렌스에 다녀온 적이 없음에도 우리는 그것들을 매우 잘 안다고 느낄 수 있다.

→ 문맥상 앞의 문장과 역접의 의미이므로 역접 접속사[even if (~일지라도)]가 적절하다.

15 Surveillance cameras have been widely 15 used in lots of places for security ⓐ purposes. _____, their usefulness is still under discussion.

ⓐ However
ⓑ Consequently
ⓒ In contrast
ⓓ Fortunately

정답 ⓐ

해석 안전 목적으로 감시 카메라는 많은 장소에서 널리 사용되어져 왔다. 그러나 그것들의 유용성은 여전히 논란이 되고 있다.

→ 문맥상 앞의 문장과 역접의 의미이므로 역접 접속부사[however (그러나)]가 적절하다.

16 If you have only one temperature sensor for the whole plot of land, itⓑ must be an accurate one; _____, it does not provide reliable data.

ⓐ conclusively
ⓑ otherwise
ⓒ moreover
ⓓ similarly

16 정답 ⓑ

해석 만약 그 경작지 전체에 오직 하나의 온도센서가 있다면 그것은 정확한 것이어야 한다. 그렇지 않으면 믿을 만한 데이터를 제공하지 못한다.

→ 문맥상 앞의 문장과 역접의 의미이므로 역접 접속부사[otherwise (그렇지 않으면)]가 적절하다.

17 People think of lie detectors as foolproof simply because they areⓑ machines. _____, they often made errors due to many factors.

ⓐ Hence
ⓑ In fact
ⓒ In addition
ⓓ Altogether

17 정답 ⓑ

해석 거짓말 탐지기가 기계이기 때문에 사람들은 거짓말 탐지기를 완벽한 것으로 생각하고 있다. 사실상, 거짓말탐지기는 많은 요인 때문에 종종 오류가 있다.

→ 문맥상 앞의 문장과 역접의 의미이므로 역접, 강조 접속부사[in fact (사실상)]가 적절하다.

18 In the story, the rich will be totally useless greedy characters, _____ⓒ the poor will be simple, honest people whose daily work is profitable to the community.

ⓐ when
ⓑ since
ⓒ while
ⓓ whether

18 정답 ⓒ

해석 그 이야기에서 부유한 사람들은 전적으로 쓸모없고 탐욕스러운 인물들인 반면에 가난한 사람은 그들의 노동이 사회에 혜택을 주는 단순하고 정직한 사람들이기 때문이다.

→ 문맥상 부유한 사람과 가난한 사람을 대조한다. 따라서 대조접속사[while (반면에)]가 적절하다.

19 Being successful is all a matter of luck. 19 _____, those who persevere recognize ⓑ that they are ultimately responsible not just for pursuing their goals, but for setting them.

ⓐ Besides
ⓑ However
ⓒ Thus
ⓓ Afterward

해석 성공이라는 것은 전적으로 운의 문제이기 때문이다. 그러나 참고 견디는 사람들은 목표를 추구하는 것뿐만 아니라 목표를 정하는 것도 궁극적으로 자신들의 책임이라는 것을 인정한다.

→ 문맥상 앞의 문장과 역접의 의미이므로 역접 접속부사[however (그러나)]가 적절하다.

20 An updraft may start over ground that 20 is more intensely heated by the sun ⓑ than the land surrounding the area. _____, bare, rocky, or paved areas usually have updrafts above them.

ⓐ On the other hand
ⓑ For example
ⓒ Eventually
ⓓ In fact

정답 ⓑ

해석 태양에 의해 주변 지역보다 집중적으로 데워진 지역의 땅 위에서 상승기류가 시작할 수 있다. 예를 들어 벌거숭이고, 바위가 많고, 포장도로 지역에서 보통 그 위에 보통 상승기류가 있다.

→ 문맥상 앞 문장에 대한 예시가 이어지므로 예시의 접속부사[for example (예를 들면)]가 적절하다

MEMO

ANSWERS

CHAPTER 7

실전
모의고사

01 China is considered to be one of the most influential countries in the world not just socially but also economically. The China that _____ at 10 percent **for 30 years** was a powerful source of fuel for much of what drove the global economy forward.

ⓐ has grown
ⓑ were growing
ⓒ had been growing
ⓓ would grow

[정답] ⓒ

[해석] 중국은 사회적으로뿐만 아니라 경제적으로도 세계에서 가장 영향력 있는 국가들 중에 하나이다. 30년 동안 10퍼센트의 성장을 해온 중국은 세계 경제의 발전을 견인한 강력한 연료 공급원이었다.

→ 해당문장에 시제가 과거이고 기간의 부사어구[for 30 years] 있으므로 과거완료진행형이 적절하다.

02 Thunberg, 16, has become the voice of young people around the world who are protesting climate change and **demanding** that governments around the world _____ more action.

ⓐ took
ⓑ take
ⓒ taking
ⓓ have taken

[정답] ⓑ

[해석] 16세 나이의 Thunberg는 기후변화에 항의하며 세계 각국 정부의 더 많은 조치를 요구하는 전 세계 젊은이들의 목소리가 됐다.

→ 당위동사[demand (요구하다)]의 목적절은 당위절로 해당절에 동사를 반드시 동사원형으로 나타내야 한다. 따라서 [take]가 적절하다.

03 There are a lot of students looking for many kinds of jobs in the world. If you **are considering** _____ for a job overseas, seek the advice of an international employment agency first.

ⓐ being looking
ⓑ looking
ⓒ look
ⓓ to look

[정답] ⓑ

[해석] 세상에는 많은 종류의 직업을 찾는 학생들이 있다. 만약 당신이 해외에서 일자리를 찾는 것을 고려중이라면 우선 국제직업소개소의 조언을 구해라.

→ 타동사[consider (고려하다)]는 동명사를 목적어로 취하는 동사이므로 [looking]이 적절하다.

04 Bella didn't tell Russell that she had difficulties studying English grammar and vocabulary. If she _____ him about the problem, he **would have helped** her with them.

ⓐ tells
ⓑ had told
ⓒ would tell
ⓓ has told

정답 ⓑ

해석 벨라는 러셀에게 영문법과 어휘를 공부하는데 어려움이 있다는 것을 말하지 않았다. 만약 그녀가 그에게 그 문제를 이야기 했다면, 그가 그것을 도왔을 것이다.

→ 주절의 동사가 [조동사의 과거형 + have pp(would have helped)]이므로 과거의 사실에 대한 것이다. 따라서 가정절의 동사는 과거완료형[had told]가 적절하다.

05 In Mexico, the value spike of limes is attracting criminals, forcing growers _____ their limited supply of "green gold" from drug cartels.

ⓐ guarding
ⓑ to guard
ⓒ to be guarding
ⓓ having guarded

정답 ⓑ

해석 멕시코에서 라임 가격 급등은 범죄를 유인한다, 그래서 재배업자들로 하여금 마약 범죄조직으로부터 한정된 'green gold(라임)' 공급을 보호하게 했다.

→ 타동사[force (강요하다)]는 5형식 구조에서 [to]부정사를 목적보어로 취한다. 따라서 [to guard]가 적절하다.

06 Many gun-rights proponents say these statistics do not indicate a cause-and-effect relationship and note that the rates of gun homicide and other gun crimes in the United States _____ **since highs in the early 1990's.**

ⓐ are dropping
ⓑ have been dropping
ⓒ had dropped
ⓓ drop

정답 ⓑ

해석 많은 총기 소유권 지지자들은 이 통계들이 인과관계를 나타내지 못하며 총기 살인이나 다른 총기관련 범죄가 1990년대 초의 높은 기록들 이후로 줄어들고 있다고 지적한다.

→ 해당문장에 현재완료진행 부사어구[since highs in the early 1990's]가 있으므로 현재완료진행형이 적절하다.

07 The company was established in September, 1970 and _____ our business operations around Asia **ever since**.

    ⓐ had been expanding
    ⓑ would expand
    ⓒ has been expanding
    ⓓ will be expanding

정답 ⓒ

해석 기업은 1970년 9월에 창립되었다. 그 후로 아시아 쪽에서 사업영역을 넓혀 왔다.

→ 해당문장에 현재완료진행 부사어구[ever since(그 후로)]가 있으므로 현재완료진행형이 적절하다.

08 In order to allow their children to learn from their mistakes, parents _____ necessarily provide them with the freedom to make mistakes.

    ⓐ may
    ⓑ must
    ⓒ will
    ⓓ can

정답 ⓑ

해석 아이들이 자신들의 실수로부터 배우게 하기 위해서 부모들은 그들에게 실수를 할 자유를 제공해야 한다. (의무)

→ 문맥상 강한 의무이므로 [must(반드시 ~해야 한다)]가 적절하다.

09 Andy Warhol began to wear rock-star leather jackets, satin shirts and a silver-sprayed wig. His trademark use of product labels in his art first showed up as prints on **the paper dresses** _____.

    ⓐ whom he created.
    ⓑ when he created.
    ⓒ which he created.
    ⓓ whose he created.

정답 ⓒ

해석 앤디워홀은 록스타의 가죽 재킷과 새틴 셔츠, 은색 가발을 착용하기 시작했다. 자기 작품에 상표를 사용하는 그의 독보적인 기법은 그가 만든 종이 드레스 위의 프린트로 처음 선보여 졌다.

wig 가발 leather 가죽 satin 매끄러운, 광택이 나는

→ 선행사[the paper dresses]가 사물이고 뒤에 목적어가 없는 불완벽한 문장이다. 따라서 목적격 관계대명사[which]가 적절하다.

10 We had no idea that the start time of the soccer game had been changed, so we were not able to compete. If we **had known** about the rescheduling and participated in it, we _____ this much.

ⓐ were not disappointed
ⓑ would not be disappointed
ⓒ would not have been disappointed
ⓓ are not disappointed

정답 ⓒ

해석 우리는 축구경기 시작시간이 변경된 것을 알지 못해서 경기를 할 수가 없었다. 만약 우리가 일정재조정을 알고, 경기에 참여할 수 있었다면 누리는 이렇게 실망하지 않았을 것이다.

→ 가정절의 동사가 과거완료[had known]이므로 과거사건에 대한 가정법 과거완료문장이다. 따라서 주절은 [조동사의 과거형＋have pp(would not have been disappointed)]가 적절하다.

11 Following the Mass is an elaborate party, with dancing, cake, and toasts. Finally, _____ the evening, the young woman dances a waltz with her favorite escort.

ⓐ ending
ⓑ to end
ⓒ to be ending
ⓓ being ending

정답 ⓑ

해석 미사 후에는 춤, 케이크, 술을 곁들인 멋진 파티가 이어진다. 마지막으로 그 밤을 끝내기 위해 젊은 여성이 그녀가 좋아하는 남자 에스코트와 왈츠를 춘다.

→ 문맥상 주어[the young woman]보다 앞에 위치한 부사적 용법의 목적(~하기 위하여)이다. 이 경우 [to]부정사 [To end]가 적절하다.

12 The United States has the highest homicide-by-firearm rate among the world's most developed nations. _____, many gun-rights proponents say these statistics do not indicate a cause-and-effect relationship.

ⓐ Similarly
ⓑ But
ⓒ Therefore
ⓓ Besides

정답 ⓑ

해석 미국은 세계의 가장 발전된 국가들 사이에서 가장 높은 총기에 의한 살인율을 가지고 있다. 그러나 많은 총기 소유 지지자들은 이 통계들이 인과관계를 나타내지 못한다고 말한다.

→ 문맥상 앞의 내용과 역접의 흐름으로 등위접속사 [but (그러나)]이 적절하다.

13 Jane is often late for work because she doesn't have a car and has to take public transportation. If she **afforded** a car, she _____ one immediately.

ⓐ will purchase
ⓑ purchases
ⓒ will have purchased
ⓓ would purchase

【정답】ⓓ

【해석】제인은 직장에 자주 늦는다. 왜냐하면 그녀는 자동차가 없어서 대중교통을 이용해야 하기 때문이다. 만약 그녀가 자동차한대를 구매할 여력이 있다면 한 대를 즉시 구매할 것이다.

→ 가정절의 동사가 과거[afforded]이므로 현재 또는 미래사건에 대한 가정법 과거문장이다. 따라서 주절은 [조동사의 과거형 + 동사원형(would purchase)]가 적절하다.

14 The chef _____ have checked the temperature of the oven before trying to roast the chicken instead of just assuming it was hot enough.

ⓐ might
ⓑ should
ⓒ will
ⓓ can't

【정답】ⓑ

【해석】요리사는 닭고기를 굽기 전에 단순히 오븐이 충분히 뜨겁다고 생각하지 말고 오븐의 온도를 확인했어야 했다.

→ 문맥상 과거에 대한 후회와 반성[should have pp (~했어야 했다)]이므로 조동사[should]가 적절하다.

[might have pp (~였을 지도 모른다)]

15 In countries operating under the "innocent until proven guilty" system, society has decided that it is **better** that they _____ a guilty person to go free than to imprison an innocent person.

ⓐ will allow
ⓑ allow
ⓒ are allowing
ⓓ have allowed

【정답】ⓑ

【해석】무죄추정의 원칙 하에서 운영하는 나라들에선 사회는 무고한 사람을 투옥시키는 것보다 죄가 있는 사람은 풀어주는 것이 더 낫다고 결론을 내렸다.

→ 이성적 판단형용사[better (더 좋은)]의 진주어는 당위절로 항상 동사원형으로 나타내야 한다. 따라서 [allow]가 적절하다.

16 Two men on a motorcycle attacked Garry when he _____ home one evening. He spent two nights in the hospital recovering from trauma and injuries.

ⓐ walks
ⓑ was walking
ⓒ has walked
ⓓ has been walking

정답 ⓑ

해석 어느 날 저녁 집으로 가는 길이었는데 오토바이를 탄 두 남성이 게리를 공격했다. 그는 부상과 충격에서 회복하느라 이틀 동안 병원에 있어야 했습니다.

→ 해당문장의 주절[Two men on a motorcycle attacked Garry]이 과거이므로 과거진행형이 적절하다.

17 Andrew has been working as an accountant for more than ten years now. _____ the long period of working, he is not well recognised and can't earn much money. I think he had better change his career.

ⓐ Although
ⓑ Instead of
ⓒ Despite
ⓓ Owing to

정답 ⓒ

해석 앤드류는 현재 10년 넘게 회계사로 일해오고 있다. 오랜 기간 동안의 일에도 불구하고 그는 그렇게 인정받지 못하고 있고 많은 돈도 벌지 못한다. 내 생각에는 그는 직업을 바꾸는 것이 좋은 것 같다.

→ 해당문장은 바로 뒤에 명사[the long period of working]가 이어지고, 문맥상 양보의 의미이므로 양보전치사[despite (~에도 불구하고)]가 적절하다.

18 My brother and I have always dreamed of owning a fishing boat so that we can catch bigger fish. If we _____ one, we would always be in the sea, fishing and sailing whenever we can.

ⓐ had had
ⓑ had
ⓒ has
ⓓ will have

정답 ⓑ

해석 내 동생과 나는 더 큰 물고기를 잡을 수 있도록 낚시 배를 가지는 꿈을 항상 꿔왔다. 만약 우리가 한 대가 있다면 우리는 가능할 때마다 낚시하고 세일링하면서 항상 바다에 있을 것이다.

→ 주절의 동사가 [조동사의 과거형 + 동사원형(would always be)]이므로 현재 또는 미래의 사실에 대한 것이다. 따라서 가정절의 동사는 과거형[had]이 적절하다.

19 Such person will be a source of happiness and a recipient of reciprocal kindness. _____ **many people spontaneously and without effort** is perhaps the greatest of all sources of personal happiness.

ⓐ Like
ⓑ To like
ⓒ Liking
ⓓ Having liked

정답 ⓒ

해석 그런 사람은 행복의 원천이 되면 서로 친절을 주고 받으며 이런 친절을 받는 사람이 될 것이다. 많은 사람을 자발적으로 그리고 수고하지 않고서 좋아하는 것은 아마도 행복의 모든 원천 가운데 가장 큰 원천이다.

→ 본주어 자리는 동명사[Liking]가 적절하다. 즉, 해당문장의 동사[is]의 주어로 쓰인 동명사구이다.

20 One of the oldest frauds of gemstones was the sale of **water** _____, on the pretense that contact with the gem had made the water medicinal.

ⓐ whose a gemstone had been dipped into
ⓑ whom a gemstone had been dipped into
ⓒ which a gemstone had been dipped into
ⓓ when a gemstone had been dipped into

정답 ⓒ

해석 원석에 대한 가장 오래된 사기중의 하나는 보석과의 접촉은 물을 약성을 띠게 만든다는 가정하여 원석이 담겨져 있던 물을 판매하는 것이었다.

→ 선행사[water]가 사물이고 뒤에 목적어가 없는 불완벽한 문장이다. 따라서 목적격 관계대명사[which]가 적절하다.

21 Jason lost his chance to make the interviewers impressed and to get a job since he made quite a few mistakes in the job interview. If he **had prepared** the job interview more carefully, he _____ the mistakes.

ⓐ wouldn't have made
ⓑ hasn't made
ⓒ isn't making
ⓓ won't make

정답 ⓐ

해석 제이슨은 면접에서 실수를 많이 하였기 때문에 면접관들이 감명 받게 하여 직장을 얻을 기회를 놓쳤다. 만약 그가 면접을 더 세심하게 준비를 했다면, 그는 실수를 하지 않았을 것이다.

→ 가정절의 동사가 과거완료[had prepared]이므로 과거사건에 대한 가정법 과거완료문장이다. 따라서 주절은 [조동사의 과거형 + have pp(wouldn't have made)]가 적절하다.

22 West Bromwich finished at the top of the Football League Championship, which means that **next season,** Kim and the team _____ in the top division, the English Premier League.

ⓐ are playing
ⓑ have played
ⓒ will be playing
ⓓ had been playing

해석 웨스트 브롬위치는 챔피언십 리그 우승을 확정지었다. 그것은 다음 시즌에, 김과 그의 팀은 1부 리그인 영국 프리미어 리그에서 경기를 하게 될 것을 의미한다.

→ 해당문장에 미래진행부사어구[next season (다음 시즌에)]가 있으므로 미래진행형이 적절하다.

23 Russell was very interested in cooking when young, and now is a famous chef in a world class hotel. He still **enjoys** _____ new cuisines.

ⓐ to create
ⓑ creating
ⓒ to have created
ⓓ having created

정답 ⓑ

해석 러셀은 어릴 때 요리에 아주 흥미가 있었고, 지금 월드클라스 호텔의 유명한 요리사이다. 그는 여전히 새로운 요리법을 만드는 것을 즐긴다.

→ 타동사[enjoy]는 동명사를 목적어로 취하는 동사이므로 [creating]이 적절하다.

24 When Jose got up late this morning, the rest of his family had gone out for lunch. There was nothing to eat at home. If he **had woken** up earlier before they went out, he _____ them.

ⓐ joined
ⓑ was joining
ⓒ would have joined
ⓓ has joined

정답 ⓒ

해석 호세가 오늘 아침 늦게 일어났을 때, 그의 식구들은 점심 먹으로 나가고 없었다. 집에는 먹을 것이 없었다. 만약 그가 그들이 나가기 전에 좀 더 일찍 일어났다면, 그는 그들과 함께 할 수 있었을 것이다.

→ 가정절의 동사가 과거완료[had woken]이므로 과거사건에 대한 가정법 과거완료문장이다. 따라서 주절은 [조동사의 과거형 + have pp(wouldn't have joined)]가 적절하다.

25 Russell is in his last year as a medical student and is looking forward to graduation. **By the time he finishes this semester,** he _____ only leukemia and the treatments **for over five years.**

ⓐ will be studying
ⓑ will have been studying
ⓒ has studied
ⓓ would study

26 After completing its probe into why the South Korean military failed to report accurately about the North's violation of an inter-Korean maritime border last week, the Defense Ministry **recommended** that the government seriously _____ two generals and subject three other military officers to lesser punishment.

ⓐ censures
ⓑ censure
ⓒ has censured
ⓓ is censuring

01 The world population, which was almost 6 billion in 2000, is expected to double by 2050. Almost 95 percent of this growth will be in **developing countries,** _____.

ⓐ that 77 percent of the world's population lives.

ⓑ where 77 percent of the world's population lives.

ⓒ which 77 percent of the world's population lives.

ⓓ when 77 percent of the world's population lives.

정답 ⓑ

해석 2000년에 거의 60억이었던 세계 인구는 2050년까지 두 배가 될 것으로 예상된다. 이 성장의 거의 95%는 개발도상국에서 나타날 것인데, 세계인구의 77%가 이곳에 살고 있다.

→ 관계사 뒤에 문장이 완벽하고 선행사[developing countries]가 장소명사이므로 장소의 관계부사[where]가 적절하다.

02 After Francesca strongly suggested staying at home during the summer holidays, an uncomfortable silence fell on the dinner table. Robert was not sure if it was the right time for him _____ **her about his grandiose plan.**

ⓐ to be telling

ⓑ to tell

ⓒ telling

ⓓ tell

정답 ⓑ

해석 Francesca가 여름휴가 동안에 집에 있자고 강력히 제안한 후에 거북한 침묵이 저녁 식사 시간에 내려앉았다. 로버트는 지금 그녀에게 자신의 웅장한 계획에 대해서 말해야 할지 확신하지 못했다.

→ 가주어·진주어 구문에서 진주어는 [to]부정사가 온다. 따라서 [to tell]이 적절하다.

03 Developmental delays _____ manifest themselves in poor social skills, a short attention span, and difficulties with schoolwork.

ⓐ would

ⓑ may

ⓒ must

ⓓ shall

정답 ⓑ

해석 발달 지체는 사회성 부족, 짧은 집중 시간, 학업의 어려움이라는 형태로 나타날 수 있다.

→ 문맥상 추측이므로 [may (~일지도 모른다)]가 적절하다.

04 By the 18th century, the term Le Cordon Bleu became directly connected with superior cuisine, and the school _____ its prominence even **these days**.

ⓐ is keeping
ⓑ will keep
ⓒ has kept
ⓓ was keeping

정답 ⓐ

해석 18세기 무렵 '르 꼬르동 블루'라는 용어는 우수한 요리와 직접적 관련을 맺게 되었다. 그리고 이 학교는 그 명성을 심지어 지금도 유지하고 있다.

→ 해당문장에 현재진행부사어구[these days (요즘)] 가 있으므로 현재진행형이 적절하다.

05 Russel usually goes on a travel alone. But this time he joined a group tour and met such a wonderful lady, Amanda. If he _____ alone this time, he **wouldn't have met** her.

ⓐ has traveled
ⓑ is traveling
ⓒ had traveled
ⓓ would travel

정답 ⓒ

해석 러셀은 대게 혼자서 여행을 다닌다. 그러나 이번에는 그룹투어를 했는데 아만다라는 아주 멋진 여성을 만나게 되었다. 만약 그가 이번에 혼자서 여행을 했다면 그는 그녀를 만나지 못했을 것이다.

→ 주절의 동사가 [조동사의 과거형 + have pp(wouldn't have met)]이므로 과거의 사실에 대한 것이다. 따라서 가정절의 동사는 과거완료형[had traveled]가 적절하다.

06 Smith's restaurant is very popular and quite a few people love it. When Bella got to the restaurant for dinner yesterday, she had to wait in line for about an hour. Therefore I **advised** that she _____ a reservation in advance, next time she visits it.

ⓐ will make
ⓑ make
ⓒ makes
ⓓ would make

정답 ⓑ

해석 스미스 식당은 아주 유명하고 꽤 많은 사람들이 그곳을 사랑한다. 어제 벨라가 저녁을 먹으로 그 식당에 도착했을 때 그녀는 약 한 시간 동안 줄서서 기다려야 했다. 그래서 나는 다음번에 그곳을 방문할 때 미리 예약을 할 것을 조언했다.

→ 당위동사[advise (조언하다)]의 목적절은 당위절로 해당절에 동사를 반드시 동사원형으로 나타내야 한다. 따라서 [make]가 적절하다.

07 Bella bought the novel *Harry Potter and the Sorcerer's Stone* by J.K. Rowling. She began reading it yesterday evening, and hasn't been finished with the book yet. She _____ **for over 20 hours by 10 pm tonight.**

ⓐ will have been reading
ⓑ is reading
ⓒ will be reading
ⓓ had read

정답 ⓐ

해석 벨라는 J.K. Rowling이 쓴 해리포터와 마법사의 돌을 구매해서 어제 저녁에 그것을 읽기 시작했고 아직도 다 읽지 못했다. 오늘밤 10시면 그녀는 20시간 넘게 읽고 있는 중일 것이다.

→ 해당문장에 미래완료진행부사어구[for over 20 hours by 10 pm tonight (오늘 밤 10시까지 20시간이 넘는 시간동안]가 있으므로 미래완료진행형이 적절하다.

08 Assertive behavior **involves** _____ your rights and expressing your thoughts and feelings in a direct, appropriate way.

ⓐ to stand up for
ⓑ to standing up for
ⓒ standing up for
ⓓ would stand up for

정답 ⓒ

해석 적극적 행동에는 자신의 권리를 옹호하고 자신의 생각과 감정을 직접적이고 적절한 방식으로 표현하는 것이 포함된다.

→ 타동사[involve]는 동명사를 목적어로 취하는 동사이므로 [standing up for]이 적절하다.

09 Some movies explored the possibility of sustaining human life in outer space, _____ other films have questioned whether extraterrestrial life forms may have visited our planet.

ⓐ because
ⓑ while
ⓒ since
ⓓ even if

정답 ⓑ

해석 어떤 영화들이 우주에서 인간의 생명을 지속하는 가능성을 탐구했고, 반면 다른 영화들은 외계 생명체가 우리의 행성을 방문했을 지도 모른다고 의문을 가졌다.

→ 문맥상 영화를 대조의 의미이므로 대조접속사 [while (반면에)]가 적절하다.

10 Some of my friends are enjoying a music concert in Seoul right now. I really envy them. If I _____ much work to do now, I **would be** there with them and enjoy myself.

ⓐ didn't have
ⓑ don't have
ⓒ wouldn't have
ⓓ hadn't had

정답 ⓐ

해석 내 친구들 몇 명이 지금 서울에서 음악콘서트를 즐기고 있다. 나는 정말 그들이 부럽다. 만약 지금 해야 할 일이 많지 않다면, 나도 그들과 함께 그곳에서 즐기고 있을 것이다.

→ 주절의 동사가 [조동사의 과거형 + 동사원형(would be)]이므로 현재 또는 미래의 사실에 대한 것이다. 따라서 가정절의 동사는 과거형[didn't have]가 적절하다.

11 Regarding excise taxes that are under fire for distorting the economy, the minister said that the government _____ removing them **right now**.

ⓐ had considered
ⓑ was considering
ⓒ had considered
ⓓ is considering

정답 ⓓ

해석 경제를 왜곡시킨다는 비난을 받고 있는 특별소비세에 대해 장관은 정부가 지금 그것들을 폐지하는 것을 검토하고 있다고 말했다.

→ 해당문장에 현재진행부사어구[right now (바로 지금)]가 있으므로 현재진행형이 적절하다.

12 Anxiety can cause both physical and emotional symptoms, and a specific situation or fear _____ cause some or all of these symptoms for a short time.

ⓐ ought to
ⓑ can
ⓒ will
ⓓ must

정답 ⓑ

해석 불안감은 육체적, 정신적 증상을 유발하며, 특정한 상황이나 공포감은 짧은 시간 동안 이런 증상들의 일부 또는 전체를 유발할 수 있다.

→ 문맥상 가능성을 나타내므로 가능의 조동사[can (~일 수 있다)]가 적절하다.

13 Speaking up is important. Yet speaking up without listening is **like** _____ pots and pans together: even if it gets you attention, it's not going to get you respect.

ⓐ to bang
ⓑ banging
ⓒ bang
ⓓ to have banged

정답 ⓑ

해석 의견을 말하는 것은 중요하다. 그러나 듣지 않고 의견을 말하는 것은 냄비와 팬을 함께 세게 두드리는 것과 같다: 비록 그것이 당신에게 관심을 갖게는 할지라도 당신을 존중하게 하지는 못할 것이다.

→ 해당문장의 [like]는 전치사로 동명사를 목적어로 취한다. 따라서 [banging]이 적절하다.

14 The company has provided many medical products for the needy who can't afford them. _____, the company plans to build many houses for them to live for free.

ⓐ Moreover
ⓑ Therefore
ⓒ However
ⓓ In other words

정답 ⓐ

해석 그 기업은 의약품을 구입할 수 없는 사람들에게 많은 의약품을 제공했다. 게다가 그 기업은 그들이 무료로 살 수 있는 많은 집들도 지어줄 계획이다.

→ 문맥상 앞 문장에 언급한 의약품의 내용에 무료 집으로 이어지는 첨가하는 내용이므로 첨가의 접속부사 [Moreover (게다가)]가 적절하다.

15 Jason had such a tiring day in school yesterday. As soon as he got home, he went straight to bed. He _____ **for over 10 hours when Russell finally woke him up.**

ⓐ has slept
ⓑ had been sleeping
ⓒ was sleeping
ⓓ would sleep

정답 ⓑ

해석 제이슨은 어제 학교에서 피곤한 날을 보냈습니다. 그는 집에 도착하자마자 곧바로 자러갔다. 그는 러셀이 결국 그를 깨울 때까지 10시간 넘게 잠을 자고 있는 중 이었다.

→ 해당문장의 부사절[when Russell finally woke him up]의 시제가 과거시제이고, 주절에 [for over 10 hours (10시간 넘는 시간 동안)]가 있으므로 과거완료진행형이 적절하다.

16 Russell has worked so hard for a month and he think he needs to have a break. Because he has been to many foreign countries, this time he **is considering** _____ to Jeju island.

ⓐ traveling
ⓑ to travel
ⓒ to be traveling
ⓓ will travel

정답 ⓐ

해석 러셀은 한 달 동안 너무 힘들게 일해서 그는 휴식을 취할 필요가 있다고 생각했다. 그는 많은 외국에 있는 국가들은 가봤기 때문에 이번에는 그는 제주도에 여행가는 것을 고려하는 중이다.

→ 타동사[consider]는 동명사를 목적어로 취하는 동사이므로 [traveling]이 적절하다.

17 I always want to have enough money not to be worried about how much money I should spend. However, I know well that if I _____ so rich, I **wouldn't be** what I am now.

ⓐ am
ⓑ were
ⓒ had been
ⓓ has been

정답 ⓑ

해석 나는 얼마나 많은 돈을 써야하는지를 걱정하지 않을 만큼 충분한 돈을 갖기를 원한다. 그러나 만약 내가 부자라면 지금의 내가 아닐 것이라는 것을 나는 잘 알고 있다.

→ 주절의 동사가 [조동사의 과거형+동사원형(wouldn't be)]이므로 현재 또는 미래의 사실에 대한 것이다. 따라서 가정절의 동사는 과거형[were]가 적절하다.

18 I am not sure if Russell will visit us in the evening today. But I **remember** _____ me last Saturday that he would come to my place and enjoy dinner together today.

ⓐ to tell
ⓑ telling
ⓒ to have heard
ⓓ told

정답 ⓑ

해석 나는 러셀이 오늘 저녁에 우리를 방문할지 확실하지 않다. 그러나 나는 지난주 토요일에 그가 나에게 우리 집에 와서 같이 저녁을 함께 즐길 것이라고 말했던 것을 기억한다.

→ 타동사[remember]은 [to R]와 동명사를 모두 목적어로 취할 수 있다. 즉, [remember to R (~할 것을 기억하다)]와 [remember ~ing (~했던 것을 기억하다)]이다. 해당문장의 문맥상 '~했던 것을 기억하다'로 동명사[telling]가 적절하다.

19 The Moors, Arab conquerors from North Africa, ruled Spain for nearly 800 years. **The society** _____ was in its unprecedented tolerance, unique.

ⓐ when the Moors presided over in medieval Spain

ⓑ whom the Moors presided over in medieval Spain

ⓒ whose the Moors presided over in medieval Spain

ⓓ that the Moors presided over in medieval Spain

정답 ⓓ

해석 북아프리카 출신의 아랍계 정복자들인 무어인들은 거의 800년 동안 스페인을 통치했다. 무어인들인 중세 스페인에서 지배한 사회는 전례가 없는 관용이라는 점에서 독특했다.

→ 선행사[The society]가 사물이고 뒤에 전치사의 목적어가 없는 불완벽한 문장이다. 따라서 선행사가 사람이나 사물 모두 취할 수 있는 관계대명사[that]이 적절하다.

20 Last month Russell worked temporarily at a supermarket, where he accidently broke the front door and had to compensate for it. He _____ it, **had** he **been** more careful.

ⓐ wouldn't break

ⓑ will break

ⓒ broke

ⓓ wouldn't have broken

정답 ⓓ

해석 지난달에 러셀은 임시적으로 한 슈퍼마켓에서 일을 했다. 거기서 그는 우연찮게 가게 앞문을 부셨고 그것에 대한 변상을 해야 했다. 만약 그가 좀 더 조심했다면 그는 그것을 부서뜨리지 않았을 것이다.

→ 가정절의 동사가 과거완료[had been]이므로 과거 사건에 대한 가정법 과거완료문장이다. 따라서 주절은 [조동사의 과거형 + have pp(wouldn't have broken)]가 적절하다. 참고로 해당문장은 가정절의 접속사[if]가 생략된 문장이므로, 가정절의 주어와 동사가 도치[Had I]가 되어 있다.

21 The second South-North Korean summit was first scheduled to be held on August 28 to 30, but in mid-August, the North was beset by severe floods and **asked** that the meeting _____ to October.

ⓐ was postponed

ⓑ will be postponed

ⓒ be postponed

ⓓ had been postponed

정답 ⓒ

해석 두 번째 남북 정상 회담은 원래 8월 28일에서 30일에 걸쳐 열릴 예정이었지만 8월 중순에 북한이 심각한 홍수 피해를 입어 회담을 10월로 연기할 것을 요청했다.

→ 당위동사[ask (요구하다)]의 목적절은 당위절로 해당절에 동사를 반드시 동사원형으로 나타내야 한다. 따라서 [be postponed]가 적절하다.

22 A Korea-China-Japan summit is to be held in Seoul **later this month,** and people _____ whether it will bring a breakthrough in the comfort women issue.

ⓐ have watched
ⓑ will be watching
ⓒ were watching
ⓓ will have been watching

해석 이달 말께 한·중·일 정상회의가 서울에서 열릴 것이고, 우리는 그 회의가 위안부 문제에 대한 해결책을 이끌어낼 것인지를 볼 것이다.

→ 해당문장에 미래진행부사어구[later this month (이달 말께)]가 있으므로 미래진행형이 적절하다.

23 I am glad to have my English teacher, Russell, who is always passionate and makes English easy to learn. If it _____ for him, I **might be studying** another language, not English.

ⓐ had not been
ⓑ were not
ⓒ is not
ⓓ has not been

정답 ⓑ

해석 나는 항상 열정적이고 영어를 배우기 쉽게 만들어주는 영어선생님, 러셀이 있어서 기쁘다. 그가 없다면 나는 영어가 아니라 다른 언어를 공부하고 있을 것이다.

→ 주절의 동사가 [조동사의 과거형 + 동사원형(might be studying)]이므로 현재 또는 미래의 사실에 대한 것이다. 따라서 가정절의 동사는 과거형[were not]가 적절하다.

24 Because Julia arrived at the theater after the movie started, my friend and I missed the beginning part of the movie. We _____ for about 30 minutes before she finally appeared.

ⓐ were waiting
ⓑ have been waiting
ⓒ will have waited
ⓓ had been waiting

정답 ⓓ

해석 줄리아는 영화가 시작하고 극장에 도착했다. 내 친구와 나는 영화의 시작부분을 놓쳤다. 우리는 그녀가 마침내 나타나기까지 약 30분 동안 그녀를 기다려 오는 중이었다.

→ 해당문장의 부사절[before she finally appeared]의 시제가 과거시제이고, 주절에 [for about 30 minutes (대략 30분 동안)]가 있으므로 과거완료진행형이 적절하다.

25 Yesterday Jack bought two movie tickets to get a date with his girl friend. But she didn't make it so he had to watch the movie alone. If he **had known** that she couldn't make it, he _____ the two tickets.

ⓐ hadn't bought
ⓑ wouldn't have bought
ⓒ buys
ⓓ bought

[정답] ⓑ

[해석] 어제 잭은 그녀의 여자 친구와 데이트를 하기 위해서 영화티켓을 두 개를 구매했다. 그러나 그녀는 영화를 볼 수가 없어서 혼자서 영화를 봐야했다. 만약 그가 그녀가 올 수 없다는 것을 알았다면 그는 영화티켓을 구재하지 않았을 것이다.

→ 가정절의 동사가 과거완료[had known]이므로 과거사건에 대한 가정법 과거완료문장이다. 따라서 주절은 [조동사의 과거형 + have pp(wouldn't have bought)]가 적절하다.

26 Lino A. Saputo, chair and CEO of the company, said, "Treating people with respect and without discrimination is one of our basic principles, and it is **imperative** that we _____ to uphold this in everything we do.

ⓐ have continued
ⓑ continue
ⓒ will continue
ⓓ are continuing

[정답] ⓑ

[해석] 이 회사의 회장이자 CEO, 리노 A 사푸토는 "사람을 존중하고 차별 없이 대하는 것은 우리의 기본 원칙 중 하나이며, 우리가 하는 모든 일에 있어서 이를 계속 유지하는 것이 중요합니다."라고 말했다.

→ 이성적 판단형용사[imperative (필수적인)]의 진주어는 당위절로 항상 동사원형으로 나타내야 한다. 따라서 [continue]가 적절하다.

01 Although Jack tries to save enough money to buy a house here, he doesn't think he can however hard he may work. _____ **a house**, he must have at least two jobs and spend little money.

ⓐ Buying
ⓑ To have bought
ⓒ To buy
ⓓ Having bought

정답 ⓒ

해석 비록 잭은 이곳에서 집을 구매하기 위한 충분한 돈을 모으려고 시도하지만 그는 아무리 열심히 일하더라도 그렇게 할 수 있다고 생각하지 않는다. 집을 구매하기 위해서는 그는 최소 두 개의 직장이 있고 돈도 거의 쓰면 안 된다.

→ 해당문장의 주어[He]보다 앞에 위치한 부사적 용법의 목적(~하기 위하여)이다. 이 경우 [to]부정사 [To buy]가 적절하다.

02 It's already 8 o'clock in the evening, and I am still working in the office because of a lot of paper work to complete by today. I think I _____ here **until midnight**.

ⓐ will be staying
ⓑ will have stayed
ⓒ have been staying
ⓓ would have been staying

정답 ⓐ

해석 이미 저녁 8시인데 오늘까지 처리할 많은 서류작업이 있어서 나는 여전히 일을 하고 있다. 내 생각에 자정까지 이곳에 있을 것 같다.

→ 해당문장에 미래진행부사어구[until midnight (자정까지)]가 있으므로 미래진행형이 적절하다.

03 A majority of voters did not support the mayor as in the previous election. If the mayor **had been** more sympathetic to their concerns, they _____ for him.

ⓐ would have voted
ⓑ had voted
ⓒ will vote
ⓓ would vote

정답 ⓐ

해석 대다수의 유권자들은 이전 선거에서처럼 그 시장을 지지하지 않았다. 그들의 관심사에 시장이 좀 더 동조를 했더라면 그에게 표를 던졌을 것이다.

→ 가정절의 동사가 과거완료[had been]이므로 과거사건에 대한 가정법 과거완료문장이다. 따라서 주절은 [조동사의 과거형 + have pp(would have voted)]가 적절하다.

04 Russell tends to deal with even minor tasks in person to make everything correctly done. One of his colleagues **advises** that he _____ some of his work to his staff so that he can focus more important task.

ⓐ allocate
ⓑ is allocating
ⓒ allocates
ⓓ has allocated

정답 ⓐ

해석 러셀은 모든 것이 올바르게 마무리되게 하기 위해서 심지어 중요하지 않은 일까지 직접 처리하는 경향이 있다. 그의 동료중의 한명은 그가 좀 더 중요한 일에 집중할 수 있도록 그의 업무 중의 일부를 직원에게 할당해라고 조언한다.

→ 당위동사[advise (조언하다)]의 목적절은 당위절로 해당절에 동사를 반드시 동사원형으로 나타내야 한다. 따라서 [allocate]가 적절하다.

05 The company Mr Smith works for is currently having a hard time. He _____ as an accountant of the company **for around 15 years now** and is considering moving to another company.

ⓐ is working
ⓑ has been working
ⓒ works
ⓓ are working

정답 ⓑ

해석 스미스씨가 일하는 기업이 현재 어려운 시간을 보내고 있다. 그는 그 회사 회계사로서 약 15년 동안 일해오고 있다. 그는 다른 기업으로 이직하는 것을 고려하고 있다.

→ 해당문장에 현재완료진행부사어구[for around 15 years now (지금까지 약 15년 동안)]가 있으므로 현재완료진행형이 적절하다.

06 The Minister of Employment and Labor said yesterday that companies are willing to cooperate with employees for their job security. _____, it must not hamper labor flexibility.

ⓐ Therefore
ⓑ In fact
ⓒ To sum up
ⓓ Even so

정답 ⓓ

해석 기업들은 고용 안정을 위해서 직원들과 기꺼이 협력할 것이다. 그렇다 할지라도 그것이 노동시장 유연성을 방해해서는 안 된다 라고 고용노동부 장관이 어제 말했다.

→ 문맥상 양보의 의미이므로 양보의 접속부사[even so (그렇다 할지라도)]가 적절하다.

07 You _____ place more value on one over the other, because they are all needed to form the whole. That's called synergy, meaning that the whole is more than the sum of the individual parts.

ⓐ shall not
ⓑ should not
ⓒ can not
ⓓ might not

해석 둘 중의 어느 하나에 더 많은 가치를 두어서는 안 되는데, 그들 모두 전체를 이루는 데 필요하기 때문이다. 그 것은 시너지 효과라고 하는데, 전체는 개별 부분의 총합보 다 크다는 의미이다. (조언)

→ 문맥상 조언이나 충고이므로 조언, 충고의 조동사 [should not(~하지 말아야 한다)]가 적절하다.

08 If the United States **had pursued** its comparative advantage in accordance with market principles, it _____ fish, fur, agricultural products, etc..

ⓐ would export
ⓑ was exporting
ⓒ will have exported
ⓓ would have been exporting

정답 ⓓ

해석 만약, 미국이 시장 원칙에 맞추어 비교 우위를 추구 했더라면, 미국은 생선, 모피, 농산물 등을 수출하고 있을 것이다.

→ 가정절의 동사가 과거완료[had pursued]이므로 과거사건에 대한 가정법 과거완료문장이다. 따라서 주절은 [조동사의 과거형 + have pp(would have been exporting)]가 적절하다.

09 Ross never saw the car running over an old lady on the road. If he _____ the car accident, he **wouldn't have said** that in such a careless way.

ⓐ has witnessed
ⓑ would witness
ⓒ had witnessed
ⓓ was witnessing

정답 ⓒ

해석 로스는 그 자동차가 그 도로에서 한 나이든 숙녀를 치는 것을 결코 보지 못했다. 만약 그가 그 사고를 목격했 다면 그는 그렇게 부주의하게 말하지 않았을 것이다.

→ 주절의 동사가 [조동사의 과거형 + have pp(wouldn't have said)]이므로 과거의 사실에 대한 것이 다. 따라서 가정절의 동사는 과거완료형[had witnessed] 가 적절하다.

10 With the effect of its power saving demonstrated, GS Retail, which runs GS25 convenience stores, _____ the number of its stores adopting the technology **since last year**.

ⓐ is increasing
ⓑ increased
ⓒ has been increasing
ⓓ will increase

정답 ⓒ

해석 전력을 절약하는 효과가 검증됨으로써 GS25를 운영하는 GS리테일은 지난해부터 점차 이 기술을 적용하는 매장의 수를 늘려오고 있는 중이다.

→ 해당문장에 현재완료진행부사어구[since last year (작년 이후로)]가 있으므로 현재완료진행형이 적절하다.

11 The report **suggested** that the government _____ a favorable environment for companies to adopt various safety nets for management protection, while keeping a watchful eye on foreign investors.

ⓐ create
ⓑ created
ⓒ was creating
ⓓ had created

정답 ⓐ

해석 이 보고서는 정부가 외국인 투자자를 면밀히 지켜보는 가운데, 기업이 경영권 보호를 위해 여러 가지 안전망을 채택할 수 있는 우호적인 환경을 조성해야 한다고 제안했다.

→ 당위동사[suggest (제안하다)]의 목적절은 당위절로 해당절에 동사를 반드시 동사원형으로 나타내야 한다. 따라서 [create]가 적절하다.

12 The English essay Jane wrote for his English composition class is very similar to mine. It has even similar grammar errors. But she firmly **denies** _____ my essay.

ⓐ to copy
ⓑ copied
ⓒ will copy
ⓓ copying

정답 ⓓ

해석 제인이 영작문 수업을 위해 작성한 영어 에세이는 나의 것과 아주 흡사했다. 심지어 비슷한 문법 오류도 가지고 있었다. 그러나 그녀는 나의 에세이를 카피했다는 것을 단호하게 부인했다.

→ 타동사[deny (부인하다)]는 동명사를 목적어로 취하는 동사이므로 [copying]이 적절하다.

13 Schooling is compulsory for all children in the United States. _____ the age range for which school attendance is required varies from state to state.

ⓐ However
ⓑ Hence
ⓒ Eventually
ⓓ Moreover

정답 ⓐ

해석 학교 교육은 미국에 있는 모든 아이들에게 의무이다. 그러나 학교 출석이 요구되는 나이 범위는 주마다 다르다.

→ 문맥상 앞문장과의 역접의 의미이므로 역접의 접속부사[however (그러나)]가 적절하다.

14 When Russell was a high school student, he wished that he could speak Spanish. But he ended up studying English though. If he **were given** another opportunity, he _____ to study Spanish.

ⓐ would choose
ⓑ will choose
ⓒ is choosing
ⓓ chooses

정답 ⓐ

해석 러셀이 고등학생일 때 그는 스페인어를 말할 수 있기를 바랬다. 그러나 그는 영어를 공부하게 되었다. 만약 그에게 또 다른 기회가 주어진다면 그는 스페인어를 공부하는 것을 선택할 것이다.

→ 가정절의 동사가 과거[were given]이므로 현재 또는 미래사건에 대한 가정법 과거문장이다. 따라서 주절은 조동사의 과거형[would choose]가 적절하다.

15 A pandemic disease has prohibited many people from traveling to foreign countries for over a year. When the situation ends, people won't be able to **resist** _____ to other countries for vacation.

ⓐ flocking
ⓑ to flock
ⓒ to have flocked
ⓓ having flocked

정답 ⓐ

해석 유행병 때문에 많은 사람들이 1년 넘게 외국으로 여행을 갈 수 없었다. 이 상황이 끝나면 사람들은 휴가차 외국으로 몰려가는 것을 거부할 수 없을 것이다.

→ 타동사[resist (거부하다, 저항하다)]는 동명사를 목적어로 취하는 동사이므로 [flocking]이 적절하다.

16 Drivers often forget renewing their driver's license. Drivers are advised to renew their driver's license on time as they may be required _____ the written and driving tests past the expiration date.

ⓐ retaking
ⓑ are retaking
ⓒ to retake
ⓓ would retake

해석 운전자들은 종종 운전면허증을 갱신하는 것을 잊는다. 유효기간이 지나면 필기시험과 행행시험을 다시 쳐야할지도 모르기 때문에 운전자들은 제 때에 운전면허를 갱신하도록 충고 받는다.

→ 타동사[require]의 수동2형식 문장이다. 즉, [be required to R (~해야 하다. ~할 것을 요구받다)]로 [to] 부정사 [to retake]가 적절하다.

17 When I was finished with homework yesterday, it was too late to go out. That's why I just stayed home then. If I **had finished** it earlier, I _____ out for dinner.

ⓐ went
ⓑ would have gone
ⓒ have gone
ⓓ did go

해석 어제 내가 숙제를 마쳤을 때, 외출하기에는 너무 늦었다. 그래서 나는 집에 그냥 있었다. 만약 숙제는 더 일찍 마쳤다면, 나는 저녁 먹으러 외출했을 것이다.

→ 가정절의 동사가 과거완료[had finished]이므로 과거사건에 대한 가정법 과거완료문장이다. 따라서 주절은 [조동사의 과거형 + have pp(would have gone)]가 적절하다.

18 According to the Office of Health and Safety, odors _____ come from chemicals inside or outside an office space, or even from the construction of a building.

ⓐ will
ⓑ might
ⓒ would
ⓓ shall

해석 Office of Health and Safety (보건안전국)에 따르면 악취는 사무실 실내외의 화학물질이나 심지어 건물의 공사장에서 기인할지도 모른다.

→ 문맥상 추측이므로 추측 조동사[might(~일지도 모른다)]가 적절하다.

19 Jack likes watching soap opera so much that he is called 'couch potato'. There is no doubt that he _____ on the sofa and watching soap opera **right now**.

ⓐ is sitting
ⓑ sat
ⓒ has sat
ⓓ will sit

정답 ⓐ

해석 잭은 드라마를 보는 것을 너무 좋아해서 그는 'couch potato(소파에 앉아서 TV만 보는 사람)'로 불린다. 지금 그는 소파에 앉아서 드라마를 보고 있는 것이 분명하다.

→ 해당문장에 현재진행부사어구[right now (바로 지금)]가 있으므로 현재진행형이 적절하다.

20 In a 2008 decision confirming an individual right to keep and bear arms, the court struck down Washington, D.C. *laws* _____ and required those in the home to be locked or disassembled.

ⓐ who banned handguns
ⓑ that banned handguns
ⓒ when banned handguns
ⓓ whose banned handguns

정답 ⓑ

해석 2008년의 무기를 소유하고 휴대할 수 있는 개인의 권리를 확인하는 결정에서 법원은 권총을 금지하고 권총을 가정에서 안전장치를 해 두거나 분해해 둘 것을 규정하는 워싱턴 DC의 법을 기각했다.

→ 선행사[laws]가 사물이고 뒤에 주어가 없는 불완벽한 문장이다. 따라서 선행사가 사람이나 사물 모두 취할 수 있는 관계대명사[that]이 적절하다.

21 There will surely be a huge crowd at the airport after the global pandemic ends. Therefore, if you prefer to travel abroad with a tight budget, it is **best** that you _____ about three to four months after the pandemic finally ends.

ⓐ will leave
ⓑ are leaving
ⓒ leave
ⓓ have left

정답 ⓒ

해석 세계적인 전염병이 끝난 이후 엄청난 군중이 공항에 몰릴 것이다. 그러므로 만약 빠듯한 예산으로 해외로 여행하기 원한다면 최종적으로 전염병이 끝난 3~4개월 이후에 떠나는 것이 최고다.

→ 이성적 판단형용사[best (가장 좋은)]의 진주어는 당위절로 항상 동사원형으로 나타내야 한다. 따라서 [leave]가 적절하다.

22 When my parents moved in Busan some 60 years ago, there were few buildings there. However, **since then,** the city _____ so fast that it has become one of the most modern cities in the world.

ⓐ developed
ⓑ has been developing
ⓒ had been developing
ⓓ develops

정답 ⓑ

해석 나의 부모님께서 약 60년 전에 부산으로 이주했을 때, 그곳에는 거의 어떤 건물도 없었다. 그러나 그때 이후로 그 도시는 아주 빠르게 발전하여 세계에서 가장 현대적인 도시 중에 하나가 되었다.

→ 해당문장에 현재완료진행부사어구[since then (그때 이후로)]가 있으므로 현재완료진행형이 적절하다.

23 Martin enjoys fishing very much, but has never gone fishing for over three months because he has been so busy working on the project. If he hadn't been that busy, he _____ fishing several times.

ⓐ would have gone
ⓑ would go
ⓒ goes
ⓓ will be going

정답 ⓐ

해석 마틴은 낚시를 많이 좋아하지만 3달 넘게 한 번도 가지 못했다. 왜냐하면 프로젝트에 일한다고 아주 바빴기 때문이다. 만약 그가 그렇게 바쁘지 않았다면 그는 몇 번은 낚시를 갔을 것이다.

→ 가정절의 동사가 과거완료[hadn't been]이므로 과거사건에 대한 가정법 과거완료문장이다. 따라서 주절은 [조동사의 과거형 + have pp(would have gone)]가 적절하다.

24 This mold is impossible to remove and can ruin the fabric. To prevent it, you need to waterproof the canvas. _____ **blocks of wax on your canvas** can make it naturally waterproof.

ⓐ Rubbing
ⓑ To rub
ⓒ Being rubbing
ⓓ To rubbing

정답 ⓐ

해석 이 곰팡이는 제거하기 불가능하여 그 천을 못 쓰게 할 수 있다. 그것을 예방하기 위해서 캔버스 그 천을 방수처리 할 필요가 있다. 캔버스 천에 왁스 덩어리들로 문지르는 것으로 그 천을 자연스럽게 방수처리 할 수 있다.

→ 본주어 자리는 동명사[Rubbing]가 적절하다. 즉, 해당문장의 동사[can make]의 주어자리이다.

25 As the stream continues down the mountain, the steepness of the slope decreases, which results in fewer **rapids** _____ and becomes oxygenated.

ⓐ when the water tumbles over rocks
ⓑ where the water tumbles over rocks
ⓒ whose the water tumbles over rocks
ⓓ whom the water tumbles over rocks

정답 ⓑ

해석 개울이 산 아래로 계속 내려가면서 경사면의 가파름은 감소하고, 그것은 물이 바위 위로 떨어져 내리면서 산소화 되는 급류의 수가 더 줄어들게 한다.

→ 관계사 뒤에 문장이 완벽하고 선행사[fewer rapids (급류)]가 장소명사이므로 장소의 관계부사[where]가 적절하다.

26 One of my colleagues, Jane, had prepared her audition so enthusiastically. Unfortunately, while she _____ on the stage, **the power went out suddenly,** so her performance had to be rescheduled.

ⓐ performed
ⓑ was performing
ⓒ has performed
ⓓ will be performing

정답 ⓑ

해석 나의 동료중의 한명인 제인은 그녀의 오디션을 아주 열정적으로 준비했다. 불행히도 그녀가 무대에서 공연을 하고 있을 때 갑자기 전기가 나가서 그녀의 공연은 일정이 재조정되어야 했다.

→ 해당문장에 주절[the power went out suddenly]이 과거시제이므로 시간부사절은 과거진행시제가 적절하다

01 Currently we are expanding our business for your convenience to include traveling to repair your vehicle. For the last 20 years, our Automotive Center _____ the finest automotive supplies, including cleaning tools, batteries, car accessories and much more.

ⓐ is providing
ⓑ provided
ⓒ had been providing
ⓓ has been providing

정답 ⓓ

해석 현재 저희는 당신의 자동차를 수리하기 위해 출장을 가는 것을 포함시키면서 당신의 편의성을 높이는 방향으로 사업을 확장하고 있습니다. 지난 20년 동안 우리 자동차 센터는 청소도구, 건전지, 자동사 액세서리 등을 포함한 가장 좋은 자동차 부품을 제공해 왔습니다.

→ 해당문장의 현재완료부사어구[For the last 20 years]가 있으므로 현재완료진행[has been providing]가 적절하다.

02 It is generally agreed that fossil fuels are a limited resource. One day they will run out. All countries need _____ on alternatives to fossil fuels to avoid major disruption to out daily lives.

ⓐ working together
ⓑ to work together
ⓒ to have worked together
ⓓ worked together

정답 ⓑ

해석 화석연료가 한정된 자원이라는 것에 일반적으로 동의된다. 언젠가 화석연료가 고갈될 것이다. 우리 일상생활의 커다란 혼란을 피하기 위해서 화석연료의 대체물에 대해서 모든 나라가 협력할 필요가 있다.

→ 동사[need]는 [to R]를 목적어로 취하는 동사이므로 [to work together]가 적절하다. [need]은 완료부정사 [to have worked together]를 목적어로 취하지 않는다.

03 The Battle of Saratoga in 1777, led by General Arnold, was considered a pivotal victory for the Americans. History may not remember this now, but America's war effort _____ successful if it had not been for his early contributions.

ⓐ might not have been
ⓑ have not been
ⓒ wasn't
ⓓ might not be

정답 ⓐ

해석 1777년에 아놀드 장군이 지휘했던 사라도 전투는 미국인들에게는 중요한 승리로 기억되어 있다. 지금은 역사가 기억하지 못할지라도, 아놀드의 초창기 기여가 없었더라면 미국의 전쟁에 대한 노력은 성공하지 못했을 것이다.

→ [if]절 내의 동사가 과거완료시제[had not been]라서 해당문장은 가정법 과거완료문장이다. 따라서 주절은 과거에 대한 사실을 나타내는 [조동사의 과거형 + have pp]가 적절하다.

04 The stress associated with retraining and new work routines _____ lead to a higher risk of heart disease, high blood pressure, as well as other health issues. The study could help social workers advise seniors about their job opportunities.

ⓐ shall
ⓑ would
ⓒ must
ⓓ can

정답 ⓓ

해석 재교육과 새로운 업무 루틴과 관련된 스트레스는 심장병, 고혈압 및 다른 건강상의 위험으로 이어질 수 있다. 이 연구는 사회복지사들이 고령자들에게 일자리에 대한 상담을 해 줄 때 도움을 줄 수 있다.

→ 해당문장은 문맥상 [~할 가능성이 있다]라는 가능성의 조동사[can]이 적절하다.

05 My wife and sons saw my move-out as an act of abandonment, and my divorce came less than a year later. I know now that if your children or your wife ask you to stay, it is best that you _____ hard about where your priorities lie.

ⓐ think
ⓑ will think
ⓒ to think
ⓓ are thinking

정답 ⓐ

해석 제 아내와 아들들은 나의 이사를 가정을 팽개치는 행위로 보았고, 1년이 채 되지 않아 저는 이혼을 하고 말았습니다. 이제 저는 만일 당신의 아이들이나 아내가 당신에게 머물 것을 요구한다면, 당신의 우선순위가 어디에 있는지를 곰곰이 생각해 보는 것이 가장 좋다는 것을 압니다.

→ 당위형용사[best]로 구성된 가주어·진주어 구문이다. 이 경우 진주어는 당위종속절이므로 절 내 동사는 반드시 동사원형[think]가 와야 한다.

06 Please wash the vegetables before peeling them, and then slice them into small pieces. While you are doing that, I get some pasta from the refrigerator. When I come back, I _____ you how to cook and blend the ingredients so that your sauce turns our smooth and creamy.

ⓐ have shown
ⓑ have been showing
ⓒ will be showing
ⓓ showed

정답 ⓒ

해석 야채는 껍질을 벗기기 전에 씻은 다음 얇게 썰어 주세요. 여러분께서 그렇게 하시는 동안, 저는 냉장고에서 파스타를 꺼내오겠습니다. 돌아오면, 제가 재료를 넣고 어떻게 요리해야 소스가 잘 섞이고 크림 같이 되는지 보여드리겠습니다.

→ 시간부사절[when I come back]에서 동사[come]는 현재시제이나 문맥상 미래를 의미한다. 따라서 주절은 미래진행시제[will be showing]가 적절하다.

07 Please look the photos over and, in your reply, let me know which one you think would be best for our work needs. I am willing _____ my own money if the one with the most votes is beyond our means.

ⓐ to be contributing
ⓑ contributing
ⓒ contributed
ⓓ to contribute

정답 ⓓ

해석 사진들을 살펴보신 후, 회신에 우리 업무용으로 가장 적절한 것이 어떤 것인지 알려주시기 바랍니다. 마지막 한 가지가 있습니다. 만약 가장 많은 표를 받은 것이 예산을 넘는다면 저는 기꺼이 제 돈을 찬조하겠습니다.

→ [be willing to R (기꺼이 ~ 하다)]구문으로 [to R]가 적절하다.

08 In the analysis of the course survey results, students' dissatisfaction seems to come down to one thing. If students _____ how difficult the course would be, they might not have registered. In the future, it will be necessary to ensure they are aware of what will be required.

ⓐ knew
ⓑ had known
ⓒ have known
ⓓ know

정답 ⓑ

해석 강의에 대한 설문조사결과를 보면 학생들의 불만이 결국 한 가지로 귀착되는 것 같습니다. 만약 학생들이 이 과정이 얼마나 어려울지 알고 있었더라면, 아마 등록을 하지 않았을 것입니다. 앞으로는 무엇이 요구될 지를 학생들이 반드시 알고 있도록 하는 것이 필요합니다.

→ 해당문장은 가정법 과거완료 문장이다. 구체적으로 [if]절의 동사는 주절의 동사[might not have registered]을 고려하여 과거완료시제[had known]가 적절하다. 즉, 과거사건에 대한 것을 설명하고 있다.

09 China's appetite for turtle has emptied the streams across Asia of their terrapin populations. The terrapin population decrease _____ since 1990s when the traditional association between reptile meat and longevity was reemphasized.

ⓐ is doubling
ⓑ had been doubling
ⓒ has been doubling
ⓓ will be doubling

정답 ⓒ

해석 중국의 거북에 대한 식욕 때문에 아시아 전역의 개울들에서 식용 거북의 씨가 마르고 있다. 식용 거북의 개체 수 감소는 파충류 고기와 장수 사이의 전통적인 연관성아 다시 한 번 강조되었을 때인 1990년대 이후로 두배가 되었다.

→ 해당문장에 현재완료부사어구[since ~]가 있으므로 현재완료시제[has been doubling]가 적절하다.

10 The drugs or substances categorized in schedule A are mostly narcotic, have no current acceptance for medical use, and _____ not be prescribed. On the other hand, drugs assigned in schedule B through F have accepted medical use.

ⓐ will
ⓑ may
ⓒ ought to
ⓓ would

해석 항목 A로 분류된 약물들은 대개 마약 성분이 있어 의약적으로 사용을 위해서 현재 승인되지 않고 또한 처방받을 수 없다. 반면에 항목 B부터 F로 분류된 약품들은 의약적 사용이 승인되었다.

→ 문맥을 고려하면 '처방하지 못한다'라는 의미의 허락이나 금지의 의미를 지니는 조동사[may]가 적절하다.

11 James was sick with covid-19 for two weeks. Therefore he could hardly do any school work. For instance, he wasn't able to read any book or write its book report. If he had not gotten sick, he _____ the book.

ⓐ had surely read
ⓑ would have surely read
ⓒ was surely read
ⓓ has surely read

해석 제임스는 코비드 19로 2주간 아팠다. 그래서 그는 어떠한 학교 공부를 할 수가 없었다. 예를 들면 그는 어떤 책도 읽을 수도 그것에 대한 독후감도 쓸 수 없었다. 만약 그가 아프지 않았다면 그는 분명히 책을 읽었을 것이다.

→ [if] 가정절 내의 동사가 과거완료이므로, 가정법 과거완료문장이다. 따라서 주절은 [조동사의 과거형 have + pp]가 와야 한다. 즉, [would have surely read]가 적절하다.

12 As Hurricane Hilda makes her way north, we advise you to garage your vehicles, and to avoid being outside whenever possible until everything has blown over, _____.

ⓐ when should be around midnight tonight
ⓑ what should be around midnight tonight
ⓒ which should be around midnight tonight
ⓓ that should be around midnight tonight

해석 허리케인 힐다가 북상함에 따라, 차량은 차고 안에 넣어두시고, 가능하면 강한 바람이 모두 지나가는 오늘 자정 무렵까지는 외출을 삼가시는 것을 권합니다.

→ 선택지에서 관계사 뒤에 주어가 없는 불 완벽한 절을 고려할 때 관계부사[when]은 적절하지 않다. 또한 콤마[,]가 있어서 [that] 역시 적절하지 않다. [what]은 선행절이 있으므로 적절하지 않다. 따라서 [which]가 적절하다.

13 Traffic today is expected to be unusually slow on the Capital beltway heading out of the city. We urge that you _____ in an additional 90 minutes for traffic delays until around 7 this evening.

ⓐ have built
ⓑ building
ⓒ build
ⓓ are building

정답 ⓒ

해석 오늘 시내 밖으로 빠져나가는 캐피탈 순환도로의 교통상황이 평소보다 정체될 것으로 예상됩니다. 교통정체로 인해 오늘 저녁 7시 정도까지 약 90분 정도 더 예상하시길 바랍니다.

→ 당위동사[urge]의 목적절은 당위종속절이므로 [that]절 내의 동사는 반드시 동사원형[build]가 적절하다.

14 According to firsthand accounts from many of his peers, Beethoven was difficult _____ with and to understand. He would often arrive late for dinner and would frequently appear in public unshaven and unkempt.

ⓐ getting along
ⓑ to get along
ⓒ to have got along
ⓓ gets along

정답 ⓑ

해석 그의 많은 동료들의 직접 증언에 따르면 베토벤은 친하게 지내거나 이해하기가 어려웠다고 한다. 그는 종종 만찬에 늦게 도착했고, 면도하지 않고 깔끔하지 못한 모습으로 대중 앞에 나타나는 경우도 많았다.

→ 형용사[difficult]를 수식하는 [to R]의 부사적용법이다. 따라서 [to get along]이 적절하다.

15 He was talking about strong, smart, hardworking entrepreneurs. They woke up motivated every day and _____ their best to make their lives and their family's lives better.

ⓐ are doing
ⓑ has done
ⓒ had been doing
ⓓ were doing

정답 ⓓ

해석 그는 힘세고, 똑똑하며 열심히 일하는 기업가들에 대해 이야기 하고 있었다. 그들은 매일 의욕적으로 일어나서, 그들의 삶과 그들 가족의 삶을 더 낫게 만들기 위해 최선을 다하는 사람들이었습니다.

→ 위 글의 모든 시제가 과거동사이고, 문맥상 단순과거진행시제[were doing]가 적절하다.

16 People often associate entertainment with city life. _____, people enjoy eating out, night-clubbing, going to bars or ballet, opera and symphony orchestras. Cities offer choices that aren't possible in smaller towns.

    ⓐ For example
    ⓑ In contrast
    ⓒ Even though
    ⓓ Besides

정답 ⓐ

해석 사람들은 오락과 도시 생활을 연결시킨다. 예를 들자면, 사람들은 외식과 나이트클럽, 술집, 발레, 오페라와 교향악단 공연에 가는 것을 즐긴다. 도시는 작은 타운에서 가능하지 않은 선택들을 제공한다.

ⓐ 예를 들면　ⓑ 대조적으로
ⓒ 비록 ~이지만　ⓓ 게다가

→ 문맥을 고려하면 앞의 문장에서 언급한 도시와 오락에 대한 예시가 이어진다. 따라서 예시의 접속부사[For example]이 적절하다. 참고로, [Even though]는 접속사로 의미와 관계없이 문법적으로 올수 없다.

17 Benedict Arnold, the general of the American Revolutionary War, became America's most notorious traitor. _____, people forget that up until he changed sides and joined the British, Arnold had a very distinguished record for the American side.

    ⓐ Therefore
    ⓑ However
    ⓒ Indeed
    ⓓ In addition

정답 ⓑ

해석 미국 독립전쟁의 장군인 베네딕트 아놀드는 미국에서 가장 악명 높은 반역자가 되었다. 그러나 사람들은 그가 영국군에 합류할 때까지는 아놀드가 미국편에서 아주 뛰어난 업적이 있었다는 것을 잊는다.

ⓐ 그러므로　ⓑ 그러나
ⓒ 정말로　ⓓ 덧붙여

→ 앞의 문장은 베네딕트 아놀드가 반역자라 언급을 하고, 뒤의 문장은 미국을 위해서 많은 업적을 쌓았다는 의미로, 문맥상 역접의 의미를 지닌다. 따라서 [however]가 적절하다.

18 Because of his tight financial budget this year, Jack won't be able to afford a Christmas tree for his children this holiday. He would immediately buy it if he _____ enough money, which isn't meant to be this year.

    ⓐ had
    ⓑ would have
    ⓒ had had
    ⓓ has

정답 ⓐ

해석 그의 빡빡한 올해의 재정예산 때문에 잭은 이번 휴일에 아이들을 위한 크리스마스트리를 구매할 여력이 없을 것이다. 만약 그가 충분한 돈이 있으며 즉시 그것을 구매할 것이지만 올해는 그렇게 되지 않을 것이다.

→ 주절의 동사[would immediately buy]를 고려하면 현재 또는 미래사실에 대한 내용이다. 따라서 [if] 가정절의 동사역시 과거동사[had]가 적절하다.

19 City officials are cautioning pet owners to be extra careful about _____ their animals stay outside for extended periods of time. With temperatures regularly in the low 90s, this summer heat is expecially dangerous to animals with thick coats of fur.

ⓐ letting
ⓑ to let
ⓒ let
ⓓ having let

해석 시 공무원들은 애완동물 주인들에게 오랜 시간동안 야외에 동물들이 나와 있지 않도록 각별히 조심해 달라고 주의를 주고 있습니다. (화씨) 90도를 약간 넘는 기온이 지속되는 이번 여름의 더위는 두터운 털을 갖고 있는 동물들에게 특히 위험합니다.

→ 전치사[about]의 목적어로 동명사[letting]이 적절하다.

20 Dubbed the world factory, over the last decades, China _____ more industrial goods than any other country. The communist country has helped fuel its high-speed economic growth that is expected to surpass 8 percent this year.

ⓐ had been rapidly producing
ⓑ has been rapidly producing
ⓒ was rapidly producing
ⓓ will have rapidly produced

정답 ⓑ

해석 세계의 공장이라고 불리고 있는 중국은 지난 수십 년 동안 그 어떤 나라보다도 많은 산업재를 급격히 생산해 왔다. 그 공산국가는 올해 8%를 초과할 것으로 예상되는 초고속 경제성장의 촉진을 도왔다.

→ 해당 문장에 현재완료부사어구[over the last decades(지난 수십 년간)]가 있으므로 현재완료진행 시제가 적절하다.

21 These latest findings are supported by many experts, _____ that the theory of a Darwinian link between Ida and humans has been unconvincing.

ⓐ what have argued from the beginning
ⓑ who have argued from the beginning
ⓒ that have argued from the beginning
ⓓ when have argued from the beginning

정답 ⓑ

해석 이번의 최근발견은 많은 전문가들에 의해서 지지를 받고 있는데, 이들은 처음부터 아이다와 인간 사이의 진화론적인 연결 이론이 설득력이 없다고 주장해 왔습니다.

→ 선행사가 사람[many experts]이고 동사[have argued]가 이어지는 것을 고려하면 주격 관계대명사[who]가 적절하다. 관계대명사[that]은 콤마[,]때문에 적절하지 않다.

22 Before you leave the bus, you should be aware of a few basic safety procedures as you tour the construction site. It is really important that we _____ anyone working as guests here. Also, make sure you wear your hard hat at all times.

ⓐ not disrupting
ⓑ don't disrupt
ⓒ not to disrupt
ⓓ <u>not disrupt</u>

정답 ⓓ

해석 버스에서 내리기 전에, 여러분은 공사 현장을 둘러볼 때 지켜야 할 기본적인 안전수칙 몇가지를 알고 있어야 합니다. 이곳에서 방문객으로써 작업하는 사람들을 방해하지 않는 것이 중요합니다. 또한 항상 안전모를 반드시 착용하십시오.

→ 당위형용사[important]로 구성된 진주어 가주어 구문이다. 진주어는 당위절로 반드시 동사원형[not disrupt]가 적절하다.

---

23 According to the investigation report of the serious car crash which occurred last night, if only the driver of the tourist bus had refrained from speeding and kept the minimal safe distance between vehicles, it _____ the collision.

ⓐ had avoided
ⓑ could avoid
ⓒ <u>could have avoided</u>
ⓓ has avoided

정답 ⓒ

해석 지난밤에 일어난 심각한 자동차 충돌사고에 대한 수사보고서에 따르면, 만약에 관광버스의 운전자가 과속을 삼가고 차량 간의 최소한의 안전거리를 유지했더라면 충돌은 피할 수 있었을 것이다.

→ [if] 가정절의 동사[had refrained]을 고려하면 가정법 과거완료임을 알 수 있다. 이 경우 주절은 과거사건을 설명하는 [조동사의 과거형 + have pp]로 나타내야 한다. 따라서, ⓒ [could have avoided]가 적절하다.

---

24 Half of the people invited to the meeting showed up late. Combined with the other problems yesterday, that really made Jane angry. She started _____ her fingers on the table, glaring at the latecomers.

ⓐ <u>drumming</u>
ⓑ will drum
ⓒ having drummed
ⓓ to have drummed

정답 ⓐ

해석 회의에 초대된 사람들 중의 절반이 늦게 나타났다. 어제 있었던 다른 문제들과 더불어, 그것이 제인을 정말 화나게 만들었다. 그녀는 늦게 온 사람들을 노려보면서, 테이블을 자신의 손가락으로 쳐서 둥둥 소리를 냈다.

→ 동사[start]는 [to R]와 [~ing] 둘 다 목적어로 취할 수 있다. 그러나 선택지에는 동명사[drumming]만 있으므로 ⓐ [drumming]이 적절하다.

25 Almost all the current movies revolve around romantic love in which a main character meets his or her counterpart of ideal. Although it is an impossible situation, the implausible situation _____ to be projected on the big screen nowadays.

ⓐ has been continuing
ⓑ is continuing
ⓒ has continued
ⓓ continued

해석 거의 대부분의 최근 영화들은 주인공이 이상형을 만나게 되는 낭만적 사랑을 다루고 있습니다. 그것은 실현 불가능한 상황인데, 요즘에 이러한 믿기 어려운 상황이 큰 스크린에서 계속 상영되어 있습니다.

→ 해당문장에 현재시제 부사어구[nowadays]가 있으므로 현재진행시제[is continuing]가 적절하다.

26 Mr. Park, the CEO of JR Electronic, was found guilty of the embezzlement for the last five years. If he offered his resignation and gave the money back immediately, he _____ to jail.

ⓐ would go
ⓑ will go
ⓒ goes
ⓓ would have gone

해석 JR전장 CEO인 박씨는 지난 2년간의 횡령으로 유죄 선고를 받았다. 그가 즉시 사임 하고 돈을 돌려주더라도 그는 감옥에 갈 것이다.

→ [if]절의 동사가 과거시제[offered]이므로 가정법 과거구문이다. 따라서 주절은 현재 또는 미래사건에 대한 내용이므로 주절이 동사는 [조동사의 과거형 + 동사원형]이 적절하다. 즉, ⓐ [would go]가 적절하다.

01 Robert Novak, director of clinical education in audiology at Purdue University, said he has been increasingly seeing too many young people with "older ears on younger bodies," a trend that _____ since the portable Walkman made its debut a few decades back.

ⓐ builds
ⓑ has been building
ⓒ had been building
ⓓ will have build

정답 ⓑ

해석 퍼듀 대학의 청각학 임상교육 담당자인 로버트 노박은 휴대용 워크맨이 몇 십 년 전에 나타난 이래로 증가하고 있는 경향인 "젊은 육체에 늙은 귀"를 가진 젊은이들이 점차적으로 늘어나고 있다고 말했다.

→ 현재완료부사어구[since]가 있으므로 현재완료시제[has been building]가 적절하다.

02 A tourist bus fell off the motorway this morning. If only the builders of the bridge _____ guardrails of concrete instead of iron plates, the bus might have not fallen off the 10-meter-high motorway to the construction site below.

ⓐ have made
ⓑ had made
ⓒ will make
ⓓ make

정답 ⓑ

해석 관광버스 한 대가 오늘 아침에 고가도로에서 떨어졌다. 만약에 교량 건설사가 가드레일을 철판이 아니라 콘크리트로 만들었더라면, 버스는 10미터 높이의 고가도로에서 그 아래 공사장으로 떨어지지 않았을 지도 모른다.

→ 주절의 동사[might have not fallen]을 고려하면 과거사건임을 알 수 있다. 따라서 [if] 가정절 역시 과거사건에 대한 것이어야 한다. 따라서 과거완료시제[had made]가 적절하다.

03 Secretary Ken Watters was reportedly seen leaving a hotel Monday with a young woman. The secretary _____ denied any wrongdoing to reporters. His wife was also asked about the supposed affair this morning but offered no comment.

ⓐ whom has been married for 23 years
ⓑ which has been married for 23 years
ⓒ what has been married for 23 years
ⓓ that has been married for 23 years

정답 ⓓ

해석 켄 와터스 비서관은 젊은 여성과 함께 월요일 한 호텔에서 나오는 것이 목격되었습니다. 결혼한 지 23년이 된 이 비서관은 기자들에게 어떠한 범죄행위에 대해서도 부인했습니다. 그의 아내 또한 이 불륜 소문에 대해서 오늘 아침 질문을 받았지만, 아무런 말도 하지 않았습니다.

→ 관계대명사 뒤에 주어가 없는 불완벽한 절[has been married for 23 years]이 오고 선행사가 사람[The secretary]이므로 관계대명사[that]이 적절하다. 참고로 [whom]은 목적격으로 뒤에 동사가 이어지지 않는다.

04 Anger is a natural response to frightening or threatening situations. Parents should help their children learn to express anger constructively. _____ constructive anger shows children how to convey their feelings in an assertive but unaggressive manner.

ⓐ Expressing
ⓑ To express
ⓒ Having expressed
ⓓ To have expressed

정답 ⓐ

해석 분노는 두렵거나 위협적인 상황에 대한 자연스러운 반응이다. 부모들은 자녀가 건설적으로 분노를 표현하는 방법을 배우도록 도와야 한다. 건설적인 분노 표출 방법은 자녀들에게 단호하지만 공격적이지 않은 방식으로 자신의 감정을 전달하는 방법을 보여준다.

→ 동사의 주어자리에는 동명사만 주어가 될 수 있다. 따라서 해당문장은 동사[shows]의 주어이므로 동명사[Expressing]이 적절하다.

05 When Russell saved enough money to buy a house, both he and his wife breathed a sigh of relief as they have been wanting to purchase a house since they got married. When he buys a house this year, they _____ for more than 10 years.

ⓐ will have been waiting
ⓑ have been waiting
ⓒ had waited
ⓓ are waiting

정답 ⓐ

해석 러셀이 집을 살만큼의 충분한 돈을 모았을 때, 그와 그의 아내는 안도의 한숨을 쉬었다. 왜냐하면 그들은 결혼 후부터 집을 구매하기를 원해왔기 때문이다. 그가 올해 집을 구매할 때는 그들은 10년 이상 기다려 온 것이 된다.

→ [When]절의 현재동사[buys]는 미래사건을 의미하고 시간의 범위[for more than 10 years]가 있으므로 미래완료진행시제[will have been waiting]가 적절하다.

06 Five-star restaurant La Verona was temporarily shut down last night due to continual overcrowding. The local fire marshal ordered that the famed eatery _____ after it had ignored several previous warnings.

ⓐ to close
ⓑ closed
ⓒ close
ⓓ might close

정답 ⓒ

해석 5성 레스토랑 라 베로나가 상습적인 정원 초과로 지난밤 일시적으로 물을 닫았습니다. 그 지역 소방서장은 그 레스토랑이 앞선 두세 번의 경고를 무시한 후, 그 유명한 음식점의 영업중단을 명령했습니다.

→ 당위동사[order]의 목적절은 당위종속절이다. 이 경우 [that]절의 동사는 반드시 동사원형[close]가 적절하다.

07 Russell's family was going to have a grand birthday party for Bella last Sunday. While Russell was preparing the food, Bella couldn't resist _____ at the kitchen due to the delicious smell coming from there.

ⓐ peeking
ⓑ to peek
ⓒ to have peeked
ⓓ peeked

정답 ⓐ

해석 러셀의 가족은 지난 일요일에 벨라는 위한 성대한 깜짝 생일파티를 열 것이었다. 러셀이 음식을 준비하는 동안 벨라는 부엌에서 나는 맛있는 냄새 때문에 부엌을 훔쳐보지 않을 수 없었다.

→ 동사[resist]는 동명사를 목적어로 취하는 동사이다. 따라서 동명사 ⓐ[peeking]이 적절하다.

08 Cholera was believed to be transmitted by gas or vapor. _____, according to the 1854 Cholera Map of London by Dr. John Snow, the cases were centered on a particular water pump used by all residents. Based on this observation, Snow concluded that water was the carrier of cholera, not gas.

ⓐ Besides
ⓑ Hence
ⓒ However
ⓓ That's why

정답 ⓒ

해석 콜레라는 기체나 증기에 의해서 전염된다고 여겨졌다. 그러나 존 스노 박사의 1854년 런던 콜레라 지도에 따르면 모든 주민들이 사용했던 특정한 수도 펌프에 발병 사례들이 집중되어 있음을 보여주었다. 이러한 관찰을 바탕으로, 스노는 기체가 아니라 물이 콜레라의 매개체라고 결론을 내렸다.

ⓐ 게다가 ⓑ 따라서
ⓒ 그러나 ⓓ 그래서

→ 앞의 문장의 내용은 콜레라가 기체에 의해서 전염된다는 내용이고, 뒤의 내용은 기체에 의한 전염이 아니라는 내용이므로 역접의 접속부사[However]가 적절하다.

09 One needs to be versatile and easygoing to be a teacher. They should be comfortable around with kids. Hence, it is strongly suggested that potential teachers _____ a variety of social activities.

ⓐ have joined
ⓑ joining
ⓒ will join
ⓓ join

정답 ⓓ

해석 선생님이 되기 위해서는 다재다능하고 편안한 성격을 지녀야 한다. 그들은 아이들과 함께하는 것에 편안함을 느껴야 한다. 따라서, 교사가 될 사람들은 다양한 사회 활동에 참여할 것을 강력히 제안한다.

→ 해당 문장은 동사[suggest]의 당위종속절이다. 따라서 동사원형[participate]가 적절하다.

10 Jack was supposed to meet one of his friends, Russell, at the study cafe at 5 pm on Sunday for the regular meeting. But it slipped his mind, causing he not to make it on time. If he _____ the appointment down on his calendar, he would have arrived on time.

ⓐ could have written
ⓑ wrote
ⓒ had written
ⓓ has written

정답 ⓒ

해석 잭은 정기모임으로 일요일 5시에 스터디 까페에서 친구, 러셀을 만나기로 되어 있었다. 그러나 그는 깜빡 잊었고 제시간에 도착하지 못했다. 만약 그가 그 약속을 일정표에 적어 놓았다면 그는 제 시간에 도착했을 것이다.

→ 주절의 동사[would have arrived]를 고려하면 과거사실에 대한 내용이다. 따라서 [if] 가정절의 동사역시 과거완료동사[had written]이 적절하다.

11 Contrary to popular belief, _____ a cellular phone does not seem to increase brain cancer risk, a new study has revealed. The study involved over ten thousand people, making it the largest analysis of its kind ever conducted.

ⓐ use
ⓑ using
ⓒ to use
ⓓ to have used

정답 ⓑ

해석 일반적인 생각과는 반대로, 휴대폰을 사용하는 것이 뇌종양의 위험을 증가시키는 것으로는 보이지 않는다고 새로운 연구가 밝혔다. 그 연구는 지금까지 실시된 같은 종류 중에서 가장 큰 분석 연구로 만 명이상의 사람들을 참여시켰다.

→ 동사[does not seem ~]의 주어자리이므로 동명사[using ~]가 적절하다.

12 On account of traffic jam, I am stuck on the road and literally crawling at the speed of five kilometers per hour. By the time I get to the office located near Seoul station, I _____ there for over two hours.

ⓐ have driven
ⓑ will drive
ⓒ had been driving
ⓓ will have been driving

정답 ⓓ

해석 교통정체 때문에 나는 도로에서 꼼짝 못하고 실질적으로 시속 5km의 속도로 기어가고 있습니다. 내가 서울역 근처에 위치한 사무실에 도착했을 무렵쯤이면 나는 두 시간 이상 그곳으로 운전했을 것이다.

→ 시간부사절내의 현재동사[get]은 미래사건에 대한 것이다. 또한 시간의 범위[for over two hours]가 있으니 미래완료진행시제[will have been driving]가 적절하다.

13 Conventional rockets generate thrust by burning chemical fuel. Electric rockets, _____, propel space vehicles by applying electric or electromagnetic fields to clouds of charged particles to accelerate them.

ⓐ in short
ⓑ consequently
ⓒ furthermore
ⓓ by contrast

〔정답〕 ⓓ

〔해석〕 재래식 로켓은 화학연료를 연소시킴으로써 추진력을 생성한다. 대조적으로, 전기 로켓은 전기장 또는 전자기장을 하전입자에 걸어 속도를 높여 우주선을 앞으로 나아가게 한다.
ⓐ 요약하면 ⓑ 결과적으로
ⓒ 더구나 ⓓ 대조적으로

→ 해당문장은 재래식 로켓과 전기 로켓을 대조 설명하는 내용이다. 따라서 대조의 접속부사[by contrast]가 적절하다.

14 Those who are willing to go through much physical pain and stress possess unique personalities. These people tend _____ achievers who set high standards for themselves not only in sports but also in general.

ⓐ to become
ⓑ becoming
ⓒ become
ⓓ having become

〔정답〕 ⓐ

〔해석〕 많은 신체적 고통과 스트레스를 기꺼이 겪어내려는 사람들에게는 독특한 성격이 있다. 이 사람들은 스포츠에서뿐만 아니라 전반적으로 스스로에게 높은 기준을 세우는 성취자가 되려는 경향이 있다.

→ 동사[tend]는 [to R]를 목적어로 취하는 동사이다. 따라서 ⓐ[to become]가 적절하다.

15 When Russell tried to pay for the drink in a local bar yesterday, he realized that he had forgot his purse. If only he had been more careful, he _____ embarrassed there.

ⓐ will not be
ⓑ was not
ⓒ would not have been
ⓓ would not be

〔정답〕 ⓒ

〔해석〕 어제 러셀이 로컬 바에서 술값을 지불하려고 할 때 그는 지갑을 두고 온 것을 깨달았다. 만약 그가 좀 더 주의했더라면, 그는 그곳에서 당혹스럽지 않았을 것이다.

→ [if]절의 동사가 과거완료시제[had been]이므로 가정법 과거완료구문이다. 따라서 주절 또한 과거사건에 대한 내용이므로 주절의 동사는 [조동사의 과거형 + have + pp]가 적절하다. 즉, ⓒ [would not have been]이 적절하다.

16 The government has been criticized for changing the curriculum too frequently, causing confusion and trouble to students. It should no longer play with short-sighted education policies. Instead, policymakers _____ stress what the essential requirements in the curriculum are in the longer run.

ⓐ might
ⓑ must
ⓒ can
ⓓ would

해석 정부가 교과과정을 너무 자주 바꿔 학생들에게 혼란과 갈등을 주고 있다는 비판을 받아왔다. 정부는 더 이상 근시안적인 교육정책으로 학생들을 농락해서는 안 된다. 오히려, 정책입안자들은 교과과정에서 반드시 요구되는 바가 무엇인지를 장기적인 관점에서 강조를 해야 한다.

→ 문맥상 교육정책 입안자가 해야 할 것을 언급하는 내용으로 의무의 조동사[must]가 가장 적절하다.

17 If you send personal emails on your office desktop, there is a high possibility that the boss is keeping an eye on you. In a survey of approximately 1,000 companies, nearly 70% of them admitted _____ a rang of surveillance methods to monitor their employees.

ⓐ used
ⓑ to have used
ⓒ to use
ⓓ using

정답 ⓓ

해석 만약 당신이 회사 컴퓨터로 개인적인 이메일을 발송한다면 당신의 상가가 당신을 감시할 가능성이 매우 크다. 대략 1,000개의 회사들을 대상으로 한 조사에서 거의 70%가 그들의 직원들을 감시하기 위해서 일련의 감시 방법들을 사용하고 있다고 인정했다.

→ 동사[admit]는 동명사를 목적어로 취하는 동사이므로 ⓓ[using]이 적절하다.

18 A new study says the rates of breast cancer mortality _____ across much of the world. Declines in breast cancer deaths are most prominent in developed countries, with England and Wales experiencing the biggest drops.

ⓐ currently drop
ⓑ are currently dropping
ⓒ were currently dropping
ⓓ had currently dropped

정답 ⓑ

해석 새로운 연구에 따르면 유방암 사망률이 전 세계 여러 지역에서 감소하고 있다. 유방암 사망률 감소는 선진국들에서 아주 뚜렷한데, 잉글랜드와 웨일스가 가장 큰 폭의 감소를 보이고 있다.

→ 선택지내 현재시제부사[currently]를 고려하면 현재진행시제[are currently dropping]이 적절하다.

19 A friend of mine, Jessica, is worried about her son since he has a financial problem for his business. If Jessica _____ the money to spare for his business, she would help her son right away.

ⓐ had
ⓑ would have
ⓒ has
ⓓ has had

해석 나의 친구 중 한명인 제시카는 그녀의 아들을 걱정한다. 왜냐하면 그는 그의 사업에 있어 재정문제를 겪고 있기 때문이다. 만약 제시카가 그녀 아들의 사업을 위한 여유돈을 가지고 있다면, 그녀는 바로 그를 도와줄 것이다.

→ 주절의 동사[would help]를 고려하면 현재 또는 미래사실에 대한 내용이다. 따라서 [if] 가정절의 동사역시 과거동사[had]가 적절하다.

20 When the U.S. Weather Service released its latest hurricane warning, workers _____ the finishing touches to the preparations for the July 4th celebrations at the governor's mansion. Nevertheless, the much-awaited party was canceled because of the weather condition.

ⓐ had been just putting
ⓑ have just put
ⓒ just put
ⓓ were just putting

해석 미국 국립 기상청이 최신 허리케인 경고를 발표했을 때, 인부들은 주지사이 저택에서 독립기념일 기념행사를 위한 마무리 작업을 하고 있는 중이었다. 그럼에도 불구하고 기상조건 때문에 많이 기다려온 파티가 취소되었다.

→ [When]시간부사절 내의 동사[released]가 과거시제이므로 주절 역시 과거진행시제[were just putting]가 가장 적절하다.

21 Tension thickened last week when Washington hinted it may consider referring North Korea's nuclear issue to the U.N. Security Council. In the meantime U.S. media reported over the weekend that North Korea _____ be preparing for its first nuclear test.

ⓐ shall
ⓑ might
ⓒ will
ⓓ must

해석 미국이 북한 핵문제를 유엔 안보리에 회부하는 것을 고려할 수 있다는 것을 암시한 지난주에 긴장이 고조되었다. 그러는 동안 미국 언론은 지난 주말 북한이 최초의 핵실험을 준비하고 있을 지도 모른다는 보도를 냈다.

→ 문맥을 고려하면 북한이 핵실험을 준비하고 있을지도 모른다는 추측을 드러내고 있다. 따라서 추측의 조동사[might]가 가장 적절하다.

22 Russell is thought to be a very lovely and friendly man. Handsome with a smart, polite personality, indeed he is every woman's desired man. If Jane had the opportunity to hang out with him, she _____ happy.

ⓐ would be
ⓑ is
ⓒ would have been
ⓓ was

정답 ⓐ

해석 러셀은 사랑스럽고 다정한 남자라고 한다. 똑똑하고 공손한 성격의 잘생긴 그는 모든 여성들이 원하는 남자이다. 만약 제인이 그와 함께 시간을 보낼 기회를 갖는다면 그는 기쁠 것이다.

→ [if]절의 동사가 과거시제[had]이므로 가정법 과거 구문이다. 따라서 주절 또한 현재 또는 미래사건에 대한 내용이므로 주절의 동사는 [조동사의 과거형 + 동사원형]이 적절하다. 즉, ⓐ [would be]가 적절하다.

23 Some people may still be haunted by an embarrassing incident _____. Indeed, a memory of being made fun of as a child can do permanent damage to one's self-image.

ⓐ who occurred during their school years
ⓑ where occurred during their school years
ⓒ whose occurred during their school years
ⓓ that occurred during their school years

정답 ⓓ

해석 어떤 사람들은 학창시절에 일어났던 당혹스러운 사건에 여전히 시달릴 지도 모른다. 정말로, 아이였을 때 놀림을 받은 기억은 한 사람의 자아상에 영구적인 손상을 줄 수도 있다.

→ 주어가 없는 불 완벽한 절이 오고 선행사가 사물 [an embarrassing incident]인 경우 관계대명사[that]이 적절하다.

24 Technology comes at a price. But today many people _____ so confident that technology can provide all the answers to our problems that they overlook the fact that technology can bring about new problems.

ⓐ had become
ⓑ are becoming
ⓒ will be becoming
ⓓ became

정답 ⓑ

해석 기술은 대가가 따른다. 그러나 오늘날 많은 사람들은 기술이 우리의 문제에 대한 모든 대답을 제공할 수 있다고 너무 확신해서, 기술이 새로운 문제를 야기할 수 있다는 사실을 간과한다.

→ 현재부사[today]를 고려하면 현재진행시제[are becoming]가 적절하다.

25 Instead of dealing with the fact that a 555-meter tall building is out of the question, Lotte has suggested that the Seoul Airport runway _____ in order to make room for the skyscraper.

ⓐ to be adjusted

ⓑ be adjusted

ⓒ has been adjusted

ⓓ is adjusted

정답 ⓑ

해석 555미터 높이의 빌딩이 들어서는 것이 불가능하다는 문제에 대처하지는 않은 채, 롯데는, 고층 건물을 위한 공간을 마련하기 위해 서울 공항 활주로를 조정해 줄 것을 제안했다.

→ 당위동사[suggest]의 목적절은 당위 종속절이다. 따라서 [that]절 내의 동사는 동사원형[be adjusted]가 적절하다.

26 Even though video tapes can only be checked out from the video rental store for a three-week period, Jane kept on for over five weeks. If she _____ the video tape by the due date, a fine would not have been charged.

ⓐ had returned

ⓑ has returned

ⓒ would return

ⓓ returns

정답 ⓐ

해석 비디오테이프를 비디오 대여가게에서 2주 만 빌릴 수 있는데도 제인은 하나를 5주 넘게 가지고 있었다. 만약 그녀가 마감기한까지 그 비디오테이프를 반납했다면, 벌금이 부과되지 않았을 것이다.

→ 주절의 동사[would not have been charged]를 고려하면 과거사실에 대한 내용이다. 따라서 [if] 가정절의 동사 역시 과거사실에 대한 것을 설명하는 과거완료동사 ⓐ [had returned]가 적절하다.

MEMO

G TELP

GRAMMAR
GENIUS

G-TELP 문법의 최신 출제 경향 반영
최소 노력으로 최대 효과를 얻는 구성
왕초보를 위한 최단기 합격법 제시

G-TELP 인증점수 획득을 위한 필수 문법서

공무원, 경찰, 군무원 수험자를 위한
G-TELP 학습서
개정판

G-TELP
GRAMMAR
THEORY

PREFACE

[G-TELP GRAMMAR GENIUS (지텔프 그래마 지니어스)]는 공무원, 경찰 공무원, 군무원 시험을 준비하는 수험생만을 위해서만 집필한 책입니다. 인증점수 달성을 위한 교재입니다. 어학점수 향상을 위해서도 얼마든지 활용이 가능하지만, 지텔프 문법 해결을 위한 해결전략은 인증점수 획득에 초점을 두고 집필하였습니다.

최신 출제 경향반영

지텔프 문법의 최신 출제 경향을 반영하여 실제 출제 유형만을 집중 학습할 수 있도록 하였습니다. 출제되는 유형을 반복 제시하여 유형파악과 해결방법을 숙달할 수 있게 만들었습니다.

최소한의 노력으로 최대한의 결과

초급영어 수험자들이 목표한 인증점수를 획득하기 위해서는 많은 인내와 노력을 들일 수밖에 없습니다. 그러는 동안 많은 고민과 좌절을 겪은 후에 포기하는 수험생도 적지 않습니다. 하여 '어떻게 하면 초급수험자도 인증점수를 쉽게 획득할 수 있을까?'라는 집필동기에 충실하여 본 교재를 만들었습니다.

읽어야 하는 어려운 문제는 패스

지텔프 문법은 해석할 수 없어도 풀 수 있는 문제가 대부분입니다. 6개의 유형 중에서 2개 유형(4 문제)은 반드시 읽어서 풀어야 하는 비교적 난이도가 높은 문제이지만, 나머지 4개의 유형(22 문제)은 의미를 알지 못해도 정답을 찾을 수 있습니다. 그 22문제만 집중을 해도 인증점수 획득에 아무런 문제가 없기 때문에 그에 대한 완벽한 해결전략을 제시하며 본 교재를 집필하였습니다.

왕초보도 두 달이면 필승

올바른 전략을 제시하여 인증영어에 부담을 최소화하였습니다. 다른 수험과목에 집중할 수 있도록 속전속결방법을 제시합니다. 아무리 왕초보라 하더라도 두 달이면 가능할 수 있도록 최선을 다해서 집필하였습니다.

마지막으로..

[G-TELP GRAMMAR GENIUS (지텔프 그래마 지니어스)]가 수험생 여러분들에게 부담을 최소화해주고, 사기를 진작시키는 역할을 할 수 있었으면 하는 바램입니다.

교재를 마무리하면서 *서병석*

G-TELP(General tests of English Language Proficiency)는 국제테스트 연구원(ITSC, International Testing Services Center)에서 주관하여 University of California Los Angeles, Georgetown University, San Diego State University, Lado International College 등의 저명 교수진이 연구 개발하였고, 국내외 저명한 언어학자, 평가전문가들이 참여하여 국제적으로 시행하는 글로벌 영어능력 평가인증시험입니다.

G-TELP는 1983년부터 ITSC 주관으로 개발 검증된 이래 수년간 미국, 중국, 사우디아라비아, 일본, 대만 등 세계 여러 나라에서 표본 조사 및 시행을 통하여 개발완료 하였고, 정부기관 기업 단체에서 독해(reading), 청취(listening), 구술(speaking), 쓰기(writing) 평가를 위한 일반영어, 실용영어 활용능력 평가 교육 도구로서 기업의 채용 인사고가 해외파견, 국가공무원선발 국가자격시험, 초 중고 대학(원)입학 졸업 등 목적으로 널리 활용되고 있습니다.

우리나라에는 1986년에 G-TELP KOREA가 설립되어 ITSC's G-TELP SERVICES의 글로벌 파트너로서 G-TELP(지텔프) 시험을 운영 주관하고 있습니다. G-TELP는 듣기(listening), 말하기(speaking), 쓰기(writing), 읽기(reading) 등 언어의 4대 영역을 종합 평가하는 영어 평가 교육 시스템입니다.

일반적인 시험 구성은 paper-based test(PBT)로 문법/독해/청취를 평가하는 G-TELP Level Test(GLT), 말하기 시험인 G-TELP Speaking Test(GST), 작문시험인 G-TELP Writing Test(GWT)로 구성되어 있습니다. 기업의 비지니스 영역 평가에 특화된 말하기와 작문시험인 G-TELP Business Test(GBST/GBWT), 주니어 종합 영어평가시험인 G-TELP Jr.가 있습니다. 특수 목적형 시험인 UN. ICAO 규정 항공영어말하기자격시험인 English proficiency Test for Aviation(EPTA)가 있습니다.

G-TELP는 대한민국, 미국, 일본, 중국, 대만, 멕시코 등을 중심으로 국제적으로 활용되고 있으며 그 실용성 객관성 타당성을 인정받아 88서울올림픽, 2008 베이징 올림픽의 공식 영어 평가교육 툴(통역 안내, 자원봉사자 선발 교육)로써 지정 활용되어 영어평가 교육 방법 체계의 객관성, 타당성 그리고 우수성을 입증 받은 바 있습니다. 약200여개 회원국으로 구성된 국제민간항공기구(UN. ICAO)규정에 따라 세계적으로 의무 시행되는 항공영어말하기자격시험(EPTA)을 개발하여 보급 시행하였고, Rated Speech Sample(채점 샘플)로 보급되어 특수목적형 시험개발 운영 시행의 객관 타당성, 우수성을 입증한 바 있습니다.

TOEFL이나 TOEIC 등의 기존 테스트 방식의 대다수가 Norm referenced method로 개발된 반면, G-TELP 는 Criterion referenced method로 개발이 되었습니다. Norm referenced method란 테스트의 주목적이 A라는 수험자의 언어능력을 B라는 수험자와 단순 비교하기 위한 방식인데 비해, Criterion referenced method는 A와 B의 단순한 비교에 더하여 A와 B의 언어능력을 분석하여, A 또는 B가 무슨 일을 할 수 있는지 까지를 정확히 분석 진단하는 방식입니다. Criterion referenced method의 대표적인 예는 운전 면허 시험방식 이라 할 수 있습니다. G-TELP는 어떤 특정한 업무수행, 예를 들면 사무직, 기술직, 대학생만이 아닌, 일상생활과 관련된 일반적인 의사소통능력을 평가하는 다섯단계의 등급시험(Level Tests)과 말하기 쓰기 시험을 평가하는 별도의 독립된 말하기&쓰기(Speaking & Writing Tests)로 구성되어 있습니다.

G-TELP(General tests of English Language Proficiency)는 단순히 어떤 배운 내용을 평가하는 시험이 아 닌, 영어능력을 종합적으로 평가하는 시험이며 국제 공인 시험이 가지는 신뢰성(Reliability), 타당성(Validity), 실용성(Practicality)을 갖춘 시험으로 점수를 다른 사람과 비교할 수 있을 뿐 아니라 수험자의 영어능력을 철저 하게 분석하고 진단하여 수험자가 자신의 언어능력으로 무슨 일을 어느 정도로 잘 해낼 수 있는지를 알려줍니다.

현재 대한민국에서는 국가고시(공무원, 군무원, 소방, 경찰 등), 공무원 해외파견, 국가자격증(변리사, 회계사, 세 무사, 노무사, 감정평가사, 행정사, 관광통역안내사, 호텔경영사 등) 영어대체시험, 기업체의 신입사원 채용 및 인사, 승진 평가시험, 대학(원)교 졸업자격 및 논문 심사 영어대체시험, 초·중·고등학교 영어 평가인증 및 교육자 료로 활용되고 있습니다.

G-TELP의 시험 구성

출처: 지텔프코리아 (www.g-telp.co.kr)

구분	출제방식 및 시간	평가기준	합격자의 영어 구사 능력
Level 1	청취: 30문항/약 30분 독해 및 어휘: 60문항/70분 합계: 90문항/약 100분	Native Speaker에 준하는 영어 능력: 상담, 토론 가능	• 모국어로 하는 외국인과 거의 대등한 의사 소통이 가능 • 국제회의 통역도 가능한 수준
Level 2 공무원 군무원 자격증 등 영어대체 시험에 활용	문법: 26문항/20분 청취: 26문항/약 30분 독해 및 어휘: 28문항/40분 합계: 80문항/약 90분	다양한 상황에서 대화 가능: 업무상담 및 해외연수 등이 가능한 수준	• 일상 생활 및 업무 상담 등에서 어려움 없이 의사소통 할 수 있는 수준 • 외국인과의 회의 및 세미나 참석, 해외 연수 등이 가능한 수준
Level 3	문법: 22문항/20분 청취: 24문항/약 20분 독해 및 어휘: 24문항/40분 합계: 70문항/약80분	간단한 의사소통과 친숙한 상태에서의 단순 대화 가능	• 간단한 의사 소통과 친숙한 상태에서의 단순한 대화가 가능한 수준 • 해외 여행과 단순한 업무 출장을 할 수 있는 수준
Level 4	문법: 20문항/20분 청취: 20문항/약 15분 독해 및 어휘: 20문항/25분 합계: 60문항/약 60분	기본적인 문장을 통해 최소한의 의사소통이 가능한 수준	• 기본적인 어휘의 짧은 문장을 통해 최소한의 의사 소통이 가능한 수준 • 외국인이 자주 반복하거나 부연설명을 해주어야 이해할 수 있는 수준
Level 5	문법: 16문항/15분 청취: 16문항/약 15분 독해 및 어휘: 18문항/25분 합계: 50문항/약 55분	극히 초보적인 수준의 의사 소통 가능	• 영어 초보자 • 일상의 인사, 소개 등을 듣고, 이해할 수 있는 수준 • 말 또는 글을 통한 자기표현은 거의 불가능한 수준

G-TELP (LEVEL 2)의 시험 영역과 시간 (80문항 / 약 90분)

Section 1 _ 문법 (Grammar _ 100점 만점) - 26문항 / 20분
- 가정법(6): 가정법 과거, 가정법 과거완료 등
- 시제(6): 진행형, 완료형, 완료진행형 등
- 조동사(2): 다양한 조동사의 쓰임 및 요구/제안/명령 동사 등
- 당위종속절(3): should 생략
- 준동사(To 부정사(2)와 동명사(3)): 역할 및 목적어로 취하는 동사들 등
- 연결사(2): 종속접속사, 등위접속사, 접속부사, 전치사
- 관계사(2): 관계대명사, 관계부사 등

Section 2 _ 청취 (Listening _ 100점 만점) - 26 문항 / 30분
- 개인적인 이야기
- 어떤 결정에 이르고자 하는 비공식적인 협상 등의 대화
- 어떤 특정한 행동의 진행상황을 설명하거나 특정한 상품을 추천하는 공식적인 담화
- 일반적인 어떤 일의 진행이나 과정에 대한 설명

Section 3 _ 독해와 어휘 (Reading & Vocabulary _ 100점 만점) - 28 문항 / 40분
- 과거 역사 속의 인물, 사건이나 현시대의 이야기
- 최근의 사회적이고 기술적인 묘사에 초점을 맞춘 잡지나 신문의 기사
- 전문적인 것이 아닌 일반적인 내용의 백과사전
- 어떤 것을 설명하거나 설득하는 상업서신

G-TELP와 타시험 점수 대비표

출처: 지텔프코리아 (www.g-telp.co.kr)

G-TELP	G-TELP Level 1 대비		G-TELP Level 2 대비	
	TOEIC	TOEFL(IBT)	TOEIC	TOEFL(IBT)
99	없음	114-115	969	111-112
98	없음		962	110
97	없음		954	109
96	없음	113	947	
95	없음		940	106-108
94	없음		932	
93	없음	111-112	925	
92	없음		918	105
91	989		910	
90	984		903	
89	980	110	896	103-104
88	976		889	101-102
87	972	109	881	
86	967		874	100
85	963		867	
84	959		859	98-99
83	954	106-108	852	
82	950		845	96-97
81	946		837	
80	941		830	94-95
79	937		823	
78	933	105	815	92-93
77	928		808	

76	924		801	90-91
75	920		793	
74	916	103-104	786	88-89
73	911		779	
72	907		771	86-87
71	903	101-102	764	84-85
70	898		757	83
69	894		749	
68	890		742	81-82
67	885	100	735	79-80
66	881		720	77-78
65	877		713	
64	873		706	76
63	868		698	
62	864	98-99	691	74-75
61	860		684	72-73
60	855		676	
59	851	96-97	669	71
58	847		662	
57	842		654	69-70
56	838		647	68
55	834	94-95	640	66-67
54	830		632	
53	825		625	65
52	821	92-93	618	64
51	817		610	
50	812		603	

* 토플 CBT변환 점수는 YBM 시사닷컴을 참고하였음.

구분	TOEIC	G-TELP(LEVEL 2)
5급 공채	700	65
외교관 후보자	870	88
7급 공채	700	65
7급 외무영사직렬	790	77
7급 지역인재	700	65
국회사무처(입법고시)	700	65
대법원(법원행정고시)	700	65
국민안전처(소방 간부 후보생)	625	50
경찰청(경찰 간부 후보생)	625	50
경찰청(경찰공무원)	600	48점: 가산점 2점 75점: 가산점 4점 89점: 가산점 5점
국방부(군무원)	5급 700 7급 570 9급 470	5급 65 7급 47 9급 32
카투사	780	73
특허청(변리사)	775	77
국세청(세무사)	700	65
고용노동부(공인노무사)	700	65
국토교통부(감정평가사)	700	65
행정자치부(외국어 번역 행정사)	Writing 150점	Writing 3급
한국산업인력공단(관광통역안내사)	760	74
한국산업인력공단(호텔 경영사)	800	79
한국산업인력공단(호텔관리자)	700	66
한국산업인력공단(호텔서비스사)	490	39
금융감독원(공인회계사)	700	65

- **G-TELP Level2 정기시험은 월 2회, 전국에서 시행됩니다.**
  - 주 2회 해당 일요일 15시 (오후 2시 20분까지 입실 완료)

- **성적발표**
  - 시험일로부터 5일 후 온라인으로 확인 가능하며, 원본 성적표는 온라인 성적표를 바로 인쇄하거나, 시험일로부터 2주 이내에 기재하신 주소로 우편 발송

- **정기시험 응시료: 정기접수기간 금액 / 추가접수기간 금액**
  - 일반: 66,300원 / 71,100원
  - 졸업인증: 45,700원 / 50,600원
  - 군인할인: 33,200원 / 38,000원
  - 중·고등학생: 35,000원 (정기접수와 추가접수 금액 동일)
    (일반 응시료로 결제하고 성적 발표 후에 31,300원 / 36,100원 환급)
  - 기초생활수급자: 정상가 결제 후 환급 (31,300원 / 36,100원 환급)
    (응시구분에서 기초생활 수급자 할인체크를 할 경우에만 환급가능)
  - 수시시험 응시료: 75,020원

- **영역별 배분시간이 없다.**

- **수정테이프 가능(수정액 불가)하고, 컴퓨터 수성 사인펜(컴퓨터용 연필 불가)을 사용해야 한다.**

G-TELP
GRAMMAR
THEORY

CONTENTS

G-TELP
GRAMMAR
THEORY

CHAPTER **1**

동사의
시제

현재 진행 시제 & 현재 완료 진행 시제

1 현재진행시제 [am / are / is + ~ ing]

현재에 진행 중인 동작이나 미래부사와 결합하여 미래를 나타낸다.

- Please be quiet. Bella *is sleeping* in her room *right now*.
  → 현재시제부사[right now]가 있으므로 현재진행시제[is sleeping]가 적절하다.

  조용해 좀 해. 지금 방에서 벨라가 자고 있는 중이야.

- Russell *is playing* tennis *at the moment*.
  → 현재시제부사[at the moment]가 있으므로 현재진행시제[is playing]가 적절하다.

  러셀은 현재 테니스를 치고 있다.

※ 현재진행시제와 동반되는 어구
right now(바로지금) // now(지금) // at this (very) moment (바로 지금) // at the moment (현재) // nowadays(요즘) // these days(요즘), currently (현재) // at present(현재), etc.

- *At this very moment*, Russell and his daughter *are catching* fish.

  바로 지금 러셀과 그의 딸은 고기를 잡고 있다.

- The weather is nice. It *is not raining* nowadays.

  날씨가 좋다. 요즘에 비가 오지 않고 있다.

- Jane *is watching* TV *now*.

  제인은 지금 TV를 시청하고 있다.

- *These days*, global warming *is becoming* a serious threat to everyone.

  오늘날, 지구 온난화는 모든 사람에게 심각한 위협이 되고 있습니다.

2 현재완료진행시제 [have/has been + ~ ing]

- 과거에 시작하여 현재까지도 진행 중인 동작이나 사건을 나타낸다.
- 현재의 시점에 범위(for + 기간)가 더해지면 현재완료진행시제가 된다.

- I hope the bus comes soon. I *have been waiting* now for 20 minutes.
  → 현재시제부사[now]와 시간의 범위[for 20 minutes]가 있으므로 현재완료진행시제[have been waiting]이 적절하다.

  버스가 바로 오면 좋겠어. 나는 20분이나 기다리고 있어.

- Bella *has been painting* her room *for the last four hours*.
  → 현재완료시제부사[for the last four hours]가 있으므로 현재완료진행시제[has been painting]이 적절하다.

  벨라는 지난 두 시간 동안 방을 페인트칠해오고 있다.

※ 현재완료진행시제와 동반되는 어구
(ever) since +과거시점어구(~ 이후로), // for·over·during the past·last + 기간 (지난 ~ 기간 동안) // 현재시점 어구+for 기간 // lately(최근에)

- Russell is out of breath. He *has been jogging* now for two hours.

  러셀은 숨이 가쁘다. 그는 20시간동안 조깅을 했다.

- The boy *has been reading* over the past two hours.

  그 소년은 지난 두 시간동안 독서를 해오고 있다.

- I *have been looking* forward to meet Russell *since last year*.

  나는 지난해부터 러셀을 만나기를 고대하고 있다.

- *Lately*, he *has been coming by* just to meet my younger brother.

  최근에 그는 저의 남동생을 만나기 위해서 들려요.

EXERCISE

I 괄호 안에서 문법적으로 올바른 것을 고르시오.

01 The CEO of the company (has exercised / is exercising / was exercising) at a gym right now.

02 The owner of the company (holds / is holding / was holding) a welcoming ceremony in honor of Mr. Park at the moment.

03 The Human Resources Department (is holding / holds / has held) a special appreciation lunch for all employees these days.

04 The New Rangton Chronicles (was offering / offers / is offering) discounts to the general public in an attempt to increase its circulation at this time.

05 Private education spending (had been increasing / has been increasing) by 2 trillion won each year since 2000.

06 A team of researchers (have been studying / are studying) dolphins in Florida, the United States for 30 years now.

07 The nation (has been improving / was improving) its transparency score since 1999, when it was given a mark of 3.8 out of a possible 10 points.

08 Even though Russell (swims / swam / has been swimming / had swum) since he was 9, he has not yet perfected his strokes.

II 다음 빈칸에 들어갈 가장 올바른 것을 고르시오.

01 Currently VNC Solutions _____ for talented computer professionals who have at least three years of experiences in the programming field.

   (a) was currently looking   (b) has currently been looking

   (c) has currently looked   (d) is currently looking

02 A survey of Torino restaurants shows that Japanese restaurants _____ popularity for over five years now.

   (a) have been gaining   (b) were gaining

   (c) gained   (d) had been gaining

1 과거진행시제 [was / were + ~ ing]

과거에 진행 중인 동작이나 사건을 나타낸다.

- *Last year* Russell *was living* in Busan.
  → 과거시제부사[Last year]가 있으므로 과거진행시제[was living]이 적절하다.

  작년에 러셀은 부산에 살고 있었다.

- She *sprained* her ankle while she *was mowing* the lawn in the garden.
  → 주절의 시제가 과거[sprained]이므로 [while]절의 동사는 과거진행시제[was mowing]가 적절하다.

  그녀는 정원에서 잔디를 깎다가 발목을 삐었다.

- Bella *was walking* in the Hyde park when she *met* Russell.
  → [when]절의 시제가 과거[met]이므로 주절의 시제는 과거진행시제[was walking]이 적절하다.

  벨라는 러셀을 만났을 때 하이드 공원을 걷고 있었다.

※ 과거진행시제와 동반되는 어구
- 기간+ago(~전에) // yesterday(어제) // at that exact moment(바로그당시에), etc.
- when·while 주어+과거동사 (~했을 때·~하던 동안에)

- Russell *burned* his hand while he *was cooking* lunch.

  러셀은 점심을 요리하다가 손을 데였다.

- Russell *was studying* when Bella *came* home.

  벨라가 집에 왔을 때는 러셀은 공부를 하고 있었다.

- The man and all his family members *weren't working two weeks ago*.

  그 남자와 모든 그의 가족들은 2주전에 일을 하고 있지 않았다.

- *Six months ago*, my mother *met* a guy while she *was taking* a walk in the park.

  6개월 전쯤에 어머니는 공원을 산책하시다가 한 남자를 만났습니다.

2 과거완료진행시제 [had been + ~ ing]

- 대과거에 시작하여 기준과거에서도 진행 중인 동작이나 사건을 나타낸다.
- 과거의 시점에 범위(for + 기간)가 더해지면 과거완료진행시제가 적절하다.

- I *had been waiting for over 20 minutes* before the bus finally *came*.
  → [before]절의 동사가 과거시제[came]이고 주절에 시간의 범위[for over 20 minutes]가 있으니 과거완료진행시제[had been waiting]가 적절하다.

  버스가 마침내 왔을 때는 나는 20분 넘게 기다리고 있었다.

- Lee *had been protesting* at the front gate *for 12 hours* when he *was shot* by a tear bomb.
  → [when]절의 동사가 과거시제[was shot]이고 주절에 시간의 범위[for 12 hours]가 있으니 과거완료진행시제[had been protesting]가 적절하다.

  이씨는 정문에서 12시간 동안 시위를 최루탄에 맞았다.

- It *had been raining for two hours* when I *came* home.

  내가 집에 도착했을 때 비가 두 시간동안 내리고 있었다.

- By the time Russell *was finished* with homework, Mike *had been cleaning* the room *for almost three hours*.

  러셀은 숙제를 마쳤을 때 마이크는 거의 3시간 동안 방을 청소를 해오고 있었다.

I 괄호 안에서 문법적으로 올바른 것을 고르시오.

01 Busan had been considered the early favorite, but Jeju's chances (are increasing / were increasing) rapidly as the decision neared.

02 One research examined 10 participants who experienced the strange phenomenon while they (were watching / had watched / are watching) ASMR videos.

03 The woman's husband (was waiting / is waiting) outside the investigation room at that exact moment, and the prosecutor claims that she was the one who seduced him.

04 American Airlines (was looking for / has been looking for) a new, fuel-efficient aircraft with plenty of cargo space to handle its Caribbean routes last year.

05 When Russell finally arrived at Busan, he (has travelled / had been travelling) for over two months.

06 We (had been playing / has been playing / were playing) soccer for an hour when it started to rain.

07 Bella (had been working out / was working out / has worked out) for 30 minutes when she realized that she was in the wrong gym.

08 By the time Russell woke up this morning, he (is sleeping / had been sleeping / has been sleeping) for about 10 hours.

II 다음 빈칸에 들어갈 가장 올바른 것을 고르시오.

01 While cyber terror attacks _____ increasingly intelligent and sophisticated, an establishment of a pan-governmental control tower and reinforcement of security awareness among businesses was urgent.

(a) wold become   (b) have been becoming

(c) had become   (d) were becoming

02 Mr. Gardner is widely respected not only for his contributions to the country's economic progress but also for its involvement in the social service. He _____ in the service for over 30 years before he died last year.

(a) was participating   (b) had been participating

(c) had participated   (d) has been participating

1 미래진행시제 [will be + ~ ing]

- 미래에 진행 중인 동작이나 사건을 나타낸다. 미재시제부사어구와 동반된다.
- <u>부사절 접속사[if, when, until, by the time]절 내의 현재시제는 미래를 의미한다.</u> 따라서 주절은 반드시 미래관련 시제가 되어야 한다.

- Don't call me *after 9 pm tomorrow*. I **will be sleeping** *then*.
  - → 미래시제부사[after 9 pm tomorrow]와 문맥상 미래를 의미하는 부사[then]을 고려하여 미래진행시제[will be sleeping]이 적절하다.
    - 내일 9시 이후에 전화하지 마. 나는 그때 자고 있는 중일 거야.
- He **will be wasting** his time if he *applies* for the job this time.
  - → [if]절의 현재시제[applies]는 미래를 의미한다. 따라서 주절은 미래진행시제[will be wasting]일 적절하다.
    - 만약 그가 이번에 그 일에 지원하면 시간을 낭비하게 될 것이다.

- Russell **will be working** at the office *at 10 tomorrow*.
  - 내일 10시에 러셀은 사무실에서 일을 하고 있을 것이다.
- **Will** you **be going** away *next summer*?
  - 다음 번 여름에 여행을 갈거니?
- By the time you *arrive* in Busan, I **will be waiting** for you.
  - 네가 부산에 도착할 때쯤에는 나는 너를 기다리고 있을 것이다.

2 미래완료진행시제 [will have been + ~ ing]

- 기준미래이전에 시작하여 특정 기준미래까지도 진행 중인 동작이나 사건을 나타낸다.
- 미래의 시점에 범위(for + 기간)가 더해지면 미래완료진행시제가 적절하다.

- *This time next year*, Russell **will have been living** here *for 10 years*.
  - → 미래부사[this time next year]가 있고, 시간의 범위[for 10 years]가 있으니 미래완료진행시제가 적절하다.
    - 내년 이맘때쯤에는 러셀은 10년 동안 이곳에 살고 있는 중일 것이다.
- When you *get* to my place, I **will have been cleaning** *for two hours*.
  - → [when]절의 현재동사[get]은 미래를 의미하고, 시간의 범위[for two hours]가 있으니 미래완료진행시제가 적절하다.
    - 네가 나의 집에 도착 때쯤에는 나는 두 시간동안 청소를 하고 있는 중일 것이다.

- When Bella *arrives* at home, Russell **will have been cleaning** *for an hour*.
  - 벨라가 집에 도착할 때는 러셀은 한 시간 동안 청소를 하고 있는 중일 것이다.
- Jack **will have been watching** TV *for exactly 5 hours by 9 tonight*.
  - 잭은 오늘 밤 9시까지 정확히 5시간동안 TV를 보고 있는 중일 것이다.

EXERCISE

I 괄호 안에서 문법적으로 올바른 것을 고르시오.

01 This time next week, I (will be lying / am lying / have been lying) on the beach in Bali.

02 By the time Russell arrives tomorrow afternoon, we (will have played / are playing / will be playing) tennis.

03 The chefs (are preparing / will be preparing / were preparing) many dishes when the restaurant opens later this evening.

04 If you need to contact me, I (stay / will be staying / have stayed) at the TG hotel until Saturday.

05 By the time Russell is finished with his work, Bella (will have been cleaning / has been cleaning / will be cleaning) her room for two hours.

06 The students (will wait / will have been waiting / are waiting) for half an hour when their teacher enters the classroom.

07 By the end of the year, the company (will promote / is promoting / will have been promoting) their products for three months.

08 When Russell moves next month, he (will have been living / is living / had been living) in his house for five years.

II 다음 빈칸에 들어갈 가장 올바른 것을 고르시오.

01 By the end of the century, people _____ new technologies that we can't imagine now.

(a) had been enjoying   (b) had enjoyed

(c) will be enjoying   (d) will enjoy

02 Bella and her friends plan to work out in the gym together until 7 pm. By the time they leave, they _____ for three hours.

(a) are working out   (b) will have been working out

(c) have been worked out   (d) had worked out

01 Currently we _____ someone to oversee the construction of the new facility to ensure that the contractors do their work appropriately.

ⓐ are looking for
ⓑ will look for
ⓒ look for
ⓓ has been looking for

02 Trade with Asia's most populous country, China, _____ at a double-digit pace since such figures were compiled in 1998.

ⓐ expands
ⓑ is expanding
ⓒ has been expanding
ⓓ will expand

03 These rats _____ much concern lately because they are very destructive to their surrounding environment.

ⓐ would arouse
ⓑ have been arousing
ⓒ arouse
ⓓ will arouse

04 Last year alone some 36,000 Koreans _____ in schools in China while more than 60,000 Chinese took Korean as a second language.

ⓐ were studying
ⓑ will be studying
ⓒ have studied
ⓓ are studying

05 In the future, the government _____ on a comprehensive plan to further open the service sector to foreign competition.

ⓐ is working
ⓑ had worked
ⓒ has been working
ⓓ will be working

06 Bella who is now seventeen years old began collecting dolls when she was ten years old. By the end of this year, Bella _____ dolls for 8 years.

ⓐ has collected
ⓑ will have been collecting
ⓒ is collecting
ⓓ would collect

07 Mr. Smith immigrated to Korea with his family 10 years ago. Since last year, Mr. Smith _____ at the Seoul University in Korea.

ⓐ lectures
ⓑ has been lecturing
ⓒ had been lecturing
ⓓ will have lectured

08 Public concern about the possible paralysis of up to 100 hospitals nationwide _____ as public and private hospitals unions move to start large-scale strikes from today.

ⓐ will now rise
ⓑ was now be rising
ⓒ is now rising
ⓓ has now risen

09 According to a recent UN report, by the year 2040, 15 percent of the world's population _____ from malaria, a serious disease carried by mosquitoes which causes periods of fever

ⓐ will be suffering
ⓑ would suffer
ⓒ is suffering
ⓓ has suffered

10 Yesterday, the Bastille Day, celebrating the French Revolution, thousands of tourists _____ the last minutes of fireworks along the beaches of Nice, a popular vacation city of France.

ⓐ were watching
ⓑ have watched
ⓒ will be watching
ⓓ had been watching

11 Russell's family went on a trip to Vietnam for vacation. When they arrived at Hanoi airport, there was nobody for them. They _____ for 20 minutes before their tour guide finally arrived.

ⓐ are waiting
ⓑ will wait
ⓒ had been waiting
ⓓ have waited

12 I _____ in the train when I woke up because of the loud noise and saw a man throwing something and starting a fire.

ⓐ would have slept
ⓑ was sleeping
ⓒ have slept
ⓓ am sleeping

13 James and his team, who specialize in developing training solutions for multinational corporations, _____ with the marine experts at the London Aquarium for the last 10 years.

ⓐ had been working
ⓑ are working
ⓒ work
ⓓ have been working

14 Back in the early 1920s in the United States, radio broadcast _____ very popular, and radios were fast-selling items.

ⓐ was becoming
ⓑ becomes
ⓒ has become
ⓓ will be becoming

15 Russell has just returned from a long Education trip, and has brought a lot of teaching materials with him. I wanted to visit him, but I am concerned he _____ for classes with them, when I get to his home.

ⓐ prepared
ⓑ will be preparing
ⓒ had prepared
ⓓ prepares

16 My parents bought my little brother, Jack, a cute toy car. He started playing with the toy car and hasn't put it aside yet. He _____ for five hours by dinnertime.

ⓐ plays
ⓑ was playing
ⓒ will have been playing
ⓓ has played

17 When I wrote my thesis on cell phones, I realized everyone _____ around wormholes in his or her pockets.

ⓐ carried
ⓑ was carrying
ⓒ would carried
ⓓ will carry

18 The population of the rural areas in the country _____ rapidly since 1995, which has contributed to high levels of poverty there.

ⓐ was soaring
ⓑ will soar
ⓒ has been soaring
ⓓ had soared

19 According to the Education Ministry, these days students _____ bigger because of junk food and little exercise.

ⓐ will be becoming
ⓑ have become
ⓒ are becoming
ⓓ became

20 Nevertheless, the average retirement age _____ since 2006, when it was recorded at 56.9.

ⓐ will slowly increase
ⓑ slowly increased
ⓒ has slowly been increasing
ⓓ would slowly increase

G-TELP
GRAMMAR
THEORY

CHAPTER **2**

가정법

01 가정법 과거

현재 또는 미래 사건을 한 시제 이전으로 표기하여 현재의 상황과 반대로, 미래 사건을 반대로 가정을 한다. 가정절인 [if]에 동사를 과거시제로 나타내고, 수식을 받는 주절은 가정의 의미를 이어받아서 반드시 조동사의 과거형을 써야한다. 주절 역시 현재 또는 미래의 사건이므로 조동사 자체 시제논리에 맞추어 동사원형으로 나타낸다. 국어 해석할 때는 현재 또는 미래로 해석을 해야 한다.

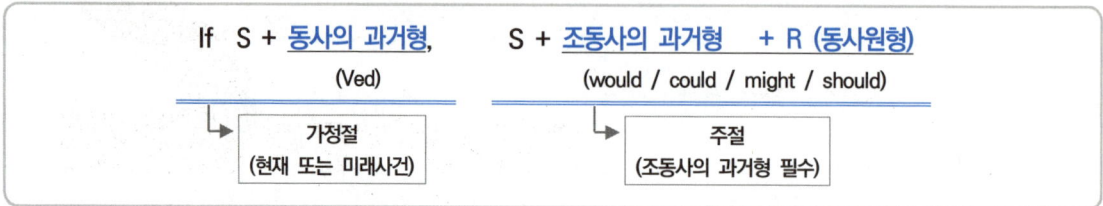

- If I *were* rich *now*, I *could buy* a building.
  - → [If] 가정절에 현재부사[now]가 있지만 가정법이 적용되어 과거시제로 나타내야 한다. 이때 be동사는 주어와 관계없이 반드시 [were]이다. 가정절에서는 [was]가 존재하지 않는다. 주절은 가정절의 불확실성을 이어받아서 완곡하게 나타내야 하므로 조동사의 과거형[could]이 있어야 하고, 시제는 가정절의 시제를 고려하면 현재이므로, 주절 역시 조동사 자체 시제 논리에 맞추어 조동사 [could] 뒤에 동사원형[buy]로 현재 또는 미래를 나타낸다.

    만약 지금 내가 부자라면 나는 건물을 하나 살 텐데.

- If she *came* here *tomorrow*, she *would get* a gift.
  - → [If] 가정절에 미래부사[tomorrow]가 있지만 가정법이 적용되어 과거시제로 나타내야 한다. 주절은 [조동사의 과거형+동사원형]이다.

    만약 그녀가 내일 여기에 온다면, 그녀는 선물을 하나 받을 것인데.

- If I *had* a car, I *would lend* you it.

  만약 내가 자동차가 있다는 너에게 빌려줄 텐데.

- If the weather *were* fine next weekend, we *would go* camping.

  다음주말에 날씨가 좋으면 우리는 캠핑을 갈 텐데.

> ※ [if] 가정절은 부사절이고 주절 뒤에 위치할 수 있다.
> - We *would go* on a picnic if it *were* not snowing heavily.
>
>   눈이 많이 내리고 있지 않다면 우리는 피크닉을 갈 텐데.
> - Bella *could buy* a luxury sedan, if she *had* enough money.
>
>   벨라가 충분한 돈이 있으면 그녀는 고급자동차를 구매할 텐데.

> ※ [if] 가정절의 조동사[could]
> - If she *could do* the work by herself, she *would not ask* me to help her.
>   - → [If] 가정절에는 조동사가 올수 없지만 능력 의미(~을 할 수 있다)의 조동사[can]의 과거형 [could + 동사원형]으로 가정법 과거문장을 구성할 수 있다.
>
>   만약에 그녀가 혼자서 그 일을 할 수 있다면, 그녀는 나에게 도움을 요청하지 않을 것이다.

Ⅰ 괄호 안에서 문법적으로 올바른 것을 고르시오.

01 If Olivia had time, she (will / would) go with us.

02 If I (know / had known / knew) the man's phone number, I might call him.

03 If I had enough money, I (will buy / would buy / would have bought) a new car.

04 If the girls came here, they (would enjoy / would have enjoyed) themselves.

05 If this room were tidy, I (could find / found / find) things easily.

06 If she were to appear at the party, everyone (would be / would have been) very surprised.

07 If my grandfather (were / had been) still alive, he would be a hundred today.

08 If I knew enough about the machine, I (would mend / mended / mend) it myself.

09 You (would know / would have known) the answer if you finished reading the book.

10 We might soon be making a profit if all (went / go) according to the plan.

Ⅱ 다음 빈칸에 들어갈 가장 올바른 것을 고르시오.

01 Jack is tired at school, which makes it hard for him to concentrate on the work. If I were him, I _____ some relax right now.

    (a) would get   (b) am getting

    (c) get   (d) had got

02 We all haven't decided to go fishing this Sunday because it is expected to rain. If the weather were not rainy, we _____ fishing.

    (a) will go   (b) go

    (c) would have gone   (d) could go

02 가정법 과거 완료

과거 사건을 한 시제 이전으로 표기하여 과거의 사건을 반대로 가정을 한다. 가정절인 [if]에 동사를 과거완료시제로 나타내고, 수식을 받는 주절은 가정의 의미를 이어받아서 반드시 조동사의 과거형을 써야한다. 주절 역시 과거사건 이므로 조동사 자체 시제논리에 맞추어 [have pp]으로 나타낸다. 국어 해석할 때는 과거로 해석을 해야 한다.

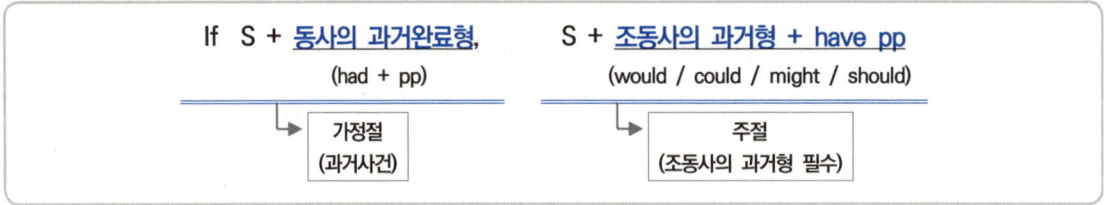

- If she *had not refused* his help *last month*, she *would have succeeded*.
  → [If] 가정절에 과거부사[last month]가 있지만 가정법이 적용되어 과거완료시제로 나타내야 한다. 주절은 가정절의 불확실성을 이어 받아서 완곡하게 나타내야 하므로 조동사의 과거형[would]가 있어야 하고, 시제는 가정절의 시제를 고려하면 과거이므로, 주절 역 시 조동사 자체 시제 논리에 맞추어 조동사[would] 뒤에 [have pp]로 과거시제를 나타낸다.
  만약 지난달에 그녀가 그의 도움을 거부하지 않았다면, 그녀는 성공했을 텐데.

※ 문제해결 조언
지텔프 가정법 문제해결에 있어서 의미는 전혀 고려대상이 아니다. 따라서 주절이든 가정절이든 부정부사 [not]은 무시해도 좋다.

- If I *had been* Russell at that time, I *would have accepted* the offer.
  그때 내가 러셀이었다면 나는 그 제안을 수락했을 텐데.
- She *wouldn't have been injured* if she *had been* more careful,
  만약 그녀가 더 조심했다면 그녀는 다치지 않았을 텐데.
- If Hitler *hadn't invaded* other European countries, World War II *might not have taken place*.
  히틀러가 다른 유럽 국가를 침략하지 않았다면 2차 세계대전은 일어나지 않았을 것이다.

※ 가정절에서 접속사[if]가 생략된 경우 주어와 동사가 도치된다.
- *If she had not refused* his help last month, she would have succeeded.
  → *Had she* not *refused* his help last month, she would have succeeded.
  만약 지난달에 그녀가 그의 도움을 거부하지 않았다면, 그녀는 성공했을 텐데.
- *Had she come* to the concert, she *would have enjoyed* it.
  그녀가 콘서트에 왔었다면 좋아했을 것이다.
- *would have eaten* something, *had I been* hungry this morning,
  내가 오늘 침에 배가 고팠다면, 나는 조금 먹었을 텐데.

EXERCISE

Ⅰ 괄호 안에서 문법적으로 올바른 것을 고르시오.

01 If the weather (was / were / had been) fine, we would have gone on a picnic.

02 If he had taken more money out of the bank, he (could have bought / bought / could buy) the shoes.

03 If he had set the alarm clock, he (wouldn't have overslept / won't oversleep / won't have overslept).

04 Had I known you were coming to Busan, I (went / would go / would have gone) to the station to meet you.

05 Tom (would have cooked / had cooked) a Thai food if he had found the proper ingredients last night.

06 Had the clerk known the great news, he (would have let / would let)you know immediately.

07 If there (had not been / weren't / wasn't) Newton, the law of gravitation would not have been discovered.

08 If it hadn't snowed, I (would go / would have gone) out with my friends then.

09 If it (hadn't rained / didn't rain) yesterday, I might not have stayed at home.

10 If I hadn't paid my electricity bill last month, I (would / will) have been in the dark.

Ⅱ 다음 빈칸에 들어갈 가장 올바른 것을 고르시오.

01 Russell quit his job three months ago and still can't get a new one. If he _____ how difficult it is to get a job, he would not have quit it in the first place.

    (a) knew   (b) had known

    (c) has known   (d) would know

02 Bella will leave for England to study English. But she is actually fonder of Spanish. If she had been given the chance to select the language to study, she _____ Spanish.

    (a) would choose   (b) chooses

    (c) would have chosen   (d) had chosen

01 John has always owned his own house. If he earned a lot of money, he _____ a house and live a happy life.

ⓐ building
ⓑ would build
ⓒ builds
ⓓ will build

02 Jenny Nelson didn't do well in school and was not interested in her study. If she had been a better student in the past, she _____ a top candidate for an entry-level position at ENR then.

ⓐ is
ⓑ was
ⓒ would be
ⓓ would have been

03 Daniel neglected equations when preparing for the math contest. Had Daniel remembered a few more equations, he _____ the math contest that he competed in last month.

ⓐ would win
ⓑ won
ⓒ would have won
ⓓ winning

04 The employees in the company had been looking forward to the company picnic. However, not many employees attended it. If Ms. Watson had distributed the flyers to all of the employees, attendance at the company picnic _____ much greater.

ⓐ would have been
ⓑ is
ⓒ being
ⓓ will be

05 Gyasa Industries would have to create a more powerful motor if it _____ to compete effectively in the lawn mower market at this stage.

ⓐ wanted
ⓑ wants
ⓒ will want
ⓓ would want

06 Please do not keep the computer printer outside. If the computer printer _____ sudden changes in the temperature, condensation might occur and result in the possibility of unsuccessful prints.

ⓐ experiences
ⓑ experienced
ⓒ experiencing
ⓓ may experience

07 If the hoses were not connected tightly, they _____, causing an enormous amount of gasoline to be spilled into the ocean and polluting plants and marine wildlife.

ⓐ broke
ⓑ break
ⓒ would have broken
ⓓ would break

08 We didn't realize that Russell had studied and conducted Marketing for over 10 years. Had we known about his extensive background in the field, we _____ him far more consideration for the position.

ⓐ are giving
ⓑ would have given
ⓒ will have given
ⓓ gave

09 If anyone spent more than usual on inventory this quarter, we _____ to reduce his or her budget by twenty percent next quarter as a punitive measure.

ⓐ would have
ⓑ have
ⓒ had had
ⓓ will have

10 There is much traffic in the rush hour around the company. If they lived closer to the company, they _____ to work instead of driving a car.

ⓐ walk
ⓑ would walk
ⓒ would have walked
ⓓ walking

11 A number of builders are against the plan to construct apartments near the river because of the weak ground. If the builders _____ able to convince the board that the site is unsuitable, the planning department would have to locate a new one.

ⓐ to be
ⓑ will be
ⓒ were
ⓓ would be

12 If one of the apartments _____ vacant before the end of next week, we would call you for an appointment to view it with one of our real estate agents.

ⓐ becomes
ⓑ became
ⓒ had become
ⓓ has become

13 Had we known that the company was going to perform so outstandingly well, we _____ our shares away at such a low price.

ⓐ hadn't given
ⓑ wouldn't have given
ⓒ haven't given
ⓓ won't have given

14 Economists are predicting that foreign investors would sell their stocks if the Indonesian economy _____ to decline.

ⓐ continues
ⓑ had continued
ⓒ is continuing
ⓓ continued

15 The current office is not attractive because it is limited and distractive. If the company had moved to its new office last year, the more spacious work areas, the upgraded cafeteria and the pleasant location _____ productivity by at least ten percent.

ⓐ were improving
ⓑ would have improved
ⓒ had improved
ⓓ would improve

16 Many small businesses are having difficulties surviving due to the recession. If the government reduced the number of small business loans and grants under this situation, many small firms _____ bankrupt before next spring.

ⓐ would go
ⓑ can go
ⓒ went
ⓓ might have gone

17 There was a report that most toys of the company had improperly been made with toxic substances. We would not have given the toys to the children at the day care center, if we _____ that they were recalled because of toxicity concerns.

ⓐ know
ⓑ had known
ⓒ would know
ⓓ knew

18 She was in two minds about running for a political office, so that she was passive about the campaign. If she _____ an aggressive campaign, she would have won the election.

ⓐ has run
ⓑ could run
ⓒ ran
ⓓ had run

19 As nursing technology continues to change rapidly, nurses need to continuously update their knowledge and skills. If they _____ such efforts, the public's health could be jeopardized.

ⓐ didn't make
ⓑ hadn't make
ⓒ haven't make
ⓓ aren't making

20 You may believe that not many of your students are interested in economics. Actually, most of them _____ an interest in that subject if they learned it in an engaging way.

ⓐ could take
ⓑ are taking
ⓒ have taken
ⓓ took

G-TELP
GRAMMAR
THEORY

관계사

주격 관계대명사 (who/which/that)

관계대명사 뒤에 바로 동사가 이어진다. 선행사가 사람이면 [who], 사물이면 [which]를 쓴다. [that]으로 대체가능하다. 주의할 것은, 콤마[,] 뒤에는 관계대명사[that]을 쓸 수 없다.

선행사가 사람일 때	선행사가 사물일 때
who (= that)	which (= that)

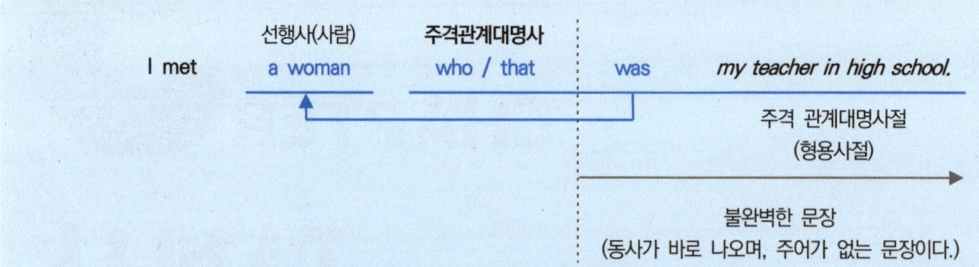

- I met *a woman* [(*who* / *that*) was my teacher in high school].

나는 고등학교시절 나의 선생님인 여성을 만났다

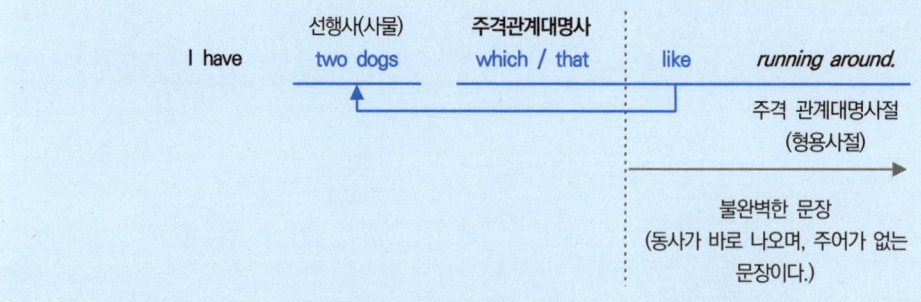

- I have *two dogs* [(*which* / *that*) like running around].

나는 이리저리 달리기를 좋아하는 개 두 마리가 있다.

- There are *a lot of people* *who / that* like the game.

그 게임을 좋아하는 많은 사람들이 있다.

- I bought *a pen* *which / that* was made in Europe.

나는 유럽에서 만들어진 펜을 하나 샀다.

※ 문제해결 조언
관계대명사[that]은 불완벽한절을 이끌고, 관계대명사 바로 앞에 콤마[,] 없으면 무조건 정답이다.

※ 관계대명사[that]은 콤마[,]뒤에는 올 수 없다.
- The student, *who* / *that* passed the exam, is planning to go abroad for pleasure.

그 학생은 시험에 합격했는데, 놀러 해외로 갈 계획이다.

- The dancer, *who* / *that* is well known to teenagers, is coming to town.

십대들에게 잘 알려져 있는 댄서가 마을로 오고 있다.

EXERCISE

I 괄호 안에서 문법적으로 올바른 것을 고르시오.

01 The river (which / who) flows through London is called the Thames.

02 About 95% of us experience jealousy at some stage in our lives. This is the basic emotion (which / who / whom) touches man in every human relationship.

03 From other countries in 1998, United States attracted more than 450,000 students, (who / that / which) poured more than $7 billion into American economy.

04 The particular stream (who / that) serves as their journey's end is almost invariably the same one in which they were born.

05 He's always a really rude man, (that / who) looks down on others.

06 The rapid melting of Arctic ice has become an undeniable phenomenon, (when / that / who / which) suggests that fear of global warming is warranted.

07 It was a rainy day, (that / which) was a great pity.

08 His brother (who / which) is just seventeen has already passed his driving test.

II 다음 빈칸에 들어갈 가장 올바른 것을 고르시오.

01 In 1863 American President Abraham Lincoln made Thanksgiving an official annual holiday, _____.

(a) which is now celebrated on the 4th Thursday of November each year

(b) who is now celebrated on the 4th Thursday of November each year

(c) when is now celebrated on the 4th Thursday of November each year

(d) that is now celebrated on the 4th Thursday of November each year

02 Money related to English teaching around the world in 1998 was about $ 10 billion. That total includes money spent for teaching, books, other materials, and tuition of students _____.

(a) who were studying in English speaking countries

(b) whom were studying in English speaking countries

(c) when were studying in English speaking countries

(d) which were studying in English speaking countries

관계대명사 뒤에 주어와 동사가 이어진다. 선행사가 사람이면 [whom], 사물이면 [which]를 쓴다. [that]으로 대체 가능하다. 주의할 것은, 콤마[,] 뒤에는 관계대명사[that]을 쓸 수 없다.

선행사가 사람일 때	선행사가 사물일 때
whom (= that)	which (= that)

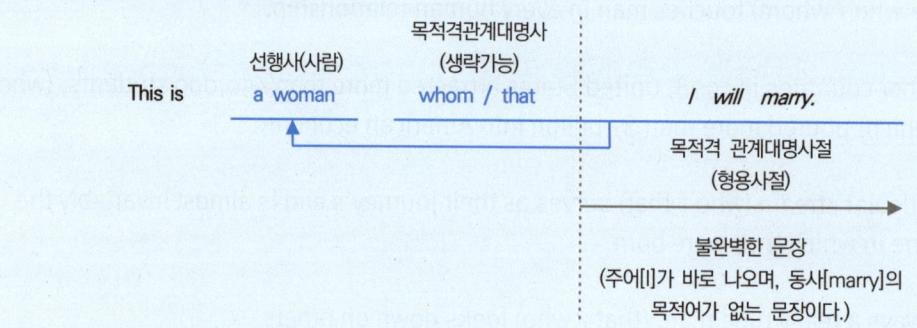

- This is *a woman* [(*whom* / *that*) I will marry].

이 사람은 내가 결혼할 여성입니다.

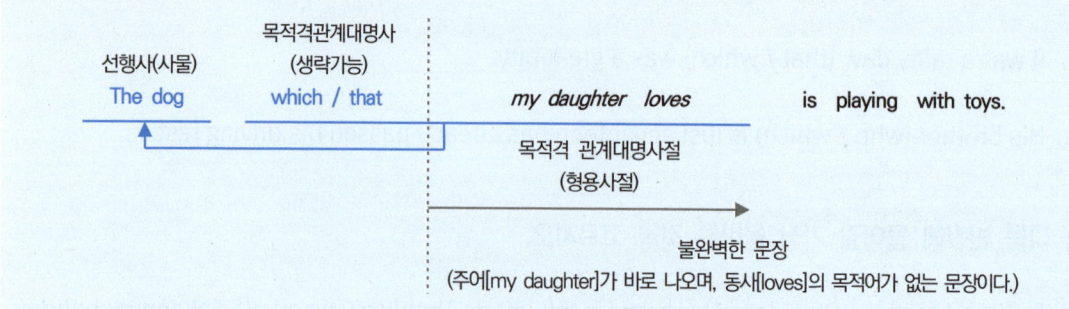

- *The dog* [(*which* / *that*) my daughter loves] is playing with toys.

나의 딸이 사랑하는 그 개는 장난감을 가지고 놀고 있다.

- Bella is *a girl* *whom / that* everyone likes.

벨라는 모든 사람들이 좋아하는 소녀이다.

- She never listens to *the advice* *which / that* I give to her.

그녀는 내가 그녀에게 하는 조언을 전혀 듣지 않는다.

※ 문제해결 조언
관계대명사[that]은 불완벽한 절을 이끌고, 관계대명사 바로 앞에 콤마[,] 없으면 무조건 정답이다.

※ 관계대명사[that]은 콤마[,]뒤에는 올 수 없다.
- Bella bought some books, [*which* / *that* she had wanted to buy].

벨라는 몇 권의 책을 구매했다. 그녀를 그것들을 구매하길 원했다.

- The building, [*which* / *that* my grandfather built 30 years ago], has been renovated.

나의 할아버지가 30전에 건설한 그 건물은 새롭게 개선되었다.

EXERCISE

I 괄호 안에서 문법적으로 올바른 것을 고르시오.

01 The man (whom / which / whose) you met yesterday on the way here is my brother.

02 They have lots of vitamin a and protein (who / whom / which) we use to prevent and delay skin from aging.

03 She is a model figure (whom / which) many Korea's future scientists look up to.

04 The car (that / whom) I can lend you right now is that yellow one.

05 I've stood at the deathbed of several famous people, (whom / which / that) you would know.

06 This means it makes a person buy a product (that / when / who) he doesn't really need — it may be a new type of telephone, or a new TV set.

07 If you compare our, perhaps, 90 years here to the age of this planet (that / who / when) we call home, you will see we are only here in a blink.

08 Watts plays an unemployed actress (whom / which / whose) King Kong falls in love with.

II 다음 빈칸에 들어갈 가장 올바른 것을 고르시오.

01 Difficulties with culture shock are often related to an individual's ability to speak the language of the country _____.

(a) when he or she is inhabiting

(b) whom he or she is inhabiting

(c) which he or she is inhabiting

(d) whose he or she is inhabiting

02 Many analysts share the view that this pattern has moved from Japan to Korea and is now in China, _____.

(a) whom a lot of fashion leaders work in

(b) which a lot of fashion leaders work in

(c) that a lot of fashion leaders work in

(d) when a lot of fashion leaders work in

03 관계부사 (when/where)

자체품사가 부사이기에 뒤에는 완벽한 절이 이어진다. G-TELP 시험에는 관계부사[why]와 [how]는 출제되지 않는다. 선행사가 시간명사인 경우에는 관계부사[when]을, 장소명사인 경우에는 관계부사[where]로 나타낸다. 주의할 것은, 선행사가 시간명사나 장소명사라고 하더라도 주어나 목적어가 없는 불완벽한 문장이 이어지는 경우에는 관계대명사[which]로 나타낸다.

선행사가 시간명사일 때	선행사가 장소명사일 때
when	where

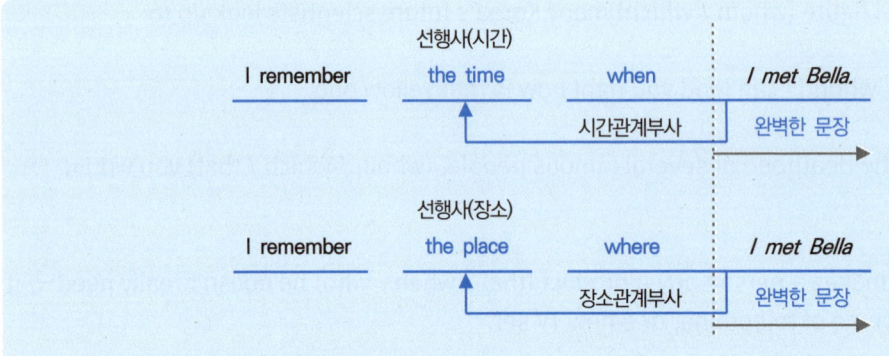

- In *the past* *when* women didn't have the right to vote there was also much racial discrimination in the world.

  여성이 투표권이 없었던 과거에는 또한 세계에서 많은 인종차별이 많이 행해지고 있었다.

- We're looking forward to *the time* *when* we can get together again.

  우리는 우리가 다시 함께할 수 있는 시간을 고대하고 있는 중이다.

- *Busan* *where* Russell and Olivia grew up is the second largest city in Korea.

  러셀과 올리비아가 성장한 부산은 한국에서 두 번째로 큰 도시이다.

- A library is *a place* where people can read books and borrow them for a designated period.

  도서관은 사람들이 책을 읽을 수 있고 지정된 기간 동안 책들을 빌릴 수 있는 장소입니다.

※ 문제해결 조언

완벽한 절이 이어지면 관계부사를, 불완벽한 절이 이어지면 관계대명사[which]로 나타내야 한다. 그러나 완벽절과 불완벽절을 구분하기 어려운 경우 관계부사가 적절할 가능성이 높다.

※ 관계부사와 관계대명사[which]의 구분

- This is *the city* [*which* / ~~where~~ all of us built together].
  → 해당문장은 관계사 뒤에 목적어가 없는 불완벽한 문장이 이어지므로 관계대명사[which]가 적절하다.

  이곳은 우리 모두가 함께 건설한 도시이다.

- This is the city [~~which~~ / *where* all of us can do anything].
  → 해당문장은 관계사 뒤에 완벽한 문장이 이어지므로 관계부사[where]가 적절하다.

  이곳은 우리 모두가 그 어떤 것이든지 할 수 있는 도시이다.

I 괄호 안에서 문법적으로 올바른 것을 고르시오.

01 A park (where / when) a number of people will enjoy themselves will have been constructed completely by next year.

02 London (where / when) there are numbers of buildings and people is one of the best cities in the world.

03 All changed in October, 1984, (where / when / that) NBC-TV showed a five-minute report on the famine.

04 We look forward to the time (where / when) the power to love will replace the love of power. Then will our world know the blessings of peace.

05 The Jeju Uprising refers to the incident on April 3, 1948, (where / when) countless Jeju citizens were killed during armed conflict.

06 As a result, human ancestors were forced to live near mountains and hills (where / when / which) there were ample sources of food and water.

07 They sold the house (where / when / who) their parents had lived for 20 years.

08 Following "Falling in Love", the girl group will be releasing a new single every month until October (where / when / which) they will release a new album.

II 다음 빈칸에 들어갈 가장 올바른 것을 고르시오.

01 Baseball games are cancelled or delayed when it rains heavily and it is difficult to play baseball during winter _____.
   (a) where the weather is cold and snowy
   (b) when the weather is cold and snowy
   (c) which the weather is cold and snowy
   (d) who the weather is cold and snowy

02 In these days when so many human beings are compelled to live in enormous cities _____, that love of nature is more necessary than ever.
   (a) which they so easily forget the fact that nature is greater than man
   (b) when they so easily forget the fact that nature is greater than man
   (c) whom they so easily forget the fact that nature is greater than man
   (d) where they so easily forget the fact that nature is greater than man

ACTUAL TEST

01 The Korean university, _____, announced Friday that the 35-year-old lawmaker-elect had committed plagiarism in his doctoral thesis.

  ⓐ which the 2004 Olympic gold medalist in taekwondo did his doctoral work in 2007

  ⓑ who the 2004 Olympic gold medalist in taekwondo did his doctoral work in 2007

  ⓒ where the 2004 Olympic gold medalist in taekwondo did his doctoral work in 2007

  ⓓ that the 2004 Olympic gold medalist in taekwondo did his doctoral work in 2007

02 Roman gladiatorial combat is thought to have originated as a religious event _____. The symbolic death of the gladiators was believed to honor the fallen.

  ⓐ when was held at funerals
  ⓑ who was held at funerals
  ⓒ where was held at funerals
  ⓓ which was held at funerals

03 A new study found a doubling of the rate of prescribing antipsychotic drugs to young patients from 2000 to 2007, _____.

  ⓐ when some patients had received a proper mental health assessment.

  ⓑ which some patients had received a proper mental health assessment.

  ⓒ where some patients had received a proper mental health assessment.

  ⓓ that some patients had received a proper mental health assessment.

04 The Anglo-Saxons eventually divided their occupied area, 'Engla Land', into seven kingdoms, _____.

  ⓐ when was eventually united as England in the tenth century

  ⓑ whom was eventually united as England in the tenth century

  ⓒ that was eventually united as England in the tenth century

  ⓓ which was eventually united as England in the tenth century

05 Come to 'Neighbors', Vancouver's trendiest new restaurant. Located in the heart of the city center, 'Neighbors' is the place _____.

ⓐ which service is as important as the food we serve

ⓑ where service is as important as the food we serve

ⓒ when service is as important as the food we serve

ⓓ that service is as important as the food we serve

06 The greatest annual domestic spending in a household with teenagers is the expense related to school, _____.

ⓐ which involves tuition fees, uniforms, books, and other equipment

ⓑ whose involves tuition fees, uniforms, books, and other equipment

ⓒ when involves tuition fees, uniforms, books, and other equipment

ⓓ who involves tuition fees, uniforms, books, and other equipment

07 People _____ believe that part-time jobs help teenagers become more responsible with money.

ⓐ whom are for teenagers having part-time jobs

ⓑ when are for teenagers having part-time jobs

ⓒ where are for teenagers having part-time jobs

ⓓ who are for teenagers having part-time jobs

08 Each of the different theme parks within Lotte World is a whirlwind of excitement, _____.

ⓐ that is going to sweep you off your feet

ⓑ which is going to sweep you off your feet

ⓒ when is going to sweep you off your feet

ⓓ who is going to sweep you off your feet

09 Before Wegener proposed the Pangaea theory, scientists believed in the existence of land bridges between America and Africa, _____.

ⓐ where had since been eroded away.

ⓑ that had since been eroded away.

ⓒ which had since been eroded away.

ⓓ who had since been eroded away.

10 At the theater playing the popular musical Cats, the people _____ in an endlessly long line wished they had come sooner to buy their tickets.

ⓐ which are waiting

ⓑ that are waiting

ⓒ whom are waiting

ⓓ where are waiting

11 The renowned watercolor painting depicts the artist's motherland with strokes ____ and reach into our senses so that we, too, can see the things his mind houses.

ⓐ when enliven each image
ⓑ where enliven each image
ⓒ that enliven each image
ⓓ who enliven each image

12 After a memorable journey, you will often want to go back to the photos taken along the way for the intensity of the feelings _____.

ⓐ where they convey
ⓑ who they convey
ⓒ which they convey
ⓓ whom they convey

13 A new term "the Hispanic paradox" was coined because Hispanics have a lower median family income than whites and are less likely than whites to have a college education – factors _____.

ⓐ who are generally associated with better health
ⓑ whom are generally associated with better health
ⓒ when are generally associated with better health
ⓓ which are generally associated with better health

14 Since foreclosure practices are similar from bank to bank, analysts now expect other lenders to follow suit and proceed with a wave of foreclosures _____.

ⓐ that could further depress the housing market
ⓑ where could further depress the housing market
ⓒ when could further depress the housing market
ⓓ whose could further depress the housing market

15 We have no choice but to try to overhaul our daycare system because the grandparents _____ now live far away.

ⓐ whose used to be around the corner
ⓑ who used to be around the corner
ⓒ where used to be around the corner
ⓓ whom used to be around the corner

16 The history of the Miss Korea contest goes back to the late 1950s, _____ after the Korean War.

ⓐ that Korea was still suffering from hardships
ⓑ when Korea was still suffering from hardships
ⓒ where Korea was still suffering from hardships
ⓓ whom Korea was still suffering from hardships

17 Afterwards, depending on the public's reaction, the playground may be developed by putting more facilities like benches and equipment _____.

ⓐ which owners and dogs can use
ⓑ who owners and dogs can use
ⓒ when owners and dogs can use
ⓓ where owners and dogs can use

18 The huge storm striking the Philippines has one confirmed fatality - a man that drowned in a river - and is expected to plunge a day later into China _____ from a coastal province.

ⓐ which authorities have evacuated 100,000 people
ⓑ that authorities have evacuated 100,000 people
ⓒ where authorities have evacuated 100,000 people
ⓓ when authorities have evacuated 100,000 people

19 The core early event was Napoleon Bonaparte's 1798 military expedition accompanied by a team of 150 scholars, _____.

ⓐ whose studied and recorded all aspects of Egypt
ⓑ whom studied and recorded all aspects of Egypt
ⓒ who studied and recorded all aspects of Egypt
ⓓ that studied and recorded all aspects of Egypt

20 Sign up for a new credit card with HCB Bank and receive up to 1,000 bonus air miles. Note that customers _____ are also eligible for lower interest rates.

ⓐ whom sign up for it before July 30
ⓑ where sign up for it before July 30
ⓒ whose sign up for it before July 30
ⓓ who sign up for it before July 30

G-TELP
GRAMMAR
THEORY

CHAPTER 4

준동사

동사가 [~ing]의 형태를 취하여 명사의 자리에 위치한다. 즉, 동명사가 적절한 자리는 본주어자리, 동명사를 목적어로 취하는 타동사의 목적어 자리, 전치사의 목적어자리가 있다.

1 본주어 자리 – 동명사의 고유용법 – To 부정사 불가

※ G-TELP에서는 본주어로 [to] 부정사는 적절하지 않다.

• *Making much money* is not easy.

큰돈을 버는 것은 쉽지 않다.

• *Seeing her again* seems impossible.

그녀를 다시 본다는 것은 불가능한 듯하다.

2 동명사만을 목적어로 취하는 타동사의 목적어자리

• Would you *mind handing* me the paper there?

⤳ Would you *mind to hand* me the paper there? (×)

→ [mind]는 동명사를 목적어로 취하는 동사이다.

거기에 있는 종이를 저에게 건네줄래요?

※ 동명사만을 목적어로 취하는 동사

mind(꺼리다), resist(저항하다), enjoy(즐기다), give up(포기하다), finish(마치다), quit(그만두다), stop(그만두다), allow(허용하다), prohibit(금지시키다), postpone(연기하다), delay(연기하다), avoid(회피하다), suggest(제안하다), recommend(추천하다), propose(제안하다), advise(조언하다), consider, reconsider(재고하다), deny(부인하다), admit(인정하다), acknowledge(인정하다), practise(연습하다), risk(위험을 무릅쓰다), experience(경험하다), involve(수반하다), entail(수반하다), include(포함하다), require(필요로 하다), keep(계속하다), etc

---

• Russell *enjoys fishing* with Bella on Sundays.

러셀은 일요일마다 벨라와 함께 낚시를 하는 것을 즐긴다.

• The politicians *avoid presenting* their opinions about the issue.

그 정치인들은 그 문제에 대해서 자신의 의견을 발표하는 것을 피한다.

3 전치사의 목적어 자리

• I am sorry *for being* late.

늦어서 죄송합니다.

• *On arriving* in Korea, he got married to her.

한국에 돌아오자마자, 그는 그녀와 결혼을 했다.

4 필수 관용어구

• can't help ~ing
  (~하지 않을 수 없다)
• go ~ing
  (~하러 가다)

• Russell *can't help thinking* about her.

러셀은 그녀를 생각하지 않을 수 없다.

• She *goes fishing* every weekend.

그녀는 매 주말마다 쇼핑하러 간다.

EXERCISE

Ⅰ 괄호 안에서 문법적으로 올바른 것을 고르시오.

01 Would you mind (turning / to turn / turned) on the radio?

02 We should postpone (deciding / to decide / decided) on the matter until we have more information.

03 The fringe benefits prevent many an employee from (to quit / quitting / quit) his or her job.

04 Night owls who sleep in late often miss the opportunity to go (having hiked / hiking / to hike) or see a beautiful sunrise.

05 (To make / Having made / Making) much money is not the aim of my life but the course.

06 The professor acknowledged (plagiarize / plagiarizing / to plagiarize) the thesis of someone else.

07 The company said that it wants to avoid (encouraging / to encourage / encourage) the killing of endangered elephants.

08 He's a bit of a fool, but I can't help (liking / like / to like) him.

Ⅱ 다음 빈칸에 들어갈 가장 올바른 것을 고르시오.

01 Aggressive behavior involves _____ your thoughts and feelings and defending your rights in a way that openly violates the rights of others.

   (a) having expressed   (b) expressing

   (c) to be expressing   (d) to express

02 Many teens play games and send messages online, which are activities that don't require _____ books.

   (a) reading   (b) to read

   (c) having read   (d) to be reading

02 [to] 부정사

동사가 [to R]의 형태를 취하여 명사, 형용사 부사의 자리에 위치한다. G-TELP에서 [to R]가 적절한 자리는 가주어·진주어구문에서 진주어자리, [to]부정사를 목적어로 취하는 타동사의 목적어 자리, 일반5형식 동사의 목적보어 자리, 부사자리에 적절하다.

1 가주어·진주어 구문에서 진주어 자리

※ 동명사는 진주어 자리에는 올수 없다.

- **It** costs a lot *to buy* a house.　집을 사는 것은 비용이 많이 든다.
- **It** is not easy *to make* much money.　큰돈을 버는 것은 쉽지 않다.

2 [to] 부정사만을 목적어로 취하는 타동사의 목적어자리

- We couldn't *afford to hire* workers any more.
  - ↗ We couldn't *afford hiring* workers any more. (×)　우리는 직원들을 더 이상 고용할 여력이 없었다.
  - → [afford]는 [to] 부정사를 목적어로 취한다.

※ **[to] 부정사만을 목적어로 취하는 동사**

want(원하다), wish(원하다), need(필요하다), decide(결정하다), choose(선택하다), prepare(준비하다), plan(계획하다), promise(약속하다), agree(동의하다), fail(~하지못하다), afford(~할 여유가 있다), offer(제의하다), refuse(거부하다), tend(~하는 경향이 있다), make sure(확실히 하다), wait (~을 기다리다), expect (~을 기대하다), etc.

- I *want to go* to America.　나는 미국에 가기를 원한다.
- She *refused to leave* for New Zealand.　그녀는 뉴질랜드로 떠나기를 거부했다.

3 일반 5형식 동사의 목적보어 자리

- The researcher *asked* all the students *to complete* a questionnaire.
  - → [ask]는 목적보어로 [to R]를 취한다.

  그 연구원은 모든 학생들이 설문지를 작성하길 요구했다.

※ **목적보어를 [to R]로 취하는 동사**

ask (요구하다), cause(유발시키다), enable(~하게 하다), allow(허용하다), require(요구하다), advise(충고하다), expect(기대하다), wish(원하다), force(강요하다), want(원하다), would like (원하다), encourage(장려하다), remind(상기시키다), etc.

- His friends *forced* him *to rob* the old lady of her purse.
  그의 친구들이 그가 그 할머니의 지갑을 강탈하라고 강요했다.
- Much snow yesterday *caused* lots of people *to slip* on the road.
  어제 눈이 많이 와서 많은 사람들이 길에서 미끄러졌다.

4 부사자리(목적: ~하기 위해서)

※ 주어 앞자리나 완벽한 문장 뒤에 오는 거의 대부분의 자리에는 [to R]가 적절하다.

- **It** costs a lot *to buy* a house.　집을 사는 것은 비용이 많이 든다.
- **It** is not easy *to make* much money.　큰돈을 버는 것은 쉽지 않다.

Ⅰ 괄호 안에서 문법적으로 올바른 것을 고르시오.

01 It no longer seems necessary (graduating / to graduate / graduate) from college to get a job in Korea.

02 (Buying / To be buying / To buy) a house, he and his wife tried to save money.

03 According to a legend, a king once placed a heavy stone in the roadway. Then he hid and waited (to see / see / having seen) who would remove it.

04 In a business, efficiency is very important and allows companies (to be / being / having been) more competitive.

05 The toy company warns you (to be keeping / kept / to keep) this toy knife away from children.

06 Many companies tend (hiring / to be hiring / to hire) people who have had previous working experience.

07 North Korea earlier refused (discussing / to discuss / to have discussed) a peace or unification agenda.

08 They say the South Korean government needs (to improve / to improving / improving) living conditions outside of Seoul.

Ⅱ 다음 빈칸에 들어갈 가장 올바른 것을 고르시오.

01 The San Francisco board of supervisors voted against Happy Meal and asked any other restaurant not _____ toys with a meal that does not meet certain nutritional requirements.

(a) having given away   (b) to giving away

(c) to give away   (d) giving away

02 This removal of both live and dead vegetation reduces the remaining plants' competition for water, sun light, nutrients, and space, allowing them _____ stronger.

(a) growing   (b) to have grown

(c) to grow   (d) having grown

1 동명사와 [to] 부정사를 모두 목적어로 취하는 동사

※ 동명사와 [to] 부정사를 의미의 변화가 없이 모두 목적어로 취하는 동사
⇒ [begin, start, hate, love, like, continue, etc]

1) remember ~ing (~한 것을 기억하다) / to R (~할 것을 기억하다)
- He *remembers sending* a letter yesterday.

  그는 어제 편지를 보낸 것을 기억한다.
- He *remembers to send* a letter tomorrow.

  그는 내일 편지를 보낼 것을 기억한다.

2) forget ~ing (~했던 것을 잊다) / to R (~할 것을 잊다)
- He *forgot sending* a letter yesterday.

  그는 어제 편지를 보낸 것을 잊었다.
- He *forgot to send* a letter yesterday.

  그는 어제 편지를 보낼 것을 잊었다.

※ 문제해결 조언
동사[try]는 지텔프에서는 거의 대부분 [to R]를 목적어로 취한다.

3) try ~ing (시험 삼아 ~ 해보다) / to R (~하려고 노력하다)
- Russell isn't here. *Try phoning* his home number.

  존은 여기 없어요. 시험 삼아 집으로 전화를 해 보세요.
- Russell *tried to get* her out of the trouble.

  러셀은 그녀를 곤란함에서 구하려고 노력했다.

2 [to] 부정사의 형용사적 용법 – [N + to R] – [~할]

※ 문제해결 조언
지텔프 문제에서는 명사뒤에는 [to R]가 온다.

- The poor boy has *someone to help* him.

  그 가난한 소년은 자신을 도와줄 누군가가 있다.
- Russell had *a chance to buy such a beautiful house*.

  러셀은 아주 아름다운 집을 살 기회가 있었다.

3 [to] 부정사의 수동 2형식 주격보어

※ 문제해결 조언
지텔프 문제에서는 수동태뒤에는 거의 대부분 [to R]가 온다.

- Russell *is required to leave* immediately.

  러셀은 즉시 떠나야 한다.
- She *is supposed to do* her homework tonight.

  그녀는 오늘 밤에 숙제를 하기로 되어 있다.

4 기타 [to] 부정사 관용표현

- be able to R
  (~할 수 있다.)
- have no choice but to R
  (~하지 않을 수 없다)
- too … to R
  (너무 …해서 ~할 수 없다)
- be willing to R
  (기꺼이 ~하다)

- Bella *is able to complete* the project in time.

  벨라는 시간 안에 그 프로젝트를 완성할 수 있다.
- The students *have no choice but to stay* in the classroom.

  학생들은 교실에 있지 않을 수 없었다.
- She is *too* careless *to handle* the work.

  그녀는 너무 부주의해서 그 일을 처리할 수 없다.
- I *am willing to help* her.

  나는 기꺼이 그녀를 도울 것이다.

EXERCISE

Ⅰ 괄호 안에서 문법적으로 올바른 것을 고르시오.

01 We must ask whether genetic information should be collected at all and who should be able (seeing / to see / to be seeing) and use it.

02 The machine's capabilities are too numerous (to list / listing / to have listed) completely.

03 When citizens are required (voting / to vote / to be voting), they become more interested in candidates and policies.

04 Russell bought many books (to read / reading / having read) during his vacation.

05 Please remember (to turn off / turning off / turn off) the TV before you go to bed.

06 The world will be willing (helped / to help / to be helping / helping) North Korea only when it genuinely tries (to come / coming / to have come) out of isolation.

07 Many people often forget (to take / taking / take / to be taking) their documents, clothes and jewelry when they got off the subway train.

08 Most people believe that all workers should be allowed (to protest / protesting / to be protesting) against unfair conditions.

Ⅱ 다음 빈칸에 들어갈 가장 올바른 것을 고르시오.

01 More and more Americans are planning to try _____ smoking because they are afraid that it may be harmful to their health.

  (a) having stopped   (b) stopping

  (c) to be stopping   (d) to stop

02 Lottery fever has hit the United States, and more and more states are beginning to use lotteries as a means of raising revenue. On the surface this seems an easy way _____ money.

  (a) to raise   (b) to have raised

  (c) raising   (d) being raising

01 City planners have been asked _____ a series of neighborhood forums that community leaders believe will increase public support for the new traffic corridor.

ⓐ initiating
ⓑ to initiate
ⓒ to be initiating
ⓓ initiated

02 The Louvre Museum in Paris added extra security to protect the Mona Lisa after someone tried _____ the priceless painting.

ⓐ to be damaging
ⓑ damaging
ⓒ being damaging
ⓓ to damage

03 After performing at three concerts in Chicago, we allowed the members of the school band some time off so that they could go _____.

ⓐ sightsee
ⓑ to sightsee
ⓒ having sightseen
ⓓ sightseeing

04 _____ worried, anxious, and nervous is a normal part of everyday life. Everyone has concerns or feels anxious from time to time.

ⓐ To feel
ⓑ Being feeling
ⓒ Feeling
ⓓ Felt

05 Central to the development of natural philosophy was the recovery of classical authors, most importantly the work of Aristotle. Humanists quickly realized the power of the printing press for _____ their knowledge.

ⓐ to spread
ⓑ to be spreading
ⓒ spreading
ⓓ having spread

06 When he was young, Bradbury enjoyed _____ books by fantasy writer Edgar Allen Poe, which influenced his later writing.

ⓐ to have read
ⓑ reading
ⓒ to read
ⓓ having read

07 Is there a simple way of easing the stress of driving? According to a new study, there is. The researchers noted that ___ to music while driving helps relieve the stress that affects heart health.

ⓐ listening
ⓑ listens
ⓒ to listen
ⓓ having listened

08 The protests became known as Fridays for Future. Since Thunberg began her protests, more than 60 countries have promised _____ their carbon footprints by 2050.

ⓐ eliminating
ⓑ to eliminate
ⓒ to be eliminating
ⓓ eliminate

09 Distinguishing between effectiveness and efficiency is much more than an exercise in semantics. Effectiveness entails _____a stated objective.

ⓐ promptly to achieve
ⓑ promptly achieving
ⓒ promptly to have achieved
ⓓ promptly achieved

10 Loneliness and lack of self-esteem are among the most obvious conditions which can be alleviated by _____ with an animal friend.

ⓐ living
ⓑ to live
ⓒ having lived
ⓓ to have lived

11 _____ responsibility to those you trust can not only make your organization run more smoothly but also free up more of your time so you can focus on larger issues.

ⓐ Giving away
ⓑ To give away
ⓒ Having given away
ⓓ To be giving away

12 Through the ages, industrious individuals have continuously created conveniences _____ life easier. From the Invention of the wheel to the light bulb, inventions have propelled society forward.

ⓐ making
ⓑ to be making
ⓒ to make
ⓓ makes

13 If you get sick yourself, keep your towels and dishes separate from everyone else's. Try _____ things that belong to others. Don't touch other people, and don't shake hands.

ⓐ not having touched
ⓑ not to touch
ⓒ not touching
ⓓ not to be touched

14 As of 2012, the Paralympic Games included events in more than 20 different sports, some of which allowed athletes _____ wheelchairs during competition.

ⓐ being used
ⓑ used
ⓒ to use
ⓓ to be using

15 Based on the updated airline policy, now passengers must remember _____ before a flight because food and drinks are not allowed onboard a plane.

ⓐ eating
ⓑ to eat
ⓒ being eating
ⓓ to have eaten

16 You respect the people with whom you're speaking and are authentically willing _____ them courteously even if you disagree with their positions.

ⓐ treating
ⓑ to treat
ⓒ to treating
ⓓ treat

17 Natural Gas World subscribers will receive accurate and reliable key facts and figures about what is going on in the industry, so they are fully able _____ what concerns their business.

ⓐ having discerned
ⓑ discerns
ⓒ discerning
ⓓ to discern

18 Have you ever tried to catch a fish under water and missed? We tend _____ of our line of sight as a straight line, but light bends due to refraction at the air-water surface.

ⓐ thinking
ⓑ to think
ⓒ to be thinking
ⓓ thought

19 The defense chief proposed _____ defense ministerial talks between the two countries every year instead of every two years and holding working-level talks twice a year.

ⓐ to hold
ⓑ holding
ⓒ having held
ⓓ held

20 Globalization leads more countries to open their markets, allowing them _____ goods and services freely at a lower cost with greater efficiency.

ⓐ trading
ⓑ to be trading
ⓒ to trade
ⓓ having traded

G-TELP
GRAMMAR
THEORY

01   may & might & can & could

1   may & might & could – 단순추측 (~일지도 모른다)

※ [can]은 단순한 추측의 의미는 없다.

※ 과거에 대한 추측
• may have + pp
• might have + pp
  ~이었을 지도 모른다.

• I haven't decided where to go on vacation.
  I *may / might / could* go to Boracay.

  나는 어디로 휴가를 갈지 결정하지 못했어. 아마도 보라카이로 갈 것 같아.

• Take a coat with you. It *may / might / could* be very cold tonight.

  코트를 가지고 가. 오늘 밤에 아주 추울 수도 있어.

• Russell *may / might / could* be at home at this time of the day.

  러셀은 이 시간에는 집에 있을 수도 있다.

2   may & can – 허락 & 허가 (~해도 된다)

• All the work has been done now. You *may / can* go home.

  이제 모든 일이 모두 완료되었다. 너는 집에 가도 된다.

• Students *may / can* not enter the building.

  학생들은 그 건물에 들어가면 안 된다.

• Bella *may / can* stay here as long as she wants.

  벨라는 이곳에서 원하는 만큼 머물러도 된다.

3   can (현재 또는 미래) & could (과거) – 능력

1) can – 현재 또는 미래 (할 수 있다)

• *Can* you speak English?

  영어를 할 수 있습니까?

• I am afraid I *can't* come to your party tonight.

  유감스럽지만 오늘 밤에 너의 파티에 갈 수 없을 것 같아.

※ 과거의 반대사실
could have + pp
~했을 수도 있었다.
(그러나 못했다.)

2) could – 과거 (할 수 있었다)

• We had a nice room in the hotel last night, so we *could* see the town.

  지난밤 호텔 방이 멋졌어. 우리는 시내를 볼 수 있었어.

• Russell played well but he *couldn't* beat Bella.

  러셀은 경기를 잘했지만 벨라를 이길 수는 없었다.

4   가능 – can (~일 수 있다) & can't (~일리가 없다)

※ 과거의 강한의심
• cannot have + pp
• couldn't have + pp
  ~이었을 리가 없다.

• The yellow table *can* fit into your study room.

  노란색 테이블이 너의 서재에 꼭 맞을 거야.

• Bella *can't* be at home right now because she went on a trip yesterday.

  벨라는 어제 여행을 떠났기 때문에 지금 집에 있을 리가 없어.

EXERCISE

Ⅰ 괄호 안에서 문법적으로 올바른 것을 고르시오.

01 Russell has been in quite a few countries. He (can / will / might) speak three languages.

02 I am looking for Bella. I think she (might / can / will) be watching TV in her room.

03 My grandmother loved music. She (could / may / will) play the violin very well then.

04 Jack says that we (can / will / must / shall) borrow his houses as long as we leave it clean and tidy.

05 Unmarried and highly paid, they (may / can / might / must) afford to spend money on luxury brand goods.

06 An adult (might / shall / would) need a translator to understand what children are talking about.

07 Currently citizens (may / would / will) visit the museum from 9 a.m. to 6 p.m. excluding Mondays.

08 When Jack gets a job, I (might / must / will) get the money back that I lent him but I am not sure.

Ⅱ 다음 빈칸에 들어갈 가장 올바른 것을 고르시오.

01 Many people worry that the next generation _____ respond wisely when others maliciously try to distort our history.

(a) shall not   (b) should not

(c) may not   (d) will not

02 When the weather is nice, all the roofs will stay opened so that spectators _____ enjoy the nice weather.

(a) might   (b) can

(c) must   (d) would

02　will & must & should

1 will - 미래 & 주어의 의지

1) 미래

- According to the weather forecast, it *will* be fine tomorrow.

　　　　　　　　　　　　　　기상예보에 따르면 내일은 날씨가 맑을 것이다.

- The bag is very well made. It *will* last a long time.

　　　　　　　　　　　　　　그 백은 아주 잘 만들어 졌어. 그것은 오래 갈 거야.

2) 주어의 의지

- I *will* invite lots of people to the party.

　　　　　　　　　　　　　　나는 파티에 많은 사람들을 초대 할 거야.

- Russell *will* not order fish because he doesn't like it.

　　　　　　　　　　　　러셀은 생선을 좋아하지 않기에 생선을 주문하지 않을 거야.

2 must - 강한 의무 & 강한 추측

1) 강한 의무 (~해야 한다)

- You *must* complete your homework before going to bed.

　　　　　　　　　　　　　　너는 자려가기 전에 숙제를 완성해야 한다.

- *Must* I join the club?

　　　　　　　　　　　　　　제가 클럽에 가입해야 하나요?

※ 과거의 강한 확신
must have + pp
~이었음이 틀림없다.

2) 강한 추측 (~임에 틀림없다, 분명히 ~일 것이다)

- Russell *must* have a lovely daughter to buy a pretty doll.

　　　　　　　　귀여운 인형을 구매하는 것을 보면 러셀은 사랑스러운 딸이 있는 것이 틀림없다.

- You have been traveling all day. You *must* be tired.

　　　　　　　　　　　　너는 하루 종일 돌아다녔어. 너는 분명히 피곤할 거야.

3 should - 충고, 조언, 권고 & 의무, 당위

※ 과거에 대한 후회/반성)
should have + pp
~했어야 했다.
(그러나 ~안했다.)

1) 충고, 조언, 권고 (~하는 것이 좋다, ~해라)

- You look tired. You *should* get some rest now.

　　　　　　　　　　　　너 피곤해 보여. 너는 지금 좀 쉬어야겠어.

- If you want to lose weight, you *should* work out regularly.

　　　　　　　　　　만약 당신이 살을 빼고 싶다면, 당신은 규칙적으로 운동을 해야 한다.

2) 의무, 당위 (~해야 한다)

- Drivers *should* consider pedestrians first of all.

　　　　　　　　　　　　운전자는 우선적으로 보행자를 고려해야 한다.

- The government *should* not let these corrupt practices happen any more.

　　　　　　　　　　정부는 더 이상 이런 부패관행이 이뤄지게 해서는 안 된다.

I 괄호 안에서 문법적으로 올바른 것을 고르시오.

01 I am too tired to walk home. I think I (will / shall / may) take a taxi.

02 To get there on time, we (will / must / might) leave home by 8, 30.

03 Bella needs a change. She (should / will / may) go away for a few days.

04 Russell (will / ought to / shall) give her another opportunity to get the suitable job.

05 We (must / will / could) do something dramatic if we want to save ourselves from going under.

06 In order to avoid such heartburn or indigestion, one (should / will / shall) try to eat regularly and slowly.

07 That man on the motorcycle isn't wearing a helmet. That's dangerous. He (should / will / may) be wearing a helmet.

08 Since there are a lot of people using smartphones and tablet PCs, webcomics (can / will / should) continue to increase in popularity.

II 다음 빈칸에 들어갈 가장 올바른 것을 고르시오.

01 For the better society, the government _____ focus on things like making more bicycle roads, putting up more lights, etc.

   (a) could   (b) should

   (c) would   (d) may

02 In order to use the playground, a dog _____ have an identification tag with the owner's contact information and the owner is responsible for cleaning up the dog's waste.

   (a) must   (b) can

   (c) will   (d) shall

당위종속절 (should 생략)

1 당위동사의 목적절

- He *asked* [that we *invest* in the property market].
  - ↝ He *asked* [that we *invested* in the property market]. (×)
  - ⋯→ 주절의 시제가 과거라고 해서 당위절의 시제를 과거로 하지 않도록 한다.

    그는 우리가 부동산에 투자를 해야 한다고 요구했다.

※ 문제해결 조언
당위동사의 [that]목적절 내의 동사는 반드시 동사원형[R]이 되어야 한다.

※ 당위동사

		당위 종속절	
제안하다	**suggest**, propose		
주장하다	insist		
요구하다	ask, require, demand, request		
권유하다	**recommend**	(that)	S + 동사원형(R)
명령하다	order, command, direct		
충고하다	**advise**		
촉구하다	urge		

- The teacher *demands* that everyone *be* in the classroom at nine.

  선생님은 모든 사람들인 9시에 교실에 있을 것을 요구하신다.

- Russell *suggested* that she *take on* the project.

  러셀은 그녀가 그 프로젝트를 맡아야 한다고 제안했다.

2 당위형용사 (당위, 의무, 중요, 당연, 적절 등의 의미를 지닌 형용사)

- It is *necessary* [that Russell *study* English hard].
  - ↝ It is *necessary* [that Russell *studies* English hard]. (×)
  - ⋯→ 종속절의 주어[Russell]이 3인칭 단수명사라서 동사에 수를 표시하지 않는다.

    러셀이 영어를 열심히 공부하는 것은 필수적이다.

※ 문제해결 조언
당위형용사로 구성된 진주어·가주어 구문에서 진주어[that]절 내의 동사는 반드시 동사원형[R]이 되어야 한다.

※ 당위형용사

It is +	important (중요한), vital (중요한), crucial (중요한), necessary (필수적인), essential (필수적인), imperative (강제적인), desirable (바람직한), natural (당연한), right (옳은), wrong (틀린), proper (적절한), appropriate (적절한), best (최고의), advisable (권할만한), etc.

(that) S + 동사원형(R)

- It is *important* that he *be* punished.

  그가 처벌을 받아야 하는 것은 중요하다.

- It is *essential* that students *not come* late for school.

  학생들이 학교에 늦지 말아야 하는 것은 필수적이다.

I 괄호 안에서 문법적으로 올바른 것을 고르시오.

01 As we become more electronically dependent, it is crucial that we (have / will have / had) the ability to feel that our information is safe

02 It is necessary that an employee (finishes / finish) his work on time.

03 It is imperative that the CEO (understand / understands) the present conditions.

04 The nurses asked that the hospital (not be / was not / won't be) closed.

05 The airline recommended we (be / were / has been) at the airport two hours before our flight.

06 It is vital that every runner (is drinking / drink / drinks) water during the marathon.

07 I forgot my daughter's birthday last year, so it is really important that I (will remember / remember / has remembered) it this year.

08 It is important that Russell (lose / lost / has lost / loses) weight for better health.

09 The police ordered that all weapons (will be / be / were) handed in immediately.

10 We insisted that the money (is / was / has been / be) available to all students in financial difficulties.

II 다음 빈칸에 들어갈 가장 올바른 것을 고르시오.

01 They advised that investors carefully _____ the current situation of the market before making any hasty investment decisions.

(a) will watch   (b) are watching

(c) watched   (d) watch

02 The members of the board strongly recommend that Russell _____ on the duties of CEO until a permanent replacement can be found.

(a) take   (b) will take

(c) has taken   (d) takes

01 The management team asked that all shipments _____ until inventories subsides to manageable levels.

ⓐ are suspended
ⓑ be suspended
ⓒ will be suspended
ⓓ have been suspended

02 Even under devastating circumstances, we _____ make our lives more pleasant by paying attention to simple amenities, such as being polite to others.

ⓐ might
ⓑ can
ⓒ will
ⓓ shall

03 The company has been prospering by selling environment-friendly products which helps make us safe. It ___ be profit-oriented, but it plays an important role in helping conserve the environment.

ⓐ will
ⓑ would
ⓒ must
ⓓ may

04 Some experts insist that expectations of growth and the models of growth in FinTech _____ a bit unrealistic, due mostly to demographics and the nature of money.

ⓐ have been
ⓑ be
ⓒ are
ⓓ would be

05 It is recommended that all the transactions involving the property _____ subject to the written approval of the committee.

ⓐ were
ⓑ will be
ⓒ be
ⓓ had been

06 It is imperative that the science communities in the 3rd worlds _____ systematized ways of amassing knowledge.

ⓐ will make
ⓑ have made
ⓒ make
ⓓ are making

07 Air Force officials believed that bad weather, mechanical problems of the ageing aircraft or pilots' suffering from vertigo _____ have led to the accidents.

ⓐ must
ⓑ should
ⓒ might
ⓓ can

08 To protect computers from malware, anti-virus programs _____ be installed and scheduled regularly to clean the computer and check for malware.

ⓐ would
ⓑ should
ⓒ will
ⓓ might

09 Farmers' interest groups like the Korean Advanced Farmers Federation have been proposing that the government _____ further protective measures against a wider rice market opening.

ⓐ has offered
ⓑ offer
ⓒ offers
ⓓ is offering

10 South Korea yesterday denied outright that the United States had requested that the Seoul government _____ a crackdown against illegal financial activities by North Korea.

ⓐ join
ⓑ is joining
ⓒ will join
ⓓ joined

11 Real fans must support celebrities through good times and bad times, and everyone _____ remember that they give us the gift of entertainment.

ⓐ can
ⓑ may
ⓒ will
ⓓ must

12 Despite the city's denial, the ruling party demanded that the mayor _____ a public apology for his remarks last Friday.

ⓐ offered
ⓑ has offered
ⓒ is offering
ⓓ offer

13 A researcher at Samsung Economic Research Institute suggested that Korea _____ on strengthening its R&D environment to attract investors.

ⓐ is focusing
ⓑ focus
ⓒ has focused
ⓓ would focus

14 Unlike teenagers who receive money from their parents, teenagers who have part-time jobs _____ save money and use it more responsibly.

ⓐ ought to
ⓑ shall
ⓒ will
ⓓ should

15 A change in the value of the 10,000 won bill, the highest-denomination banknote in the nation, shows that it is necessary that 100,000 won bills _____.

ⓐ have been issued
ⓑ will be issued
ⓒ are issued
ⓓ be issued

16 Because Asian economies have succeeded on the strength of an open international economy, it is important that they now _____ to further expand the global economic system.

ⓐ contribute
ⓑ contributed
ⓒ are contributing
ⓓ may contribute

17 The medical specialists diagnosed her with a severe form of fear of emotional attachment and recommended that they _____ her in a separate house and stop further contact.

ⓐ are placing
ⓑ have placed
ⓒ place
ⓓ would place

18 An official that if a wild boar is encountered, it is best that you _____ back from it and added the animals usually become aggressive when disturbed.

ⓐ stepped
ⓑ are stepping
ⓒ step
ⓓ have stepped

19 Our puppy, Rocky, had finally come back home. He has been missing for over two weeks. We are still wondering where he _____ have been during his absence.

   ⓐ can
   ⓑ might
   ⓒ will
   ⓓ should

20 From colonial times, unmarried women had enjoyed many of the same legal rights as men, although custom required that they _____ early.

   ⓐ were marrying
   ⓑ have been marrying
   ⓒ marry
   ⓓ married

G-TELP
GRAMMAR
THEORY

CHAPTER **6**

연결사

1 등위 접속사

단어, 구, 절 등을 모두 연결할 수 있다. 그러나 수험에서는 거의 출제가 되지 않는다.

> and(그리고), or(또는), but(그러나), so(그래서), for(왜냐하면)

2 부사절 접속사

접사속 뒤에 절[주어(S) + 동사(V)]이 이어지고, 주절과의 의미관계를 따진다.

※시간 부사절과 조건 부사절에는 미래 조동사[will]이 올 수 없다.	**시간**	when(~할때), while(~하는 동안에), until(~까지), since(~이후로), as soon as(~하자마자), before(~전에), after(~후에), whenever(~할 때마다)
	조건	if(~라면), unless(~가아니라면), in case(~라면, ~에 대비하여), once(일단 ~하면), as long as(~하는 한), provided (that)(~라면)
※[no matter how]와 [however]은 바로 뒤에 반드시 형용사나 부사가 동반된다.	**양보**	although(~이지만), though(~이지만), (even) if(~일지라도), whether(~든지 아닌지), while(~이지만, 반면에), whereas(반면에), no matter how+형용사·부사(아무리 ~일지라도), however+형용사·부사(아무리 ~일지라도), whatever(무엇이라도), wherever(어디에서라도)
	이유	because(~때문에), since(~때문에), now that(~ 때문에)
※[lest]절에는 부정어구가 올 수 없다.	**목적**	so that(~하기 위해서), in order that(~하기 위해서), lest(~하지않기 위해서, ~하지않도록, ~할까 봐)
	결과	so that(그래서 ~하다)

- *When* I meet him tonight, I will ask him why he left me.

  오늘 밤 내가 그를 만날 때, 나는 그에게 왜 나를 떠났는지 물어볼 것이다.

- *Although* she sometimes makes mistakes, she is one of the best here.

  비록 그녀는 때때로 실수를 하지만 이곳에서 최고중의 한 사람이다.

3 전치사

뒤에 명사나 동명사가 이어지고, 자신이 포함된 해당절과의 의미관계를 따진다.

	양보	despite / in spite of(~에도 불구하고), instead of(~대신에)
※[besides (게다가)] 접속부사로도 쓰인다.	**이유**	because of(~ 때문에), due to(~때문에), owing to(~ 때문에)
	시간	during(~동안에), after(~후에), before(~전에), until(~까지), since(~이후로)
	첨가	besides(~외에도), in addition to(~에 덧붙여),

- *Despite* her historic feat, her life was miserable.

  그녀의 역사적 위업에도 불구하고 그녀의 인생은 비참했다.

- All planes are grounded *because of* thick fog.

  짙은 안개 때문에 모든 비행기가 지상에 묶여있다.

I 괄호 안에서 문법적으로 올바른 것을 고르시오.

01 All drivers should carry a spare tire in good condition and an emergency kit (despite / in case / although / however) they have a breakdown.

02 Suicide rates are rapidly increasing in Korea, (while / if / once / even if) they are decreasing throughout the developed nations.

03 A number of doctors study hard (so that / afterward / unless) they can keep abreast of all the latest developments in medicine.

04 The administration's approval rating falls (in spite of / whenever / so that) the president's speech grows distant from reality.

05 Scientists have found out in a recent study that (before / wherever / no matter how / while) low-fat the milk may be, it does not affect weight loss.

06 The driver will not be able to focus on driving, (if / unless / until) you disturb the driver.

07 There can be no true liberty (unless / although / if) there is economic liberty.

08 The National Health Association approved a series of graphic anti-smoking ads, (when / during / despite / even though) the controversy surrounding them.

II 다음 빈칸에 들어갈 가장 올바른 것을 고르시오.

01 The judge is frustrated that a mistrial must be declared _____ the jury cannot reach a decision regarding the defendant's guilt or innocence.

(a) however   (b) as long as

(c) instead   (d) because

02 Firefighters are people whose job is to put out fires and rescue people. _____fires, firefighters save people and animals from car wrecks, collapsed buildings, stuck elevators and many other emergencies.

(a) While   (b) Besides

(c) Since   (d) Despite

접속사적 의미를 지니고 있지만, 접속사가 아니기 때문에 문장을 연결할 수 없다. 수험에서는 접속부사는 바로 뒤에 콤마[,]가 주로 동반된다. 또한 <u>앞 절과의 논리관계를</u> 따진다.

- Russell didn't feel well. *Nevertheless*, he went to help Bella.
  ↗ Russell didn't feel well. *Although* he went to help Bella. (×)
  ⋯→ 부사절접속사[although]는 문장을 연결하지 않으므로 적절하지 않다.
  러셀은 몸이 좋지 않았다. 그럼에도 불구하고 그는 벨라를 도우러 갔다.

※ 접속부사[however(그러나)]는 접속사[however+형/부(아무리 ~일지라도)]와 구분된다.

역접 대조 양보 however(그러나), **nevertheless**(그럼에도 불구하고), nonetheless(그럼에도 불구하고), **still**(그럼에도 불구하고), even so(그렇긴 하지만, 그런데도), otherwise(그렇지 않으면), regardless(상관하지않고), meanwhile(한편), on the contrary(대조적으로), in contrast(대조적으로), by contrast(대조적으로), on the other hand(반면에), instead(대신에·선택, 오히려), **in fact**(사실은, 실제로)

첨가 moreover(더구나), furthermore(더구나), besides(게다가), in addition(추가적으로)

강조 in fact(사실은, 실제로), as a matter of fact(사실은, 실제는), indeed(정말로, 실제로), above all(무엇보다도), first of all(우선, 무엇보다도)

결과 therefore(그러므로), hence(따라서), thus(따라서), consequently(결과적으로), as a result(결과적으로), accordingly(따라서, 그에 맞게)

비유 likewise(마찬가지로, 똑같이), similarly(마찬가지로, 이와 같이)

예시 for instance(예를 들어), for example(예를 들어)

요약 재언급 in brief(요약하면), in short(요약하면), to sum up(요약하면), in other words(다시 말하면)

결론 finally(마침내), eventually(마침내), at last(마침내), after all(마침내), in conclusion(결과적으로), altogether(대체적으로), all in all(대체로)

시간 then(그러고 나서), meanwhile(그러는 동안), in the meantime(그러는 동안), afterward(이후에), in the first place(우선), subsequently(그 뒤에, 나중에)

- You had studied English hard. *Therefore*, you passed the exam.
  너는 공부를 열심히 했다. 그러므로 당신은 시험을 통과했다.
- Bella was so hot. *Hence*, she drank something cold.
  벨라는 매우 더웠다. 그래서 차가운 것을 마셨다.

EXERCISE

I 괄호 안에서 문법적으로 올바른 것을 고르시오.

01 Bella had written many letters seeking admission to medical schools for over two years. (In addition / In other words / Finally), she was accepted by a medical school in Philadelphia.

02 The use of cameras and video cameras is permitted in all permanent collection galleries. (In other words / However / Therefore / Regardless), flash photography is not permitted inside museums.

03 People in today's society are interested in diets and eating healthily. (On the other hand / Regardless / Therefore), they refrain from eating unhealthy or high calorie foods.

04 The cruel sights touched off thoughts that, (otherwise / therefore / likewise), wouldn't have entered her mind.

05 For over 50 years, no Spanish children were born in any of the higher altitudes. (For example / On the contrary / Consequently), the Indians were fertile in the same climate.

06 The rapid growth of suburbs has created many problems. (For example / However / In contrast), numerous suburbs have had trouble raising enough money for such essential services as police and fire protection.

07 In 1857 she and her sister managed to open the first hospital for women and children. (Accordingly / Besides / In short), she established the first medical school for women.

II 다음 빈칸에 들어갈 가장 올바른 것을 고르시오.

01 In studying Chinese calligraphy, one must learn something of the origins of Chinese language and of how they were originally written. _____, except for those brought up in the artistic traditions of the country, its aesthetic significance seems to be very difficult to apprehend.

(a) Furthermore   (b) Therefore

(c) As a result   (d) However

02 Instead of asking "Am I a good person?" you may want to ask "What good do I do in the world?" Grushcow's temple puts these beliefs into action inside and outside their community. _____, they sponsored two refugee families from Vietnam to come to Canada in the 1970s.

(a) Eventually   (b) Hence

(c) For instance   (d) In conclusion

01 After Francesca made a case for staying at home _____ the summer holidays, an uncomfortable silence fell on the dinner table. Robert was not sure if it was the right time for him to tell her about his grandiose plan.

ⓐ similarly
ⓑ during
ⓒ while
ⓓ Because of

02 The world may be a different place, and you will likely be a different person. So try to anticipate these changes, both in the world and yourself, _____ you consider a job path.

ⓐ in other words
ⓑ when
ⓒ although
ⓓ because

03 Law enforcement personnel must have probable cause to believe that the owner of the property has been involved in criminal activity, _____ law enforcement personnel can search or seize private property.

ⓐ before
ⓑ while
ⓒ since
ⓓ however

04 Thunderstorms are extremely common in many parts of the world, _____, throughout most of North America. Updrafts of warm air set off these storms.

ⓐ therefore
ⓑ furthermore
ⓒ for example
ⓓ hence

05 A manuscript written by hand is a unique and unreproducible object. _____, print with its standard format and type, introduced exact mass reproduction.

ⓐ However
ⓑ Therefore
ⓒ Consequently
ⓓ Even though

06 The campaign to eliminate pollution will turn out to be absolutely futile _____ it has the understanding and full cooperation of the public who is concerned about the environmental pollution.

ⓐ if
ⓑ unless
ⓒ as soon as
ⓓ Besides

07 The white-tailed deer was one of the first animals to be protected by federal legislation. _____ unlike the passenger pigeon, white-tailed deer were not in much need of protection.

ⓐ Nevertheless
ⓑ But
ⓒ Likewise
ⓓ Hence

08 If you turn a doorknob that has always turned easily and it won't move, you will turn the knob harder, and may pull it up or push it down. _____, you may shove or kick the door.

ⓐ Eventually
ⓑ However
ⓒ Otherwise
ⓓ Accordingly

09 In what seems almost a miraculous way, poetry brightens up words that looked dull and ordinary. _____, poetry is perpetually recreating language.

ⓐ For example
ⓑ By contrast
ⓒ In other words
ⓓ Soon

10 Children are susceptible for the effects of television _____ their minds are growing, developing, and learning much faster than those of adults.

ⓐ although
ⓑ before
ⓒ because
ⓓ when

11 Aggressive drivers react foolishly in several dangerous ways. One way is to cut off another motorists and tailgate the other car. _____ cutting off and tailgating other cars, they often use rude language or gestures to show their anger.

ⓐ Therefore
ⓑ Besides
ⓒ Despite
ⓓ But

12 In our country, child labor was abrogated fifty years ago. _____, in some countries, where people are usually in a poor condition, people are still using it.

ⓐ On the other hand
ⓑ At last
ⓒ Instead
ⓓ Likewise

13 5 cents in 1972 had more market value than 5 cents today. In this situation, the actual costs can't legitimately be compared. _____, the costs have to be compared after they've been adjusted for inflation.

ⓐ For instance

ⓑ Hence

ⓒ Likewise

ⓓ Eventually

14 The Mona Lisa and Michelangelo's David are reproduced so often that we may feel we know them _____ we have never been to Paris or Florence.

ⓐ because

ⓑ when

ⓒ even if

ⓓ despite

15 Surveillance cameras have been widely used in lots of places for security purposes. _____, their usefulness is still under discussion.

ⓐ However

ⓑ Consequently

ⓒ In contrast

ⓓ Fortunately

16 If you have only one temperature sensor for the whole plot of land, it must be an accurate one; _____, it does not provide reliable data.

ⓐ conclusively

ⓑ otherwise

ⓒ moreover

ⓓ similarly

17 People think of lie detectors as foolproof simply because they are machines. ___, they often made errors due to many factors.

ⓐ Hence

ⓑ In fact

ⓒ In addition

ⓓ Altogether

18 In the story, the rich will be totally useless greedy characters, _____ the poor will be simple, honest people whose daily work is profitable to the community.

ⓐ when

ⓑ since

ⓒ while

ⓓ whether

19 Being successful is all a matter of luck. _____, those who persevere recognize that they are ultimately responsible not just for pursuing their goals, but for setting them.

ⓐ Besides
ⓑ However
ⓒ Thus
ⓓ Afterward

20 An updraft may start over ground that is more intensely heated by the sun than the land surrounding the area. _____, bare, rocky, or paved areas usually have updrafts above them.

ⓐ On the other hand
ⓑ For example
ⓒ Eventually
ⓓ In fact

G-TELP
GRAMMAR
THEORY

CHAPTER 7

실전
모의고사

01 China is considered to be one of the most influential countries in the world not just socially but also economically. The China that _____ at 10 percent for 30 years was a powerful source of fuel for much of what drove the global economy forward.

ⓐ has grown
ⓑ were growing
ⓒ had been growing
ⓓ would grow

02 Thunberg, 16, has become the voice of young people around the world who are protesting climate change and demanding that governments around the world ____ more action.

ⓐ took
ⓑ take
ⓒ taking
ⓓ have taken

03 There are a lot of students looking for many kinds of jobs in the world. If you are considering _____ for a job overseas, seek the advice of an international employment agency first.

ⓐ being looking
ⓑ looking
ⓒ look
ⓓ to look

04 Bella didn't tell Russell that she had difficulties studying English grammar and vocabulary. If she _____ him about the problem, he would have helped her with them.

ⓐ tells
ⓑ had told
ⓒ would tell
ⓓ has told

05 In Mexico, the value spike of limes is attracting criminals, forcing growers _____ their limited supply of "green gold" from drug cartels.

ⓐ guarding
ⓑ to guard
ⓒ to be guarding
ⓓ having guarded

06 Many gun-rights proponents say these statistics do not indicate a cause-and-effect relationship and note that the rates of gun homicide and other gun crimes in the United States _____ since highs in the early 1990's.

ⓐ are dropping
ⓑ have been dropping
ⓒ had dropped
ⓓ drop

07 The company was established in September, 1970 and _____ our business operations around Asia ever since.

   ⓐ had been expanding
   ⓑ would expand
   ⓒ has been expanding
   ⓓ will be expanding

08 In order to allow their children to learn from their mistakes, parents _____ necessarily provide them with the freedom to make mistakes.

   ⓐ may
   ⓑ must
   ⓒ will
   ⓓ can

09 Andy Warhol began to wear rock-star leather jackets, satin shirts and a silver-sprayed wig. His trademark use of product labels in his art first showed up as prints on the paper dresses _____.

   ⓐ whom he created.
   ⓑ when he created.
   ⓒ which he created.
   ⓓ whose he created.

10 We had no idea that the start time of the soccer game had been changed, so we were not able to compete. If we had known about the rescheduling and participated in it, we _____ this much.

   ⓐ were not disappointed
   ⓑ would not be disappointed
   ⓒ would not have been disappointed
   ⓓ are not disappointed

11 Following the Mass is an elaborate party, with dancing, cake, and toasts. Finally, _____ the evening, the young woman dances a waltz with her favorite escort.

   ⓐ ending
   ⓑ to end
   ⓒ to be ending
   ⓓ being ending

12 The United States has the highest homicide-by-firearm rate among the world's most developed nations. _____, many gun-rights proponents say these statistics do not indicate a cause-and-effect relationship.

   ⓐ Similarly
   ⓑ But
   ⓒ Therefore
   ⓓ Besides

13 Jane is often late for work because she doesn't have a car and has to take public transportation. If she afforded a car, she _____ one immediately.

ⓐ will purchase
ⓑ purchases
ⓒ will have purchased
ⓓ would purchase

14 The chef _____ have checked the temperature of the oven before trying to roast the chicken instead of just assuming it was hot enough.

ⓐ might
ⓑ should
ⓒ will
ⓓ can't

15 In countries operating under the "innocent until proven guilty" system, society has decided that it is better that they _____ a guilty person to go free than to imprison an innocent person.

ⓐ will allow
ⓑ allow
ⓒ are allowing
ⓓ have allowed

16 Two men on a motorcycle attacked Garry when he _____ home one evening. He spent two nights in the hospital recovering from trauma and injuries.

ⓐ walks
ⓑ was walking
ⓒ has walked
ⓓ has been walking

17 Andrew has been working as an accountant for more than ten years now. _____ the long period of working, he is not well recognised and can't earn much money. I think he had better change his career.

ⓐ Although
ⓑ Instead of
ⓒ Despite
ⓓ Owing to

18 My brother and I have always dreamed of owning a fishing boat so that we can catch bigger fish. If we _____ one, we would always be in the sea, fishing and sailing whenever we can.

ⓐ had had
ⓑ had
ⓒ has
ⓓ will have

19 Such person will be a source of happiness and a recipient of reciprocal kindness. _____ many people spontaneously and without effort is perhaps the greatest of all sources of personal happiness.

ⓐ Like
ⓑ To like
ⓒ Liking
ⓓ Having liked

20 One of the oldest frauds of gemstones was the sale of water _____, on the pretense that contact with the gem had made the water medicinal.

ⓐ whose a gemstone had been dipped into
ⓑ whom a gemstone had been dipped into
ⓒ which a gemstone had been dipped into
ⓓ when a gemstone had been dipped into

21 Jason lost his chance to make the interviewers impressed and to get a job since he made quite a few mistakes in the job interview. If he had prepared the job interview more carefully, he _____ the mistakes.

ⓐ wouldn't have made
ⓑ hasn't made
ⓒ isn't making
ⓓ won't make

22 West Bromwich finished at the top of the Football League Championship, which means that next season, Kim and the team _____ in the top division, the English Premier League.

ⓐ are playing
ⓑ have played
ⓒ will be playing
ⓓ had been playing

23 Russell was very interested in cooking when young, and now is a famous chef in a world class hotel. He still enjoys _____ new cuisines.

ⓐ to create
ⓑ creating
ⓒ to have created
ⓓ having created

24 When Jose got up late this morning, the rest of his family had gone out for lunch. There was nothing to eat at home. If he had woken up earlier before they went out, he _____ them.

ⓐ joined
ⓑ was joining
ⓒ would have joined
ⓓ has joined

25 Russell is in his last year as a medical student and is looking forward to graduation. By the time he finishes this semester, he _____ only leukemia and the treatments for over five years.

ⓐ will be studying
ⓑ will have been studying
ⓒ has studied
ⓓ would study

26 After completing its probe into why the South Korean military failed to report accurately about the North's violation of an inter-Korean maritime border last week, the Defense Ministry recommended that the government seriously _____ two generals and subject three other military officers to lesser punishment.

ⓐ censures
ⓑ censure
ⓒ has censured
ⓓ is censuring

01 The world population, which was almost 6 billion in 2000, is expected to double by 2050. Almost 95 percent of this growth will be in developing countries, _____.

ⓐ that 77 percent of the world's population lives.

ⓑ where 77 percent of the world's population lives.

ⓒ which 77 percent of the world's population lives.

ⓓ when 77 percent of the world's population lives.

02 After Francesca strongly suggested staying at home during the summer holidays, an uncomfortable silence fell on the dinner table. Robert was not sure if it was the right time for him _____ her about his grandiose plan.

ⓐ to be telling

ⓑ to tell

ⓒ telling

ⓓ tell

03 Developmental delays _____ manifest themselves in poor social skills, a short attention span, and difficulties with schoolwork.

ⓐ would

ⓑ may

ⓒ must

ⓓ shall

04 By the 18th century, the term Le Cordon Bleu became directly connected with superior cuisine, and the school _____ its prominence even these days.

ⓐ is keeping

ⓑ will keep

ⓒ has kept

ⓓ was keeping

05 Russel usually goes on a travel alone. But this time he joined a group tour and met such a wonderful lady, Amanda. If he _____ alone this time, he wouldn't have met her.

ⓐ has traveled

ⓑ is traveling

ⓒ had traveled

ⓓ would travel

06 Smith's restaurant is very popular and quite a few people love it. When Bella got to the restaurant for dinner yesterday, she had to wait in line for about an hour. Therefore I advised that she _____ a reservation in advance, next time she visits it.

ⓐ will make

ⓑ make

ⓒ makes

ⓓ would make

07 Bella bought the novel Harry Potter and the Sorcerer's Stone by J.K. Rowling. She began reading it yesterday evening, and hasn't been finished with the book yet. She _____ for over 20 hours by 10 pm tonight.

ⓐ will have been reading
ⓑ is reading
ⓒ will be reading
ⓓ had read

08 Assertive behavior involves _____ your rights and expressing your thoughts and feelings in a direct, appropriate way.

ⓐ to stand up for
ⓑ to standing up for
ⓒ standing up for
ⓓ would stand up for

09 Some movies explored the possibility of sustaining human life in outer space, _____ other films have questioned whether extraterrestrial life forms may have visited our planet.

ⓐ because
ⓑ while
ⓒ since
ⓓ even if

10 Some of my friends are enjoying a music concert in Seoul right now. I really envy them. If I _____ much work to do now, I would be there with them and enjoy myself.

ⓐ didn't have
ⓑ don't have
ⓒ wouldn't have
ⓓ hadn't had

11 Regarding excise taxes that are under fire for distorting the economy, the minister said that the government _____ removing them right now.

ⓐ had considered
ⓑ was considering
ⓒ had considered
ⓓ is considering

12 Anxiety can cause both physical and emotional symptoms, and a specific situation or fear _____ cause some or all of these symptoms for a short time.

ⓐ ought to
ⓑ can
ⓒ will
ⓓ must

13 Speaking up is important. Yet speaking up without listening is like _____ pots and pans together: even if it gets you attention, it's not going to get you respect.

ⓐ to bang
ⓑ banging
ⓒ bang
ⓓ to have banged

14 The company has provided many medical products for the needy who can't afford them. _____, the company plans to build many houses for them to live for free.

ⓐ Moreover
ⓑ Therefore
ⓒ However
ⓓ In other words

15 Jason had such a tiring day in school yesterday. As soon as he got home, he went straight to bed. He _____ for over 10 hours when Russell finally woke him up.

ⓐ has slept
ⓑ had been sleeping
ⓒ was sleeping
ⓓ would sleep

16 Russell has worked so hard for a month and he think he needs to have a break. Because he has been to many foreign countries, this time he is considering _____ to Jeju island.

ⓐ traveling
ⓑ to travel
ⓒ to be traveling
ⓓ will travel

17 I always want to have enough money not to be worried about how much money I should spend. However, I know well that if I _____ so rich, I wouldn't be what I am now.

ⓐ am
ⓑ were
ⓒ had been
ⓓ has been

18 I am not sure if Russell will visit us in the evening today. But I remember _____ me last Saturday that he would come to my place and enjoy dinner together today.

ⓐ to tell
ⓑ telling
ⓒ to have heard
ⓓ told

19 The Moors, Arab conquerors from North Africa, ruled Spain for nearly 800 years. The society _____ was in its unprecedented tolerance, unique.

ⓐ when the Moors presided over in medieval Spain

ⓑ whom the Moors presided over in medieval Spain

ⓒ whose the Moors presided over in medieval Spain

ⓓ that the Moors presided over in medieval Spain

20 Last month Russell worked temporarily at a supermarket, where he accidently broke the front door and had to compensate for it. He _____ it, had he been more careful.

ⓐ wouldn't break

ⓑ will break

ⓒ broke

ⓓ wouldn't have broken

21 The second South-North Korean summit was first scheduled to be held on August 28 to 30, but in mid-August, the North was beset by severe floods and asked that the meeting _____ to October.

ⓐ was postponed

ⓑ will be postponed

ⓒ be postponed

ⓓ had been postponed

22 A Korea-China-Japan summit is to be held in Seoul later this month, and People _____ whether it will bring a breakthrough in the comfort women issue.

ⓐ have watched

ⓑ will be watching

ⓒ were watching

ⓓ will have been watching

23 I am glad to have my English teacher, Russell, who is always passionate and makes English easy to learn. If it _____ for him, I might be studying another language, not English.

ⓐ had not been

ⓑ were not

ⓒ is not

ⓓ has not been

24 Because Julia arrived at the theater after the movie started, my friend and I missed the beginning part of the movie. We _____ for about 30 minutes before she finally appeared.

ⓐ were waiting

ⓑ have been waiting

ⓒ will have waited

ⓓ had been waiting

25 Yesterday Jack bought two movie tickets to get a date with his girl friend. But she didn't make it so he had to watch the movie alone. If he had known that she couldn't make it, he _____ the two tickets.

ⓐ hadn't bought
ⓑ wouldn't have bought
ⓒ buys
ⓓ bought

26 Lino A. Saputo, chair and CEO of the company, said, "Treating people with respect and without discrimination is one of our basic principles, and it is imperative that we _____ to uphold this in everything we do.

ⓐ have continued
ⓑ continue
ⓒ will continue
ⓓ are continuing

01 Although Jack tries to save enough money to buy a house here, he doesn't think he can however hard he may work. _____ a house, he must have at least two jobs and spend little money.

ⓐ Buying
ⓑ To have bought
ⓒ To buy
ⓓ Having bought

02 It's already 8 o'clock in the evening, and I am still working in the office because of a lot of paper work to complete by today. I think I _____ here until midnight.

ⓐ will be staying
ⓑ will have stayed
ⓒ have been staying
ⓓ would have been staying

03 A majority of voters did not support the mayor as in the previous election. If the mayor had been more sympathetic to their concerns, they _____ for him.

ⓐ would have voted
ⓑ had voted
ⓒ will vote
ⓓ would vote

04 Russell tends to deal with even minor tasks in person to make everything correctly done. One of his colleagues advises that he _____ some of his work to his staff so that he can focus more important task.

ⓐ allocate
ⓑ is allocating
ⓒ allocates
ⓓ has allocated

05 The company Mr Smith works for is currently having a hard time. He _____ as an accountant of the company for around 15 years now and is considering moving to another company.

ⓐ is working
ⓑ has been working
ⓒ works
ⓓ are working

06 The Minister of Employment and Labor said yesterday that companies are willing to cooperate with employees for their job security. _____, it must not hamper labor flexibility.

ⓐ Therefore
ⓑ In fact
ⓒ To sum up
ⓓ Even so

07 You _____ place more value on one over the other, because they are all needed to form the whole. That's called synergy, meaning that the whole is more than the sum of the individual parts.

ⓐ shall not
ⓑ should not
ⓒ can not
ⓓ might not

08 If the United States had pursued its comparative advantage in accordance with market principles, it _____ fish, fur, agricultural products, etc..

ⓐ would export
ⓑ was exporting
ⓒ will have exported
ⓓ would have been exporting

09 Ross never saw the car running over an old lady on the road. If he _____ the car accident, he wouldn't have said that in such a careless way.

ⓐ has witnessed
ⓑ would witness
ⓒ had witnessed
ⓓ was witnessing

10 With the effect of its power saving demonstrated, GS Retail, which runs GS25 convenience stores, _____ the number of its stores adopting the technology since last year.

ⓐ is increasing
ⓑ increased
ⓒ has been increasing
ⓓ will increase

11 The report suggested that the government _____ a favorable environment for companies to adopt various safety nets for management protection, while keeping a watchful eye on foreign investors.

ⓐ create
ⓑ created
ⓒ was creating
ⓓ had created

12 The English essay Jane wrote for his English composition class is very similar to mine. It has even similar grammar errors. But she firmly denies _____ my essay.

ⓐ to copy
ⓑ copied
ⓒ will copy
ⓓ copying

13 Schooling is compulsory for all children in the United States. _____ the age range for which school attendance is required varies from state to state.

ⓐ However
ⓑ Hence
ⓒ Eventually
ⓓ Moreover

14 When Russell was a high school student, he wished that he could speak Spanish. But he ended up studying English though. If he were given another opportunity, he _____ to study Spanish.

ⓐ would choose
ⓑ will choose
ⓒ is choosing
ⓓ chooses

15 A pandemic disease has prohibited many people from traveling to foreign countries for over a year. When the situation ends, people won't be able to resist _____ to other countries for vacation.

ⓐ flocking
ⓑ to flock
ⓒ to have flocked
ⓓ having flocked

16 Drivers often forget renewing their driver's license. Drivers are advised to renew their driver's license on time as they may be required _____ the written and driving tests past the expiration date.

ⓐ retaking
ⓑ are retaking
ⓒ to retake
ⓓ would retake

17 When I was finished with homework yesterday, it was too late to go out. That's why I just stayed home then. If I had finished it earlier, I _____ out for dinner.

ⓐ went
ⓑ would have gone
ⓒ have gone
ⓓ did go

18 According to the Office of Health and Safety, odors _____ come from chemicals inside or outside an office space, or even from the construction of a building.

ⓐ will
ⓑ might
ⓒ would
ⓓ shall

19 Jack likes watching soap opera so much that he is called 'couch potato'. There is no doubt that he _____ on the sofa and watching soap opera right now.

ⓐ is sitting
ⓑ sat
ⓒ has sat
ⓓ will sit

20 In a 2008 decision confirming an individual right to keep and bear arms, the court struck down Washington, D.C. laws _____ and required those in the home to be locked or disassembled.

ⓐ who banned handguns
ⓑ that banned handguns
ⓒ when banned handguns
ⓓ whose banned handguns

21 There will surely be a huge crowd at the airport after the global pandemic ends. Therefore, if you prefer to travel abroad with a tight budget, it is best that you _____ about three to four months after the pandemic finally ends.

ⓐ will leave
ⓑ are leaving
ⓒ leave
ⓓ have left

22 When my parents moved in Busan some 60 years ago, there were few buildings there. However, since then, the city _____ so fast that it has become one of the most modern cities in the world.

ⓐ developed
ⓑ has been developing
ⓒ had been developing
ⓓ develops

23 Martin enjoys fishing very much, but has never gone fishing for over three months because he has been so busy working on the project. If he hadn't been that busy, he_____ fishing several times.

ⓐ would have gone
ⓑ would go
ⓒ goes
ⓓ will be going

24 This mold is impossible to remove and can ruin the fabric. To prevent it, you need to waterproof the canvas. _____ blocks of wax on your canvas can make it naturally waterproof.

ⓐ Rubbing
ⓑ To rub
ⓒ Being rubbing
ⓓ To rubbing

25 As the stream continues down the mountain, the steepness of the slope decreases, which results in fewer rapids _____ and becomes oxygenated.

ⓐ when the water tumbles over rocks
ⓑ where the water tumbles over rocks
ⓒ whose the water tumbles over rocks
ⓓ whom the water tumbles over rocks

26 One of my colleagues, Jane, had prepared her audition so enthusiastically. Unfortunately, while she _____ on the stage, the power went out suddenly, so her performance had to be rescheduled.

ⓐ performed
ⓑ was performing
ⓒ has performed
ⓓ will be performing

01 Currently we are expanding our business for your convenience to include traveling to repair your vehicle. For the last 20 years, our Automotive Center _____ the finest automotive supplies, including cleaning tools, batteries, car accessories and much more.

ⓐ is providing
ⓑ provided
ⓒ had been providing
ⓓ has been providing

02 It is generally agreed that fossil fuels are a limited resource. One day they will run out. All countries need _____ on alternatives to fossil fuels to avoid major disruption to out daily lives.

ⓐ working together
ⓑ to work together
ⓒ to have worked together
ⓓ worked together

03 The Battle of Saratoga in 1777, led by General Arnold, was considered a pivotal victory for the Americans. History may not remember this now, but America's war effort _____ successful if it had not been for his early contributions.

ⓐ might not have been
ⓑ have not been
ⓒ wasn't
ⓓ might not be

04 The stress associated with retraining and new work routines _____ lead to a higher risk of heart disease, high blood pressure, as well as other health issues. The study could help social workers advise seniors about their job opportunities.

ⓐ shall
ⓑ would
ⓒ must
ⓓ can

05 My wife and sons saw my move-out as an act of abandonment, and my divorce came less than a year later. I know now that if your children or your wife ask you to stay, it is best that you _____ hard about where your priorities lie.

ⓐ think
ⓑ will think
ⓒ to think
ⓓ are thinking

06 Please wash the vegetables before peeling them, and then slice them into small pieces. While you are doing that, I get some pasta from the refrigerator. When I come back, I _____ you how to cook and blend the ingredients so that your sauce turns our smooth and creamy.

ⓐ have shown
ⓑ have been showing
ⓒ will be showing
ⓓ showed

07 Please look the photos over and, in your reply, let me know which one you think would be best for our work needs. I am willing _____ my own money if the one with the most votes is beyond our means.

ⓐ to be contributing
ⓑ contributing
ⓒ contributed
ⓓ to contribute

08 In the analysis of the course survey results, students' dissatisfaction seems to come down to one thing. If students _____ how difficult the course would be, they might not have registered. In the future, it will be necessary to ensure they are aware of what will be required.

ⓐ knew
ⓑ had known
ⓒ have known
ⓓ know

09 China's appetite for turtle has emptied the streams across Asia of their terrapin populations. The terrapin population decrease _____ since 1990s when the traditional association between reptile meat and longevity was reemphasized.

ⓐ is doubling
ⓑ had been doubling
ⓒ has been doubling
ⓓ will be doubling

10 The drugs or substances categorized in schedule A are mostly narcotic, have no current acceptance for medical use, and _____ not be prescribed. On the other hand, drugs assigned in schedule B through F have accepted medical use.

ⓐ will
ⓑ may
ⓒ ought to
ⓓ would

11 James was sick with covid-19 for two weeks. Therefore he could hardly do any school work. For instance, he wasn't able to read any book or write its book report. If he had not gotten sick, he _____ the book.

ⓐ had surely read
ⓑ would have surely read
ⓒ was surely read
ⓓ has surely read

12 As Hurricane Hilda makes her way north, we advise you to garage your vehicles, and to avoid being outside whenever possible until everything has blown over, _____.

ⓐ when should be around midnight tonight
ⓑ what should be around midnight tonight
ⓒ which should be around midnight tonight
ⓓ that should be around midnight tonight

13 Traffic today is expected to be unusually slow on the Capital beltway heading out of the city. We urge that you _____ in an additional 90 minutes for traffic delays until around 7 this evening.

ⓐ have built
ⓑ building
ⓒ build
ⓓ are building

14 According to firsthand accounts from many of his peers, Beethoven was difficult _____ with and to understand. He would often arrive late for dinner and would frequently appear in public unshaven and unkempt.

ⓐ getting along
ⓑ to get along
ⓒ to have got along
ⓓ gets along

15 He was talking about strong, smart, hardworking entrepreneurs. They woke up motivated every day and _____ their best to make their lives and their family's lives better.

ⓐ are doing
ⓑ has done
ⓒ had been doing
ⓓ were doing

16 People often associate entertainment with city life. _____, people enjoy eating out, night-clubbing, going to bars or ballet, opera and symphony orchestras. Cities offer choices that aren't possible in smaller towns.

ⓐ For example
ⓑ In contrast
ⓒ Even though
ⓓ Besides

17 Benedict Arnold, the general of the American Revolutionary War, became America's most notorious traitor. _____, people forget that up until he changed sides and joined the British, Arnold had a very distinguished record for the American side.

ⓐ Therefore
ⓑ However
ⓒ Indeed
ⓓ In addition

18 Because of his tight financial budget this year, Jack won't be able to afford a Christmas tree for his children this holiday. He would immediately buy it if he _____ enough money, which isn't meant to be this year.

ⓐ had
ⓑ would have
ⓒ had had
ⓓ has

19 City officials are cautioning pet owners to be extra careful about _____ their animals stay outside for extended periods of time. With temperatures regularly in the low 90s, this summer heat is expecially dangerous to animals with thick coats of fur.

ⓐ letting
ⓑ to let
ⓒ let
ⓓ having let

20 Dubbed the world factory, over the last decades, China _____ more industrial goods than any other country. The communist country has helped fuel its high-speed economic growth that is expected to surpass 8 percent this year.

ⓐ had been rapidly producing
ⓑ has been rapidly producing
ⓒ was rapidly producing
ⓓ will have rapidly produced

21 These latest findings are supported by many experts, _____ that the theory of a Darwinian link between Ida and humans has been unconvincing.

ⓐ what have argued from the beginning
ⓑ who have argued from the beginning
ⓒ that have argued from the beginning
ⓓ when have argued from the beginning

22 Before you leave the bus, you should be aware of a few basic safety procedures as you tour the construction site. It is really important that we _____ anyone working as guests here. Also, make sure you wear your hard hat at all times.

ⓐ not disrupting
ⓑ don't disrupt
ⓒ not to disrupt
ⓓ not disrupt

23 According to the investigation report of the serious car crash which occurred last night, if only the driver of the tourist bus had refrained from speeding and kept the minimal safe distance between vehicles, it _____ the collision.

ⓐ had avoided
ⓑ could avoid
ⓒ could have avoided
ⓓ has avoided

24 Half of the people invited to the meeting showed up late. Combined with the other problems yesterday, that really made Jane angry. She started _____ her fingers on the table, glaring at the latecomers.

ⓐ drumming
ⓑ will drum
ⓒ having drummed
ⓓ to have drummed

25 Almost all the current movies revolve around romantic love in which a main character meets his or her counterpart of ideal. Although it is an impossible situation, the implausible situation _____ to be projected on the big screen nowadays.

ⓐ has been continuing
ⓑ is continuing
ⓒ has continued
ⓓ continued

26 Mr. Park, the CEO of JR Electronic, was found guilty of the embezzlement for the last five years. If he offered his resignation and gave the money back immediately, he _____ to jail.

ⓐ would go
ⓑ will go
ⓒ goes
ⓓ would have gone

01 Robert Novak, director of clinical education in audiology at Purdue University, said he has been increasingly seeing too many young people with "older ears on younger bodies," a trend that _____ since the portable Walkman made its debut a few decades back.

ⓐ builds
ⓑ has been building
ⓒ had been building
ⓓ will have build

02 A tourist bus fell off the motorway this morning. If only the builders of the bridge _____ guardrails of concrete instead of iron plates, the bus might have not fallen off the 10-meter-high motorway to the construction site below.

ⓐ have made
ⓑ had made
ⓒ will make
ⓓ make

03 Secretary Ken Watters was reportedly seen leaving a hotel Monday with a young woman. The secretary _____ denied any wrongdoing to reporters. His wife was also asked about the supposed affair this morning but offered no comment.

ⓐ whom has been married for 23 years
ⓑ which has been married for 23 years
ⓒ what has been married for 23 years
ⓓ that has been married for 23 years

04 Anger is a natural response to frightening or threatening situations. Parents should help their children learn to express anger constructively. _____ constructive anger shows children how to convey their feelings in an assertive but unaggressive manner.

ⓐ Expressing
ⓑ To express
ⓒ Having expressed
ⓓ To have expressed

05 When Russell saved enough money to buy a house, both he and his wife breathed a sigh of relief as they have been wanting to purchase a house since they got married. When he buys a house this year, they _____ for more than 10 years.

ⓐ will have been waiting
ⓑ have been waiting
ⓒ had waited
ⓓ are waiting

06 Five-star restaurant La Verona was temporarily shut down last night due to continual overcrowding. The local fire marshal ordered that the famed eatery _____ after it had ignored several previous warnings.

ⓐ to close
ⓑ closed
ⓒ close
ⓓ might close

07 Russell's family was going to have a grand birthday party for Bella last Sunday. While Russell was preparing the food, Bella couldn't resist _____ at the kitchen due to the delicious smell coming from there.

ⓐ peeking
ⓑ to peek
ⓒ to have peeked
ⓓ peeked

08 Cholera was believed to be transmitted by gas or vapor. _____, according to the 1854 Cholera Map of London by Dr. John Snow, the cases were centered on a particular water pump used by all residents. Based on this observation, Snow concluded that water was the carrier of cholera, not gas.

ⓐ Besides
ⓑ Hence
ⓒ However
ⓓ That's why

09 One needs to be versatile and easygoing to be a teacher. They should be comfortable around with kids. Hence, it is strongly suggested that potential teachers _____ a variety of social activities.

ⓐ have joined
ⓑ joining
ⓒ will join
ⓓ join

10 Jack was supposed to meet one of his friends, Russell, at the study cafe at 5 pm on Sunday for the regular meeting. But it slipped his mind, causing he not to make it on time. If he _____ the appointment down on his calendar, he would have arrived on time.

ⓐ could have written
ⓑ wrote
ⓒ had written
ⓓ has written

11 Contrary to popular belief, _____ a cellular phone does not seem to increase brain cancer risk, a new study has revealed. The study involved over ten thousand people, making it the largest analysis of its kind ever conducted.

ⓐ use
ⓑ using
ⓒ to use
ⓓ to have used

12 On account of traffic jam, I am stuck on the road and literally crawling at the speed of five kilometers per hour. By the time I get to the office located near Seoul station, I _____ there for over two hours.

ⓐ have driven
ⓑ will drive
ⓒ had been driving
ⓓ will have been driving

13 Conventional rockets generate thrust by burning chemical fuel. Electric rockets, _____, propel space vehicles by applying electric or electromagnetic fields to clouds of charged particles to accelerate them.

ⓐ in short
ⓑ consequently
ⓒ furthermore
ⓓ by contrast

14 Those who are willing to go through much physical pain and stress possess unique personalities. These people tend _____ achievers who set high standards for themselves not only in sports but also in general.

ⓐ to become
ⓑ becoming
ⓒ become
ⓓ having become

15 When Russell tried to pay for the drink in a local bar yesterday, he realized that he had forgot his purse. If only he had been more careful, he _____ embarrassed there.

ⓐ will not be
ⓑ was not
ⓒ would not have been
ⓓ would not be

16 The government has been criticized for changing the curriculum too frequently, causing confusion and trouble to students. It should no longer play with short-sighted education policies. Instead, policymakers _____ stress what the essential requirements in the curriculum are in the longer run.

ⓐ might
ⓑ must
ⓒ can
ⓓ would

17 If you send personal emails on your office desktop, there is a high possibility that the boss is keeping an eye on you. In a survey of approximately 1,000 companies, nearly 70% of them admitted _____ a rang of surveillance methods to monitor their employees.

ⓐ used
ⓑ to have used
ⓒ to use
ⓓ using

18 A new study says the rates of breast cancer mortality _____ across much of the world. Declines in breast cancer deaths are most prominent in developed countries, with England and Wales experiencing the biggest drops.

ⓐ currently drop
ⓑ are currently dropping
ⓒ were currently dropping
ⓓ had currently dropped

19 A friend of mine, Jessica, is worried about her son since he has a financial problem for his business. If Jessica _____ the money to spare for his business, she would help her son right away.

ⓐ had
ⓑ would have
ⓒ has
ⓓ has had

20 When the U.S. Weather Service released its latest hurricane warning, workers _____ the finishing touches to the preparations for the July 4th celebrations at the governor's mansion. Nevertheless, the much-awaited party was canceled because of the weather condition.

ⓐ had been just putting
ⓑ have just put
ⓒ just put
ⓓ were just putting

21 Tension thickened last week when Washington hinted it may consider referring North Korea's nuclear issue to the U.N. Security Council. In the meantime U.S. media reported over the weekend that North Korea _____ be preparing for its first nuclear test.

ⓐ shall
ⓑ might
ⓒ will
ⓓ must

22 Russell is thought to be a very lovely and friendly man. Handsome with a smart, polite personality, indeed he is every woman's desired man. If Jane had the opportunity to hang out with him, she _____ happy.

ⓐ would be
ⓑ is
ⓒ would have been
ⓓ was

23 Some people may still be haunted by an embarrassing incident _____. Indeed, a memory of being made fun of as a child can do permanent damage to one's self-image.

ⓐ who occurred during their school years
ⓑ where occurred during their school years
ⓒ whose occurred during their school years
ⓓ that occurred during their school years

24 Technology comes at a price. But today many people _____ so confident that technology can provide all the answers to our problems that they overlook the fact that technology can bring about new problems.

ⓐ had become
ⓑ are becoming
ⓒ will be becoming
ⓓ became

25 Instead of dealing with the fact that a 555-meter tall building is out of the question, Lotte has suggested that the Seoul Airport runway _____ in order to make room for the skyscraper.

ⓐ to be adjusted
ⓑ be adjusted
ⓒ has been adjusted
ⓓ is adjusted

26 Even though video tapes can only be checked out from the video rental store for a three-week period, Jane kept on for over five weeks. If she _____ the video tape by the due date, a fine would not have been charged.

ⓐ had returned
ⓑ has returned
ⓒ would return
ⓓ returns

MEMO

서병석

- 학력
  국립 부경대학교 – 영어영문학과
  호주 Griffith University – 응용언어학(TESOL & LOTE) 석사
  호주 The University of New South Wales – 통역 & 번역학과 석사

- 약력
  울산 한국공무원학원
  울산 중앙경찰학원
  부산 한국고시학원
  부산 한국경찰학원
  부산 한국소방공무원학원

- 저서
  G-TELP Grammar Genius (배움)
  R.O.B. Grammar (배움)
  R.O.B. Reading (배움)
  VOCA BOOST UP – 실전어휘 문제 (배움)
  SEIZE 단계별 문법 집중문제 900 (배움)
  SEIZE 실전 동형모의고사 (배움)

G-TELP GRAMMAR GENIUS

ISBN 979-11-92590-64-6

발행일 | 2021年 8月 16日 초 판 1쇄
        2021年 11月 15日   2쇄
        2023年 3月 6日 개정판 1쇄
저 자 | 서병석
발행인 | 이용중
발행처 | 배움출판사
주 소 | 서울시 영등포구 영등포로 400 신성빌딩 2층 (신길동)
주문 및 배본처 | Tel 02) 813-5334 / Fax 02) 814-5334

정가 **22,000원(전 2권)**